Silent Watcher

The Hidden Horrors of the BTK Killer

Miles Donovan

Quantum Quill Media

Silent Watcher: The Hidden Horrors of the BTK Killer

Copyright © 2025 by Miles Donovan

All rights reserved. No part of this book may be reproduced, stored in a retrieval system, or transmitted in any form or by any means, electronic, mechanical, photocopying, recording, or otherwise, without prior written permission of the publisher, except in the case of brief quotations used in reviews or critical articles.

Published by **Quantum Quill Media**

This is a work of nonfiction. Every effort has been made to ensure accuracy in the presentation of facts. Some names, identifying details, or quotations may have been condensed, paraphrased, or drawn from public records, trial transcripts, or media reports for clarity. The author and publisher do not intend to glorify or sensationalize criminal acts; this book is presented for historical, educational, and journalistic purposes.

First Edition

BISAC Codes:

TRUE CRIME / Murder / Serial Killers (TRU002020)

TRUE CRIME / General (TRU000000)

SOCIAL SCIENCE / Criminology (SOC004000)

HISTORY / United States / 20th Century (HIS036060)

Contents

Introduction   1
A Monster in Plain Sight

1. Seeds of Darkness   14
   The Making of a Killer

2. Building the Mask   26
   Marriage, Church, and Community

3. The First Killings   43
   Blood on Wichita's Doorstep

4. Letters to the Police   61
   The BTK Persona

5. Blueprints of Depravity   79
   The Secret Rituals That Sustained Him

6. Beyond the Body Count   97
   The Lost Victims of BTK's Hidden Hunts

7. The Codes in the Sermons   116
   How BTK Turned Faith Into a Language of Control

8. The Boy Scout Leader's Dark Side   135
   The Oath and the Rope; How BTK Twisted Trust Into Control

9. Polaroids of a Killer   154
   The Photographs That Exposed BTK's Dual Reality

10. The Vanishing BTK   172
    The False Calm; How Dennis Rader Hid in Plain Sight for Thirteen Years

11. The Fatal Floppy Disk   189
    The Byte That Betrayed Him; How Technology Caught the Master of Control

12. Confession Without Remorse   206
    The Engineer of Evil; How BTK Turned Murder Into Method

13. The Family Torn Apart   224
    The Last Victims; How BTK's Secrets Destroyed the People Closest to Him

14. Lessons From BTK   241
    The Monster Next Door; How BTK Changed the Way We See Ordinary Evil

15. Evil in the Everyday   255
    The Banality of Horror; How BTK Turned Ordinary Life Into His Greatest Disguise

16. The Names in Silence   265
    The Victims of BTK

About the Author   272

Introduction
A Monster in Plain Sight

The morning of February 25, 2005, began like any other in Wichita, Kansas. The air was sharp and cold, carrying that gray heaviness of late winter. For most residents, it was a routine day. For Dennis Lynn Rader, it was the day his double life finally shattered. He drove toward lunch as he often did, preoccupied with his errands, his church duties, and the self-importance that came with being a local compliance officer. Then, without warning, unmarked law enforcement vehicles closed in around his car. Officers with guns drawn swarmed his truck. Commands rang out, and in seconds the man who had terrorized the city as the BTK Killer was in handcuffs. After thirty-one years of speculation, fear, and unanswered questions, the phantom had been captured, not as a shadowy drifter or an unhinged outcast, but as a 59-year-old family man from Park City who smiled at his neighbors and bowed his head in church.

The arrest stunned Wichita. For decades, people had whispered about BTK in hushed tones, warned their children not to walk alone, and speculated about whether the killer was still alive. Mothers remembered the Otero murders as if they had happened yesterday. Retired detectives carried the failure of unsolved cases like a wound that never closed. Now the face of BTK was revealed: a man who lived in their midst, lectured them about lawn ordinances, and volunteered with the Boy Scouts. The mask had been torn away, and what lay beneath was not some monstrous-looking figure but someone shockingly ordinary.

Neighbors were bewildered. Interviews broadcast that day captured the disbelief. He was described as polite, meticulous, strict but never threatening. Some found him odd, others saw him as overly authoritative in his city inspector role, but none could reconcile the man they knew with the killer he turned out to be. That was the most disturbing part, he had blended so perfectly into the background, thriving in the blindness of those around him. Evil had not come to Wichita with a terrifying face or a stranger's menace; it had come disguised as a quiet neighbor who waved while mowing his lawn.

The moment the news broke, the media descended in full force. National outlets camped in Wichita. Headlines screamed about the capture of BTK, the suburban killer who fooled everyone. The story was irresistible: a church leader by day, sadistic murderer by night. Reporters lined up side-by-side images of Rader in his church usher's jacket against the crude police sketches from the 1970s. Every detail was dissected, his family, his job, his reputation. The public consumed it all with horrified fascination. Yet even as the frenzy unfolded, much of the truth remained hidden. The grotesque realities buried in his journals, the staged photographs in women's clothing, the cold calculations of his "projects", these were not things easily broadcast in evening news segments. The simplified narrative of the "ordinary man, secret monster" left out just how profoundly disturbing his inner world truly was.

When Rader began to speak, the mask slipped further. In his confessions he recounted each murder with unnerving precision. He described how he planned, how he bound, how he strangled, and how he cleaned up after himself. Victims were reduced to "projects" and "hits." His language revealed no empathy, no recognition of humanity. Yet in moments of rare honesty he acknowledged what he was. "I'm a monster," he said, not with contrition but as a statement of fact. It was an identity he seemed almost proud of, the alter ego he had created in his communications with police and media finally merging with his real name. For years he had craved to be feared and remembered, and now, stripped of anonymity, he seemed to revel in telling the story of his reign.

Decades later, BTK still commands a grip on public imagination. Part of it lies in the longevity of his crimes and his audacity to taunt investigators. He slipped in and out of sight for decades, killing, vanishing, and then reemerging when his need for recognition outweighed his caution. But the deeper fascination lies in his ordinariness. The image of a man who lived a parallel life of such horror without detection unsettles the instinct to trust those closest to us. If Dennis Rader could be hiding behind the face of a church-going father, then what other horrors might be lurking behind polite smiles in small towns everywhere? He forces us to question the safety of the ordinary.

When police searched his home, the hidden world came into view. Stacks of documents, meticulous diaries, photographs, drawings, coded notes, he had preserved a lifetime of fantasies and crimes as if curating a museum for himself. Investigators found evidence of his obsession with binding, his staged self-portraits in grotesque costumes, his careful documentation of stalking victims who never knew they were prey. It was not just the crimes that shocked but the thoroughness with which he recorded them. He wanted BTK to live forever, not only through the headlines but through the archive he created in his own home.

Even with these revelations, there remains so much the public does not fully know. Cases remain debated, possible near-victims left in silence, and the complete contents of his diaries remain largely undisclosed. What was released was enough to confirm that the story most people knew was only the surface. The reality is far darker and stranger, filled with details that never fit into neat news packages or courtroom summaries. That is what this book aims to confront: the truths that shock not because they are exaggerated but because they are real.

The purpose here is not to glorify Rader but to strip away the myths and face the horror directly. Too often, killers like him are cloaked in narratives that turn them into dark celebrities. Myth-making makes them larger than life, feeding the ego they craved. But the reality is more unsettling: Rader was not a supervillain but an ordinary man who committed extraordinary cruelty, and his story holds lessons we cannot afford to look away from. By exposing the hidden details, the obsessions, the oversights, the chilling documents, this book seeks to reveal how easily he thrived in the silence of others.

A warning must be given at the outset: what follows is disturbing. This is not a story of redemption or catharsis. It is not about justice that erases the horror. It is about facing the unsettling reality of how one man lived two lives, how communities failed to see what was in front of them, and how the darkness of obsession can exist beneath the most ordinary of surfaces. These truths are not comfortable, but they are necessary. To understand BTK is to look directly into the mirror he holds up to us all, and to confront the terror of what it reflects.

In the weeks following Rader's arrest, Wichita felt as though it had woken from a decades-long nightmare only to discover the nightmare was real. Crowds gathered outside the Sedgwick County Courthouse, straining to catch a glimpse of the man in shackles. Some came seeking closure, others out of morbid curiosity, and still others because they simply could not believe the truth until they saw him with their own eyes. This was the face of the terror that had haunted their childhoods, their neighborhoods, their very sense of safety. People whispered that he looked too ordinary, too unremarkable to be capable of such things. And yet, it was precisely that ordinariness that had been his camouflage.

The press painted him as the classic double life: dutiful husband, strict father, respected community member, and secret sadist who had bound, tortured, and killed. But behind the sensational headlines lay details that few outside investigators and prosecutors would ever see. The boxes of journals, the binders filled with clippings and notes, the photographs hidden away in crawl spaces and storage, all of it revealed a mind that was not merely violent, but obsessed, compulsive, and disturbingly methodical. Rader had not only committed murders; he had documented them, rehearsed them, relived them through writing and photography. He had built an internal archive of horror that he revisited like a hobbyist returning to a treasured collection.

Among the most chilling discoveries were his self-staged photographs. Police uncovered images of Rader wearing women's clothing, ropes cinched around his limbs, posing in grotesque recreations of his own crimes. Sometimes he wore masks, sometimes he bound himself and set a camera on a timer, leaving himself dangling or half-buried in shallow graves he dug to simulate his fantasies. These images were never meant for the public eye; they were private trophies, evidence of a man who not only killed but consumed his own darkness repeatedly in solitude. The media alluded to these finds, but the full extent of them was too disturbing for evening broadcasts.

The fascination with the BTK case has never fully waned because it is not only a story of murder, but of deception. For thirty years, a killer existed not on the margins of society but at its very center. He attended church meetings, supervised neighborhood compliance, checked alarms in people's homes, and camped with their children. He was trusted with authority, and that trust shielded him from suspicion. The question that gnawed at Wichita after his arrest was not only how he could have done it, but how everyone else had missed it. The answer, as uncomfortable as it is, lies in the human tendency to accept appearances at face value, to believe that evil must look like evil.

There is also something deeper in why his story endures. BTK forces us to consider the uncomfortable link between fantasy and action. In his writings, Rader often referred to his "Factor X", a force he believed compelled him to kill. He gave it a name as though it were separate from himself, as though his crimes were driven by an external demon rather than his own will. Yet when investigators pored over his diaries, what they found was not a mystical force but an endless cycle of obsession: the careful stalking of potential victims, the sketches of imagined scenarios, the recordings of what he had done and what he still dreamed of doing. The killings were only one part of the life he built around violence; the fantasies were constant. The distinction between thought and action eroded until he no longer needed victims to feel power, his drawings, writings, and photographs were enough to feed the compulsion between murders.

This book is not designed to recount only the well-known crimes, the names etched in newsprint and courtroom transcripts. Those tragedies must be remembered, but they are only the beginning. Beneath them lies the untold: the survivors who narrowly escaped, the intended victims who never knew they were targets, the evidence that suggested he prowled more widely than the official record shows. The public knows the name BTK, but it does not know the full depth of the hidden world he left behind. This work seeks to pull back that curtain, to expose the truths that law enforcement, psychologists, and even his own family discovered only after the mask was gone.

There is a risk, however, in telling stories like this. True crime can blur the line between fact and spectacle, between history and myth. Serial killers are often turned into dark celebrities, their names repeated with a mixture of fear and fascination. But the danger of myth-making is that it elevates them, granting them a form of infamy they secretly crave. In Rader's case, this is especially perilous. He wanted attention; he fed on the fear he created; he relished being known. To turn him into a legend is to give him exactly what he sought. That is why this book does not seek to glorify or romanticize. The aim is to strip away the mystique and present him as he was: not a genius predator, but a compulsive, ordinary man whose evil thrived in the spaces where society looked away.

What follows will be disturbing. It cannot be otherwise. To understand Dennis Rader is to confront scenes of cruelty, to read his words in their cold matter-of-factness, to see the artifacts he created as evidence of his compulsions. Some details will shock because they are unfamiliar, others because they dismantle the simplistic narrative of a neat double life. The truth is messier, uglier, and more unsettling than any headline ever captured. If it makes the reader uncomfortable, it is because it should.

This introduction is a threshold. On the other side are the chapters that will peel back the layers of Rader's life, crime by crime, fantasy by fantasy, revealing how he lived two lives for so long, and how the world around him failed to see. To enter is to accept the weight of knowing, and to understand that some monsters do not come with warning signs. They live among us, wave from their driveways, and bow their heads in church pews, until the day their mask finally slips.

When investigators finally opened the hidden compartments of Rader's life, they discovered more than evidence of murders; they unearthed a private museum of obsession. Boxes and binders contained meticulous notes on surveillance, detailed sketches of homes, coded writings, and staged photographs that blurred the line between reality and fantasy. He had written about his "projects" in chillingly casual terms, noting when he followed them, how he might bind them, when he could strike, and even why he had decided to abort an attempt. For law enforcement, the scale of what he preserved was staggering. They had expected evidence of crimes already known; instead, they found glimpses of an entire hidden universe of terror that stretched far beyond the official count.

The public never saw most of these records. Some were described during court proceedings, others leaked in fragments to the press, but the full contents remained sealed, partly out of respect for the victims' families and partly because they revealed the grotesque banality of Rader's daily fixations. He drew crude bondage sketches during lunch breaks, cataloged women he watched from his car, and rehearsed scenarios in notebooks that read like stage directions. These documents stripped away the myth of the criminal mastermind and exposed what he truly was: a compulsive predator who could not stop feeding his fantasies, even when he was not killing.

For years afterward, Wichita wrestled with the reality that what they had feared was only part of the story. Many residents believed the narrative presented in news broadcasts and courtroom summaries: that BTK was a terrifying but rare aberration, a monster who lived in their midst but whose evil was neatly contained between 1974 and 1991. But the diaries suggested otherwise. They showed that even during his so-called dormancy, Rader never stopped stalking, never stopped planning, never stopped imagining. The killings may have ended, but the compulsion never did. He had only learned to feed it differently. That fact unsettled many more than the murders themselves, because it suggested that the monster never truly went away.

And yet, much of this remains unknown to the broader public. Outside of Wichita, BTK is often remembered in shorthand: the killer who bound, tortured, and killed; the man caught through a floppy disk and a careless question to police. The surface facts have become legend, but the deeper truths, that he staged crime-scene reenactments with himself as both victim and killer, that he meticulously chronicled his obsessions for decades, that he lived inside a fantasy world more elaborate than the crimes themselves, remain largely obscured. This book seeks to drag those truths into the light, not for spectacle, but because history cannot be properly understood if it is incomplete.

The purpose of this work is to reveal those hidden dimensions, to tell the story that is often flattened in retellings. It is not enough to say that Dennis Rader was a family man with a secret life. The horror lies in the details of how he constructed that secret life, how he nurtured it, and how it survived undetected for so long. By examining the overlooked evidence, the forgotten victims, the chilling photographs, and the diaries that lay buried in his house, we confront not just what he did but how he was able to do it for three decades without exposure.

There is a danger in this undertaking. True crime has long walked a line between education and exploitation, between telling history and feeding morbid curiosity. When a killer becomes infamous, the temptation is to frame him as larger than life, as if his cunning or cruelty elevated him into something mythic. But that very myth-making is what men like Rader desire most. In his letters, he boasted, demanded recognition, even offered suggestions for what his "brand name" should be. To glorify him, even indirectly, would be to give him exactly what he wanted. The challenge, then, is to strip away the myth and show him for what he was: not a genius predator, not an unstoppable phantom, but a deeply ordinary man whose compulsions found expression in extraordinary cruelty.

The truth is far more shocking than the myth. The truth is that he could be the neighbor who waves from his driveway, the man who fixes alarms in your home, the Scout leader teaching your children how to tie knots. He survived not because he was brilliant, but because the world around him did not believe someone like him could exist within their community. His camouflage was not in darkness but in daylight, not in disguise but in the plain view of normal life. That realization is more terrifying than any headline or police sketch.

What follows in these pages is not an easy story to read. It will disturb, anger, and sicken. It should. The only way to understand how a man like Dennis Rader thrived for so long is to confront the details, even when they are grotesque. To sanitize them is to miss the truth. To sensationalize them is to betray it. This book will do neither. It will present the record as it is, weaving together what is known, what has been documented, and what has too often been forgotten. The goal is not to elevate Rader, but to force us to look squarely at the uncomfortable reality that he represents.

For in the end, the BTK case is not only about one man's evil. It is also about the silences, the oversights, the ways a community can be lulled into believing that monsters only live elsewhere. It is about the fragility of safety and the blindness that comes with trust. The disturbing nature of what follows is not only in the crimes themselves, but in what they reveal about us, about how easily we can look past the warning signs, how deeply we want to believe that danger always wears a face we can recognize.

As the years passed after Rader's sentencing, the fascination never dimmed. Documentaries, news specials, and even fictionalized stories returned again and again to his name, often reducing the enormity of his crimes into a handful of memorable soundbites: the Otero family murders, the taunting letters, the final floppy disk. The shorthand became the story. Yet those who looked deeper, the detectives who sifted through his files, the psychologists who listened to his interviews, the victims' families who lived with the aftermath, knew that the real story was darker and more complex than most people wanted to hear. The truth was not that of a master criminal hiding behind brilliance, but of an obsessive, petty, and disturbingly ordinary man who built his entire identity around control and cruelty.

It is tempting to think of killers like Rader as monsters in the sense of being otherworldly, inhuman, outside of what ordinary people could ever understand. But to do so creates a dangerous distance. It allows us to imagine that such people could never exist among us, that they would stand out like predators in a crowd. What makes Rader so unsettling is that he did not stand out. He was the man who nodded politely in the grocery store aisle, who prepared Sunday sermons for his congregation, who took his children camping with the Scouts. To acknowledge him as both neighbor and murderer is to acknowledge that evil does not always look like evil. It can disguise itself in ordinariness, which is precisely why it thrives.

The documents, diaries, and photographs seized from his home ensure that his secret life can no longer be hidden. They also serve as proof that the surface story, told in quick news reports and simplified documentaries, barely scratches at the reality. He did not stop being BTK when the killings ceased. He never retired from his obsession. His entire life was lived in two dimensions: the one people saw, and the one he kept locked in boxes under his roof. The distance between those two worlds was not as wide as people would like to think.

This book is written with a specific purpose: to confront the truths that remain largely unseen. It does not glorify Dennis Rader, nor does it attempt to turn him into the kind of dark celebrity he always dreamed of becoming. Instead, it seeks to dismantle the myths, to strip away the legend and reveal the reality. By examining not only the murders but also the diaries, the evidence, the failures of law enforcement, and the silences of the community, it will show how a man like Rader could exist for so long undetected. To do so requires a willingness to look directly at details that are disturbing, even grotesque. It requires an acknowledgment that the world is sometimes more frightening than we admit to ourselves.

There is always a risk in telling stories of serial killers. They attract a morbid kind of attention, an uneasy mix of horror and fascination. But the greater danger lies in simplifying them into neat archetypes or legends. Rader himself longed to be remembered in exactly that way, his crimes framed as the work of a mastermind, his letters quoted as if they were poetry of fear. To grant him that would be to let him win even in defeat. The reality is more instructive, and more unsettling: he was an ordinary man who committed extraordinary acts of cruelty, and he thrived because no one wanted to see what was right in front of them.

The pages ahead are not easy. They will detail killings carried out with cold precision, fantasies recorded with chilling clarity, and a lifetime of deception that left a community blind. They will also explore the aftermath, the families broken, the city scarred, the investigators haunted by years of frustration. To read them is to step into uncomfortable territory, but that discomfort is necessary. Without it, the lessons of BTK are lost, and the warning he represents fades into myth.

As you move forward into this story, consider the words Rader himself once used to describe his secret identity: "I'm a monster." It was perhaps the truest statement he ever made, though not in the way he believed. He was not a creature of brilliance or myth, but a man who chose cruelty, who built his life around control and domination, who wore his mask so tightly that even those closest to him never suspected. The monster was not hiding in shadows but standing in the light of everyday life, waving from his driveway, sitting in church pews, walking among the unsuspecting. That is what makes him terrifying. That is why his story still matters. And that is why the disturbing truths you are about to read demand to be faced.

Chapter One
Seeds of Darkness
The Making of a Killer

Dennis Lynn Rader was born on March 9, 1945, in Pittsburgh, Kansas, the first of four sons in a working-class family. His parents, William and Dorothea, were strict but not abusive by most outward accounts. His father worked long hours as a lineman for Kansas Gas & Electric, leaving little time for home life. His mother juggled the burden of raising four boys, and Dennis often felt overlooked in the chaos. Later, he would claim that he resented the lack of attention, describing himself as lonely and detached, a child who learned to retreat into his own imagination. Whether this was the seed of something darker or simply the ordinary grumblings of a neglected boy remains unclear. What is undeniable is that from an early age, Dennis Rader developed habits and fantasies that foreshadowed the horrors to come.

Neighbors in his childhood recalled nothing unusual beyond his quietness, but subtle signs emerged even in his early years. He admitted later, with a detached calm, that as a boy he tortured small animals. Cats, dogs, and even birds became victims of his curiosity and cruelty. He bound them, strangled them, and sometimes hanged them from makeshift nooses. To most, such acts would have been unthinkable; to young Dennis, they were experiments, rehearsals for desires he did not yet understand. He discovered something within himself when he watched the life drain from those creatures: a rush of power, a sense of control that filled the emptiness he carried inside. It was here, in the quiet cruelty of a Kansas boy's backyard, that the template for BTK was first drafted.

By adolescence, his fascination with bondage and control had taken root. Rader confessed later that he fantasized about tying up girls in his neighborhood, imagining scenarios where they were completely at his mercy. He drew crude sketches of women bound and gagged, hiding the drawings in secret places. His fantasies were not fleeting curiosities but persistent obsessions. When other boys thought about sports or cars, Dennis thought about ropes and restraints. He began stealing women's underwear from clotheslines, an early manifestation of the fetish that would haunt his entire life. He would dress himself in the stolen garments, binding himself with ropes, staging his own mock scenarios in the secrecy of his bedroom or in the fields beyond his home.

Religion played a complicated role in his development. Raised in a conservative Lutheran household, Rader attended church regularly, learning early the importance of rules, ritual, and authority. He internalized the outward performance of faith while privately nurturing fantasies that stood in grotesque opposition to it. Later in life, he would draw upon scripture in his writings, weaving religious language into his letters to police, as if binding his sins to sacred words gave them a darker legitimacy. As a boy, however, church was less about belief and more about structure, a place where he learned the value of appearances. His faith was never about salvation; it was about conformity, a lesson he carried with him long after childhood.

During his teenage years at Wichita Heights High School, Rader appeared unremarkable to classmates. He was not a loner in the dramatic sense, but he was quiet, withdrawn, and socially awkward. Teachers remembered him as average, a student who did what was required but showed little ambition. Behind the mask of ordinariness, however, his private fantasies grew more elaborate. He developed what he would later call his "bondage daydreams," scenarios where he stalked, captured, and tied up women. These fantasies became a refuge, a place where he was powerful, admired, feared. He created an internal world he called "Factor X," an imagined force that he claimed compelled him to kill. In reality, Factor X was nothing more than the name he gave to his compulsions, a way of externalizing what was entirely within him. Yet even as a teenager, he began to believe, or at least to tell himself, that his fantasies were driven by something greater than himself.

College did little to change him. Rader briefly attended Kansas Wesleyan University but struggled academically. He drifted, working odd jobs and failing to find direction. In 1966, he enlisted in the United States Air Force, a decision that gave him structure and discipline but did not cure his darker urges. Stationed overseas and later in Texas, he blended into military life as he always had elsewhere, competent, quiet, unremarkable. Yet even then, the fantasies persisted. He read detective magazines, studied crime stories, and imagined himself in scenarios of domination and control. He told no one, of course. To his fellow servicemen, he was simply another airman fulfilling his duty.

When he returned to Kansas in 1970, he married Paula Dietz, a quiet, churchgoing woman who had known him from their neighborhood. To friends and family, they seemed an ordinary young couple, building a modest life together. They moved to Park City, where Rader worked at various jobs, including at the Coleman Company and later at ADT Security, where he installed alarm systems in people's homes, a chilling irony, considering his own career as a burglar and murderer. The marriage gave him stability and the outward appearance of respectability, but it did nothing to quell the hunger within him. His fantasies only grew more vivid, fueled now by the challenge of hiding them beneath the veneer of domestic life.

Rader's childhood and young adulthood illustrate the unsettling ordinariness of his beginnings. There were no catastrophic traumas, no glaring abnormalities that could explain his evolution into a serial killer. Instead, there was a quiet accumulation of obsessions, a steady nurturing of cruelty, and an increasing confidence in his ability to hide in plain sight. His early life was a rehearsal stage, where he tested boundaries with animals, built fantasies around bondage, and discovered the thrill of secrecy. Each act reinforced his belief that he was different, chosen somehow by what he called Factor X, destined to pursue the fantasies that consumed him.

By the time Dennis Rader reached adulthood, the mask was firmly in place. To the world, he was a husband, a worker, a churchgoer, a man of no particular distinction. To himself, he was something else entirely: an emerging predator, waiting for the moment when fantasy would no longer be enough. The seeds had been planted long ago in the quiet cruelty of his childhood, and now they were ready to bear their terrible fruit.

When Dennis Rader married Paula Dietz in 1971, he stepped further into the disguise of normalcy. Paula was quiet, reserved, and rooted in the same Lutheran values that Dennis outwardly professed. Their marriage seemed ordinary, stable, unremarkable. To Paula and those who knew them, Dennis was attentive, if somewhat rigid, a man who liked structure and routine. He worked, he attended church, he mowed his lawn with precision, and he seemed committed to the rituals of suburban life. Yet within him, the fantasies that had haunted his childhood continued to evolve, demanding more than drawings or private role-play.

His first real opportunity to nurture those fantasies came when he took a job at ADT Security Services in 1974. The work involved installing alarm systems in homes and businesses across Wichita. To most, it was honest work, but for Rader it became something far darker. He entered people's homes under the guise of protection, studying layouts, learning where bedrooms were located, observing habits of families. He was invited into living rooms, trusted with securing doors and windows. To him, this was surveillance disguised as labor, a way to practice control while gathering information. The irony was profound: the man who installed alarms for others was the same man who would one day bypass them to kill.

During this period, his obsession with stalking deepened. He prowled neighborhoods, sitting in his car for hours while watching women he found attractive. He took notes, mapping their routines, timing their comings and goings. These were his "projects," a word he used to reduce human lives into tasks of domination. Each project was carefully considered. He kept lists and journals, creating scenarios in his mind of how he might bind and capture them. Sometimes he followed them home, imagining how he might break in. He rarely acted, but each time he stalked, the fantasies grew stronger.

At home, Paula had no idea. She thought her husband was simply detail-oriented, perhaps too strict at times, but faithful and hardworking. He maintained their home with pride, took part in church activities, and gave every appearance of a steady suburban husband. Even as he began to explore his darkest fantasies more aggressively, he never let the mask slip.

The transition from fantasy to action did not happen suddenly. It was a slow erosion of barriers. Rader began testing himself, escalating the thrill of stalking by breaking into homes when the occupants were away. He would steal small items, women's underwear, photographs, personal mementos, and later use them in his private rituals. He staged himself in women's clothing, bound with ropes, taking photographs with a timer to freeze his fantasies into reality. He buried these trophies in boxes, creating an archive that grew year by year. Each successful intrusion gave him confidence. Each time he was not caught, he believed more firmly that Factor X was guiding him, protecting him, compelling him.

His job and his domestic life helped camouflage these darker urges. He and Paula welcomed children in the years that followed, and Rader leaned into the role of father and husband. He was proud of his reputation for discipline and order, expecting obedience from his family, his co-workers, and his church peers. But beneath the surface, the hunger persisted. His "projects" occupied his mind as much as sermons or family dinners. He perfected the art of compartmentalization, learning to separate his public face from his private obsessions.

By the early 1970s, Rader's fantasies had reached a breaking point. He no longer wanted to merely imagine scenarios of bondage and domination; he wanted to feel them unfold in real time. He began planning in earnest, moving from stalking to strategizing actual murders. He scouted homes, studied routines, and devised entry methods. He prepared his "hit kit," a set of tools that included ropes, bindings, tape, and weapons. He rehearsed in his mind exactly how he would subdue his victims, bind them, and take control of their lives.

The concept of Factor X became his justification. He later told police and psychologists that Factor X was the external force that drove him, a dark compulsion he could not resist. He described it almost like a demon, an entity that whispered commands. But in truth, Factor X was Dennis Rader himself, his desires, his fantasies, his lack of empathy crystallized into an excuse. By giving it a name, he allowed himself to believe he was powerless against it, when in fact he chose every step.

Even as he built his domestic life, the fantasies escalated to the point where inaction was no longer enough. His journals from this period reveal that he had already identified potential victims, neighbors and strangers alike, whom he labeled as projects. He studied their homes, their schedules, and their vulnerabilities. To him, these people were not human beings but challenges, puzzles to be solved, opportunities to fulfill his fantasies. He began carrying his hit kit in his car, ready at any moment to act if opportunity presented itself.

It was inevitable that he would eventually cross the line. For years, he had tested the boundaries with animals, break-ins, and staged rituals. Now he was ready for a human victim. In his mind, he had prepared for this moment all his life. To the outside world, he remained the quiet husband, the churchgoing man, the worker in a blue-collar job. But internally, Dennis Rader was ready to step fully into the role of BTK. The seeds planted in childhood, watered through years of fantasy and obsession, had grown into something that demanded action. The ordinary mask was intact, but behind it, the killer was waiting.

By January of 1974, Dennis Rader was thirty-eight years old, outwardly an ordinary man with a wife, a job, and responsibilities. But inside him the fantasies had been boiling for years. He had stalked, broken into homes, stolen clothing, and rehearsed his scenarios countless times. He had tested himself in smaller acts, but they no longer satisfied. The pressure of his obsession had built to the point that only the real experience of binding and killing could release it. He told himself that Factor X demanded it, that the force inside him required blood. In truth, he wanted it. He had always wanted it.

The Otero family became his first chosen victims. Joseph and Julie Otero lived in a modest home on Edgemoor Street with their children. They were an ordinary military family, disciplined, close-knit, and unaware that they had been placed on Rader's secret list of projects. For weeks he watched them, timing their routines. He noticed when they left for school, when Joseph went to work, when Julie was at home. He mapped the house in his mind, rehearsing entry points and methods of control. By the time he finally acted, he had convinced himself that he knew them well enough to dominate them completely.

On the morning of January 15, 1974, Rader carried his hit kit to the Otero home. He expected Julie and the children to be alone. What he did not anticipate was that Joseph would be home that morning as well. Yet instead of retreating, Rader adapted, fueled by adrenaline and determination. He forced his way inside and brandished a pistol, announcing that he was a fugitive who only wanted money and a car. He tied up the family one by one, assuring them that if they cooperated they would not be harmed. It was a lie.

What unfolded inside that house was brutality that still haunts Wichita to this day. Rader methodically bound Joseph, Julie, and their children, Josephine and Joseph Jr. He tightened ropes around their wrists and ankles, gagged them, and used his strength to dominate every move. The children cried, terrified, as their parents tried to reassure them. But Rader was in complete control. One by one, he strangled them. Joseph fought hard, but the bindings held. Julie pleaded for her children, but she too was silenced. The children suffered last. When it was over, four lives had been extinguished in a suburban home on an ordinary morning, and Dennis Rader walked away exhilarated.

Later he would describe this moment in chillingly calm detail, recounting how he experimented with different knots, how he watched their final moments with fascination. He admitted that he felt disappointment at times, his techniques did not always go as planned, but overall, the experience gave him exactly what he wanted: the sense of power, of ultimate control. He had transformed his fantasy into reality, and it was everything he imagined it would be.

For Wichita, the Otero murders were an earthquake. The crime scene shocked investigators. Four bodies bound and strangled, the work of someone who had taken his time. There was no clear motive, no robbery, no sexual assault in the traditional sense. Just domination, cruelty, and death. The randomness of the crime terrified the community. If such horror could happen to an ordinary family in their own home, it could happen to anyone.

For Rader, the Oteros marked the beginning. He later admitted that he relived the crime for years afterward, replaying the images in his mind, returning to the thrill of control. He collected souvenirs from the home to remind himself of the morning when fantasy became real. In his journals, he cataloged the crime as if it were a project completed, noting what had gone right, what could be improved, and how it had felt. He was not horrified by what he had done; he was satisfied, eager to refine his methods for the next time.

The Otero case also marked the birth of BTK as a persona. Rader craved recognition for his work. He did not want the murders to disappear into the files of unsolved crimes. He wanted his name, or at least the name he created, to live on. Within months, he wrote his first letter to the press, describing details only the killer could know. He named himself "BTK", Bind, Torture, Kill, a brand as grotesque as it was unforgettable. With that letter, he announced to the world that Wichita had a predator in its midst, and that he intended to be remembered.

The murder of the Oteros was not just an act of violence; it was a declaration. It was Dennis Rader stepping fully into the role he had fantasized about since childhood. The quiet boy who tortured animals, the teenager who sketched women in bondage, the airman who devoured detective magazines, the husband who stole underwear from clotheslines, all of it had led to this moment. In his mind, Factor X had spoken, and he had answered. To Wichita, it was a tragedy without sense. To Dennis Rader, it was the beginning of his life's true calling.

In the days after the Otero murders, Dennis Rader returned to his ordinary routines as if nothing had happened. He went to work, attended church, spent time with Paula, and maintained the outward mask of the dutiful husband and neighbor. He knew the city was in panic, newspapers filled with speculation, police urged vigilance, and residents began locking their doors for the first time in years, but he felt strangely detached from the chaos. The fear that gripped Wichita was the fear he had created. In his private mind, he savored it. He had not just killed a family; he had changed an entire city.

Rader had proven to himself that he could kill and remain invisible. This realization emboldened him. He had walked into a family's home in broad daylight, murdered four people, and then disappeared back into suburban life without detection. There had been no knocks on his door, no suspicion from friends or neighbors. The police were searching for a phantom, not a man who trimmed his lawn and sang hymns on Sunday. To Dennis, this confirmed what he had always believed: he was chosen, guided by Factor X, protected by forces greater than ordinary men. In truth, he had simply been lucky, but luck felt like destiny to a man who needed to believe he was special.

The Otero murders also gave him a system. In his journals and later confessions, he described the crime almost as a rehearsal, analyzing what had worked and what had not. He noted that binding multiple victims at once was difficult, that controlling an entire family was risky, and that he needed to refine his methods to be more efficient. He cataloged these observations as if preparing a manual for himself, a playbook for future attacks. Each detail, from the way he cut cords to the order in which he subdued his victims, was committed to memory for later use. He was not only reliving the crime in his fantasies, he was learning from it, improving, perfecting.

At the same time, he felt the need to announce himself. When no one connected the murders to a larger pattern, when no credit was attributed to him, his ego grew restless. He had risked everything to kill, and now the world seemed ready to move on. That, to him, was unacceptable. He wanted recognition, fear, and above all, the satisfaction of knowing that the police were aware of his presence. His first letter to the press, in which he revealed details only the killer could know, was a calculated act of self-promotion. By naming himself "BTK", Bind, Torture, Kill, he was not only describing what he did; he was branding himself. He wanted Wichita to have a name to whisper in terror.

Meanwhile, at home, Paula remained unaware. She had no reason to suspect her husband. He was attentive enough, strict in his expectations of family life, but never outwardly abusive. She saw him as serious, perhaps controlling, but reliable. His ability to compartmentalize was extraordinary. One moment he could be standing in church, reciting prayers with his wife; the next he was crouched in his basement, staging photographs of himself in stolen underwear, ropes tied around his body, rehearsing his fantasies again and again. The mask did not slip, not even slightly.

What is most unsettling about this period is how seamlessly Rader wove murder into the fabric of his daily life. There was no dramatic break, no collapse of his ordinary world. He did not spiral outward in the wake of the Otero killings. He simply folded them into his routine, filing away souvenirs, writing notes, and preparing for the next time. Killing had not disrupted his life; it had completed it. He now had two worlds that ran in parallel: the life everyone saw, and the life only he knew.

The investigation into the Otero murders was intense, but it yielded no suspects. Detectives were baffled by the brutality and the lack of clear motive. Rumors swirled about drug connections, family disputes, and military involvement, but none pointed toward Dennis Rader. He followed the coverage obsessively, clipping articles and saving them for his collection. Each headline was a trophy, each unsolved lead a reassurance that he remained beyond suspicion. For Rader, this was intoxicating. Not only had he killed successfully, he had confounded the authorities.

And so the seeds planted in his childhood, the cruelty to animals, the fantasies of bondage, the obsession with control, had now borne fruit in reality. The Oteros were the first victims of a man who had spent his life preparing for that moment, rehearsing it in countless ways until it became inevitable. The ordinary boy who once drew sketches of bound women, the teenager who tied himself up in stolen underwear, the young husband who prowled neighborhoods with his hit kit, he had finally crossed the line. And once crossed, there was no going back.

For the city of Wichita, the Oteros marked the beginning of a reign of terror that would span three decades. For Dennis Rader, they marked the fulfillment of his destiny as he imagined it, the proof that Factor X was real, that he was chosen to bind, torture, and kill. And with that belief, he prepared to continue, certain that he could kill again and again while hiding behind the mask of ordinariness that no one seemed able to see through.

Chapter Two
Building the Mask
Marriage, Church, and Community

When Dennis Rader looked in the mirror each morning, he saw not a killer, but a craftsman of appearances. The reflection staring back at him was carefully constructed: short hair parted neatly, collared shirt pressed flat, the faint glint of wire-frame glasses giving the impression of calm intelligence. Everything about his appearance was designed to project order and control. His wife, Paula, saw in that reflection the man she had married, a quiet, responsible husband, a provider who valued hard work and discipline. What she could not see, what no one could, was the other man who lived behind the eyes.

Their marriage had begun simply enough. Paula was drawn to his stability. Dennis was attentive, steady, polite, the kind of man her parents approved of. They married in 1971, settling into a modest house on Independence Street in Park City, Kansas. It was the sort of neighborhood where lawns were trimmed to perfection and everyone knew everyone else's name. Their life looked like something out of a Midwestern advertisement: two hardworking people building a future together.

In public, Rader played his role with conviction. He took pride in being dependable, the kind of man who showed up early to work and volunteered for committees at church. At home, he was quiet but firm, a husband who valued order and expected it in return. Paula, who was deeply religious, appreciated his seriousness. She thought of him as intense, perhaps too much so at times, but fundamentally good. She had no idea that the man who kissed her goodbye each morning was reliving scenes of murder in his mind, replaying every scream, every struggle, every tightening of rope.

When their children were born, Dennis embraced fatherhood as another performance. He liked the image of being a family man, a provider, a protector. He coached, he disciplined, he showed up for school events. To his neighbors, he was the sort of father people admired, structured, serious, devoted. Inside, however, the role was mechanical. He could mimic affection, but not feel it deeply. His emotions existed behind glass: visible but unreachable. His mind drifted constantly to his "projects," to the rituals and fantasies that fueled his hidden life.

His work life complemented the persona he was building. After leaving ADT, Rader became a compliance officer for Park City. The position suited him perfectly. It gave him authority without scrutiny, power cloaked in bureaucracy. He could issue citations, enforce rules, and exercise small dominations under the guise of civic duty. Residents described him as meticulous to the point of obsession, insisting on exact lawn lengths, measuring property lines, reprimanding homeowners for trash violations. He relished it. Every time someone flinched under his authority, he felt a faint echo of the control he had experienced in his murders.

At church, he was equally respected. He attended services faithfully at Christ Lutheran Church, where he eventually became council president. He read scripture aloud, planned community events, and chaired meetings. His fellow parishioners described him as serious but sincere, a man of faith with a strong sense of right and wrong. They mistook his rigidity for righteousness. Rader, ever the performer, understood how to exploit that perception. His life became an intricate illusion, each public act of service a brick in the wall that concealed his depravity.

By the late 1970s, Rader's position in the community had become almost untouchable. He was a father, a husband, a church leader, and a civic official. His face appeared in neighborhood bulletins and church newsletters. He attended potlucks, led prayers, and shook hands with the same people whose homes he sometimes stalked after dark. The dichotomy thrilled him. The more respectable his public image became, the more satisfying his private crimes felt. He didn't just hide in plain sight, he thrived there.

Rader's involvement with the Boy Scouts added another layer to his disguise. As a scout leader, he taught boys how to build fires, tie knots, and respect authority. Parents trusted him implicitly. They saw a man giving his time to help children learn responsibility and survival skills. But for Dennis Rader, scouting was not service, it was theater. The uniforms, the rules, the structure, all of it appealed to his need for order and control. And beneath that, it offered him something darker: proximity to vulnerability and trust.

The duplicity of Rader's existence was almost mathematical in its precision. He compartmentalized his life into neat boxes, each one sealed from the others. There was the husband and father, the city inspector, the church leader, the Scoutmaster, and then there was BTK, the shadow he carried everywhere but never allowed to surface in daylight. He managed his identities the way an accountant manages ledgers: meticulously, without overlap. If a thought of his victims flickered while he was in church, he simply filed it away to be revisited later in the privacy of his rituals. If a flash of guilt arose while kissing his children goodnight, he smothered it under the weight of habit and routine.

This ability to separate his lives made him invisible. The community's blindness was his armor. Wichita had grown accustomed to thinking of BTK as a specter, a faceless monster who had vanished into the past. No one imagined he might be the man measuring their fence height or reading scripture at the pulpit. Rader's very normalcy protected him. In small towns, familiarity breeds trust, and trust breeds blindness. He understood that better than anyone. He cultivated it deliberately, knowing that the more visible he was, the safer he became.

He took particular pride in how easily people accepted the mask. At church, women brought him baked goods and thanked him for his leadership. Parents in the Scouts praised his discipline. City residents called him "Officer Rader" and respected his attention to detail. He would go home from these interactions and write in his journals about the thrill of deception, the pleasure of fooling everyone around him. He described the feeling as an addiction, an intoxicating sense of superiority. "Nobody really knew Dennis," he later said, and he was right. Nobody did.

In truth, even he didn't fully know himself. The boundaries between his two worlds had blurred so deeply that he began to think of BTK not as a separate identity but as an extension of his truest self. The mask wasn't something he wore; it was part of him, fused to his existence. In one moment, he could scold a neighbor about weeds growing too high, and in the next, drive across town to photograph a potential victim's house. Both acts came from the same source, a hunger for control, an obsession with order, and a deep, cold emptiness that could never be filled.

His family noticed none of it. To them, Dennis was demanding but dependable, a man who insisted on doing things the right way. He attended his children's recitals, paid bills on time, and bowed his head during grace. The idea that their father could have been the phantom killer who haunted

Wichita decades earlier was unthinkable. It would remain unthinkable for thirty years.

The mask worked because Dennis Rader was not pretending to be normal, he was normal, at least on the surface. The performance was not an act he switched on and off; it was a continuous state of being. He could genuinely enjoy a family meal, then spend the evening writing about binding victims. The contradiction did not trouble him. It exhilarated him. The tension between his public virtue and private evil gave him a sense of balance, as if one justified the other. The more righteous his image became, the deeper his darkness could go.

It is this duality that makes his story so chilling. Dennis Rader did not live in the shadows; he lived under the sun, surrounded by people who trusted him, respected him, even admired him. Every rule he enforced, every sermon he read, every knot he tied with a Scout troop, each was an affirmation that his disguise was perfect. He was not just hiding from the world. He was performing for it, confident that no one would ever look behind the mask.

And for nearly thirty years, no one did.

For Dennis Rader, daily life became an exercise in choreography. Every action, every smile, every conversation was part of the performance. He understood that the mask had to be maintained with precision, that even a small crack could expose the darkness underneath. So he built a routine that would protect him, a pattern of ordinary behavior so predictable that no one would ever question it.

Each morning began the same way. He woke early, shaved, dressed neatly, and greeted his wife with mechanical warmth. The coffee maker gurgled in the kitchen, the sound as comforting as the hum of normal life. He liked mornings because they gave him structure, and structure was his camouflage. It kept the chaos contained. He went to work on time, returned home for dinner, attended church events, balanced his checkbook. He lived by a rhythm that made him indistinguishable from any other middle-aged man in the Midwest. That was the genius of his disguise, he didn't stand out; he blended in perfectly.

At work, Rader's obsession with control flourished. As Park City's compliance officer, he patrolled the quiet streets in his city-issued vehicle, clipboard in hand, measuring grass, inspecting fences, and issuing citations. He was proud of his authority. The job fed the same part of his mind that once tightened ropes around victims. Each violation he corrected, each rule he enforced, was a small act of domination. When residents protested, he relished their discomfort. Power made him feel alive. He wrote down their names, their addresses, and their offenses, filing them away with satisfaction. The mask of bureaucracy hid the predatory satisfaction beneath.

His co-workers found him peculiar but harmless. He was rigid, humorless, sometimes condescending, but he did his job efficiently. No one suspected that the man who argued over garbage placement and untrimmed hedges was also the phantom killer whose name still sent shivers through Wichita's older residents. The city had long believed BTK was gone, dead, imprisoned, or simply retired. The murders had stopped, and life had moved on. Rader was safe behind the anonymity of normal life.

At home, he maintained his image as a family man. He was stern with his children but attentive in the ways that mattered to appearances. He insisted on manners at the dinner table, on respect for elders, on hard work and discipline. He helped with homework, attended school programs, and made sure the family was seen at church every Sunday. Neighbors called them a wholesome household. He wanted them to. Every public gesture was calculated to reinforce the illusion. The idea that behind that modest house lived one of the most infamous killers in American history was unthinkable.

Yet Rader's private life remained steeped in his obsessions. Late at night, when Paula and the children slept, he would retreat to the basement or garage, pulling out his hidden boxes. Inside were his trophies: photographs, drawings, clippings, and stolen items from victims. He would handle them reverently, like sacred relics. He revisited each memory with ritualistic focus, sometimes reenacting scenes from his crimes, sometimes writing about them in coded language. These moments were his true self emerging from beneath the façade. They were the fuel that sustained him, the proof that BTK still lived.

His role in the church deepened his illusion of virtue. As council president, he chaired meetings, read scripture, and organized volunteer events. He was meticulous about attendance and order, often quoting rules from the church's constitution to assert his authority. His fellow congregants saw him as a man of principle, perhaps overly serious, but reliable. They trusted him implicitly. No one noticed how his eyes lingered on certain women during services, or how his notes and bulletins were saved not for spiritual reflection but as keepsakes in his private files. The church gave him legitimacy, respect, and cover, a fortress of morality in which he could hide his immorality completely.

Then there were the Boy Scouts. Rader's involvement began as a gesture of fatherhood, a way to bond with his son. But it quickly became another instrument of control. The uniform, the hierarchy, the structure, it all appealed to his need for authority. He taught the boys knot-tying, camping, and first aid, skills that mirrored the mechanical precision of his crimes. Parents saw only dedication and discipline. They didn't notice the deeper satisfaction behind his eyes when he demonstrated how to tie a perfect slipknot. To Dennis, the Scouts were more than community service, they were a theater of obedience, a mirror of the world he craved: orderly, rule-bound, submissive.

He thrived on the duplicity of it all. The more people admired him, the greater his private exhilaration became. To deceive the world so completely was its own form of dominance. In his mind, he controlled not only his victims but his entire environment. Everyone around him, his wife, his children, his neighbors, his co-workers, was unknowingly part of his illusion. It was a secret stage play, and he was both the actor and the director.

This duplicity gave him a sense of invincibility. He believed that God himself had blessed his ability to deceive, that his mask was a divine shield. He wrote later that he often prayed after his crimes, not for forgiveness, but in thanks for being spared from capture. His faith was not repentance, it was justification. He used scripture to reinforce his sense of destiny, interpreting verses about power and authority as validation of his control over others. To him, the world was divided between those who ruled and those who were ruled, between order and chaos. He saw himself as the enforcer of both.

The compartmentalization of his double life was almost flawless. He separated every part of himself into categories: "Family," "Work," "Church," "BTK." He kept mental ledgers, tracking details with precision. He had learned long ago that guilt could not survive if it was filed away. So he buried it beneath order. The more organized his life appeared, the safer he felt. It was as if structure itself could keep the darkness contained. But beneath that illusion, BTK never slept. He lingered in the quiet moments, in the pauses between sermons and Scout meetings, whispering through the hum of everyday life.

The blindness of the community enabled him. Wichita was not a city built on suspicion. People waved to their neighbors, trusted their pastors, and believed that evil came from elsewhere, from distant cities, from strangers, from the kind of men who didn't attend church or volunteer with children. Rader exploited that innocence. He understood that people see what they expect to see. They expected kindness, respectability, decency, and that was exactly what he showed them. He knew how to smile the right way, speak with authority, and project calm sincerity. It was his greatest weapon, more powerful than any rope or gun.

And so the years passed. The man once known as BTK became, in the eyes of everyone around him, simply Dennis, a husband, a father, a man of the community. His mask was no longer something he wore; it had become his identity. The predator had learned to live among the flock, not as an intruder but as one of them. The true horror was not in what he did, but in how effortlessly he did it, how seamlessly he moved between prayer and perversion, between civic duty and murder, between Sunday righteousness and private evil.

He lived two lives, and the world believed only one of them.

The mask that Dennis Rader built did more than hide him, it defined him. It gave him purpose. Each layer of normalcy he added to his public life became another wall shielding his secret world. But walls, even the strongest, eventually show cracks. Beneath the calm exterior, the pressures of secrecy and ego began to shift and strain.

By the mid-1980s, Rader had mastered the art of dual living. He could glide between personas effortlessly, husband, father, church leader, Scoutmaster, inspector. Each role gave him the illusion of control, the feeling that he was the center of a finely tuned machine. But control, for Rader, was never enough. He wanted recognition. He wanted to be seen as a man of authority, a figure to be respected and feared. The same impulse that once drove him to kill now expressed itself in subtler but no less disturbing ways.

At home, he grew more domineering. Paula had long accepted his strictness as part of his nature, but in later years, it hardened into something colder. He demanded precision in everything: the way the house was kept, the way the children spoke, the way dinner was served. Minor infractions, an untidy room, a missed chore, became grounds for lectures and punishments. His voice, measured and calm, carried the weight of quiet menace. He never raised his hand, but his authority was absolute. The house, like his victims, existed under his rules.

The church, too, became an outlet for his hunger for dominance. As council president, Rader often turned meetings into lectures about discipline and accountability. He quoted bylaws, corrected others publicly, and inserted himself into decisions far beyond his remit. He saw the church as a miniature world that needed order, and he was its enforcer. Parishioners began to find him overbearing, though few dared say it. In his mind, he was doing God's work, maintaining control, preserving structure, keeping chaos at bay.

At work, his reputation for inflexibility grew. Residents called him "by-the-book Rader." Some resented his citations for minor infractions, the way he measured lawn heights with a ruler or photographed unpainted fences. His authority was petty, but it satisfied the same craving that once drew him to bind his victims. Every rule enforced, every citation issued, gave him a small jolt of power. He was, as one co-worker later described, "the kind of man who enjoyed telling people no."

Rader's need for control extended into every corner of his life. He scheduled his days with precision, logging tasks in notebooks, making lists for everything from grocery shopping to house maintenance. Even his leisure time was regimented. When the family watched television, he dictated what they watched. When they went on vacations, he planned the itinerary to the minute. He lived in constant motion, driven not by joy but by compulsion. His mind could not rest. When he wasn't enforcing rules in the real world, he was revisiting them in his fantasies.

Those fantasies never left him. Though years had passed since his last known murder, BTK remained alive in his imagination. He revisited his victims through photographs and notes, sometimes writing about them as if they were old acquaintances. He crafted new scenarios, sketching women in bondage, plotting imaginary crimes he never carried out. These private rituals were his way of feeding the darkness without exposing it. He had learned how to satisfy the hunger without risking discovery. But the hunger never diminished; it only changed form.

The longer he maintained his façade, the more confident he became. He began to see himself not as a man living a double life, but as someone uniquely chosen to bear two natures. He believed that his mask was not deceit but destiny, that God had given him the ability to walk in both light and shadow. In his journals, he referred to himself as "dual," as though the existence of BTK and Dennis Rader were two halves of a divine balance. It was self-deception, but it made him feel powerful, untouchable.

Rader's arrogance crept into his interactions with others. He corrected people unnecessarily, lectured neighbors, and scolded fellow parishioners. His tone was always polite, but his words carried the edge of superiority. He enjoyed making others uncomfortable, asserting his quiet dominance through rules and moral posturing. Those who encountered him often left feeling chastised, though they couldn't quite explain why. To him, these moments were small rehearsals of control, reminders of the power he still possessed.

His neighbors noticed that he always seemed to be watching. He had a way of appearing suddenly, at the end of a driveway, near a yard fence, standing quietly while someone trimmed their hedges. He liked to know what everyone was doing. He knew who came and went, who broke local ordinances, who left their trash cans out too long. He recorded details in notebooks, just as he had once recorded his victims' routines. To outsiders, it seemed like civic diligence. In truth, it was voyeurism disguised as order. He thrived on proximity, on the subtle pleasure of observing without being observed.

The duplicity that once filled him with exhilaration now began to feel like pressure. The older he became, the more his two worlds collided in small, imperceptible ways. Sometimes, while talking to parishioners, fragments of his other life drifted into his thoughts. A name. A smell. A moment from a crime scene. He would pause mid-sentence, recalibrate, and continue as though nothing had happened. Other times, while issuing a citation at work, a flash of his victims' faces would surface in his mind, not as guilt but as satisfaction. He controlled himself outwardly, but inwardly, he was slipping.

At home, Paula occasionally saw flashes of something she didn't understand, a look in his eyes that was neither anger nor sadness, but something colder, emptier. He dismissed it with excuses about work stress or church politics, and she accepted them. After all, he was reliable, faithful, always present. Her trust was absolute, and he depended on it. That trust was the last layer of his mask, the one that made him invisible.

The thrill of hiding in plain sight became its own addiction. The more successful he was at deceiving people, the more powerful he felt. He tested boundaries, not just in his fantasies but in small, real-world provocations, leaving clues, making ambiguous comments, hinting at hidden depths no one would ever believe. It excited him to know that he could stand in front of a congregation, speak about morality, and no one would suspect the blood on his hands. He began to see himself as superior not just to his victims, but to everyone around him. They lived in ignorance; he lived in mastery.

"Nobody really knew Dennis," he said years later, and that statement was truer than anyone realized. His wife knew his habits but not his heart.

His children knew his discipline but not his demons. His church knew his devotion but not his blasphemy. His neighbors knew his face but not his soul. Even the police, who still kept dusty BTK files in drawers, knew the horror but not the man. The separation between these worlds was so complete that when the truth finally came out decades later, no one could reconcile them. The shock was not only that Dennis Rader was BTK, it was that BTK had always been Dennis Rader, hidden in plain sight, living next door, shaking hands, praying, laughing, enforcing the rules.

He had built his mask so perfectly that even he forgot where it ended.

By the end of the 1980s, Dennis Rader's mask was complete. To the world, he was the model citizen, dependable, methodical, and deeply moral. To himself, he was the perfect predator, capable of existing among the unsuspecting without raising an eyebrow. The years since the Otero murders had not erased the darkness in him; they had refined it. The killings had slowed, but the hunger had not. The mask had simply become more convincing.

Rader's life now moved according to a rhythm that would have looked comforting to anyone on the outside. Weekdays were for work, weekends for family, Sundays for church. There were barbecues, neighborhood conversations, small-town gossip. He attended Scout meetings, civic events, and city council gatherings with equal precision. He shook hands, exchanged pleasantries, and made lists of things to fix or enforce. He was not a man apart from the world, he was woven into its fabric. And that, more than any weapon or rope, was his greatest advantage.

People trusted him because he looked trustworthy. The glasses, the polite speech, the pressed shirts, all contributed to a carefully curated aura of decency. Even his job title lent weight to the illusion. As Park City's compliance officer, Rader's work revolved around upholding order, enforcing the small laws that made life predictable. When he knocked on doors to discuss grass heights or stray dogs, residents saw a civil servant doing his job. They had no reason to fear the clipboard in his hand, though it might as well have been a confession. Behind every rule he enforced lay the same psychological thread that tied his crimes together: control.

He loved the authority his position granted. When residents protested his citations, he remained calm, even smug. The tension thrilled him. It mirrored, in miniature, the feeling he once had when victims pleaded and struggled under his bindings. It was power sanitized, made acceptable by bureaucracy. The difference was only in degree. Every rule he enforced, every reprimand he issued, was a small echo of the domination that had once consumed him completely.

At home, life appeared stable. Paula and the children saw nothing beyond the surface. He was strict, but he provided. He mowed the lawn with geometric precision, pruned trees into symmetrical shapes, kept his tools arranged like surgical instruments. He read the newspaper cover to cover, discussed local politics, and attended family gatherings. To his family, he was reliable to a fault, sometimes dull, often rigid, but safe. The truth was that he was safest only when the mask stayed intact.

In the quiet hours after everyone slept, he shed that mask and revisited his secret world. He took out his boxes of clippings and photographs, his stolen trinkets, his sketches and notes. They were relics of a life few could imagine, but to him, they were sacred. He arranged them methodically, reviewing each item like a priest conducting a ritual. Sometimes he would dress himself in women's clothing, recreating his fantasies in front of a mirror. The reflection that stared back was grotesque and yet familiar, the truer face beneath the one he showed the world. He would take photographs of himself bound and gagged, then carefully hide the evidence again, locking it away beneath floorboards or behind false panels. It was his confessional, his private church of depravity.

The most disturbing part of this period was how easily he coexisted with his two selves. There was no torment, no battle between good and evil. The family man and the killer lived side by side, taking turns with casual ease. On Saturday, he might attend a Scout camping trip; on Sunday, he would lead a prayer at church; and on Monday night, he might prowl a neighborhood, watching windows from the darkness. The mask didn't restrain him, it empowered him. It gave him access. It gave him freedom.

The community, for its part, enabled him through its blindness. In small towns, people are accustomed to thinking they know one another. Evil, in their minds, is something foreign, an intrusion from elsewhere. They saw Rader's tidy home, his wife, his well-behaved children, and concluded he was one of the good ones. They mistook his rigidity for morality, his rules for righteousness. Even when his behavior bordered on invasive, when he took photographs of other people's yards or berated residents over trivial violations, they brushed it off. "That's just Dennis," they said. Every excuse they made for his arrogance, every blind spot they indulged, became another brick in the wall that hid the truth.

In a strange way, Rader's very mediocrity protected him. He was not charismatic or charming like other serial killers who drew attention to themselves. He was plain. Forgettable. His ordinariness was his camouflage. People remembered him as the man with the clipboard, the one who quoted city codes, the guy who talked too much about lawn maintenance. No one remembers monsters who look like bureaucrats. That was his genius, he never looked like a threat.

And so the illusion of safety persisted. Wichita moved on, convinced that BTK was a ghost from another era. Families who remembered the terror of the 1970s grew older, their memories fading into the kind of fear that feels almost imaginary in hindsight. Young people grew up hearing the stories as if they were urban legends. Even the police files gathered dust, the case numbers growing stale. BTK was a name without a face, a nightmare that had long since passed. All the while, Dennis Rader walked among them, carrying groceries, attending meetings, waving from his driveway.

The irony was profound: the more time passed, the safer he became. Every year without another murder reinforced the myth of his innocence. He no longer needed to kill to feel powerful. The fact that he could live undetected gave him an even greater thrill. The mask had become its own reward. It was a constant test of his superiority, the idea that he was smarter than everyone else, that he could deceive an entire city for decades. He often wrote in his journals about the "game," as he called it, the endless performance that only he knew was happening.

When he looked around Park City, he saw not a community but a stage. Every person he interacted with was a character in his play, each serving the role he assigned them. Paula was the loyal wife. His children were the symbols of respectability. His church peers were the audience. And he was both actor and director, orchestrating the illusion down to the smallest gesture. It wasn't just deception anymore, it was art. He took pride in the perfection of it.

What no one could have known was that beneath that performance, BTK was only dormant, not dead. The desires still pulsed inside him, the fantasies still flickered. His obsession with control was a hunger that never left. He had learned to feed it quietly, in secret rituals and private reenactments, but it was always there, whispering, waiting. Every sermon he delivered, every citation he issued, every polite nod to a neighbor was another turn of the screw tightening the mask against his skin.

For nearly three decades, he lived this way, an unbroken illusion of decency wrapped around a hollow core. When the truth finally surfaced, when the mask was torn away, the shock would be seismic. People would look back and realize that the signs were always there, hidden in plain sight. But by then, it would be too late.

Nobody really knew Dennis Rader. Not his wife. Not his children. Not his church. Not even himself. The mask had become him. And behind that mask, BTK never stopped watching.

Chapter Three
The First Killings
Blood on Wichita's Doorstep

On the morning of January 15, 1974, the city of Wichita woke beneath a low winter sun. The air was brittle with frost, lawns glazed with a thin crust of ice, and the streets still half asleep. Inside a modest home on Edgemoor Street, the Otero family began their day as they always did, coffee brewing, schoolbooks packed, children putting on their coats. They could not have known that by midmorning, every heartbeat in that house would be stilled.

For Dennis Rader, it was the culmination of years of obsession. He had selected the Oteros after weeks of reconnaissance, a quiet surveillance operation conducted from his car and during fabricated "errands" for work. He knew their routines, the father's job at an airbase, the mother's habits, the children's school schedules. He had driven past their home so many times that it felt familiar, almost intimate. He believed he could predict every movement inside it. The night before, he laid out his tools: a pistol, ropes, cords, tape, and a roll of plastic. He called it his "hit kit," as though murder were simply another task on his list.

The plan was simple in his mind: enter, subdue, bind, control, and kill. But even the most rehearsed fantasies collapse against the chaos of real life.

When he approached the Otero home that morning, he expected only Julie and the children to be there. Instead, he saw signs that Joseph Otero, the father, had not yet left for work. The risk was enormous, an entire family inside, including a grown man who might fight back. For a moment, he considered leaving. Then the other voice spoke, the one he later called Factor X. It whispered that this was destiny, that backing out now would be weakness. He slipped on gloves, pulled his weapon from his belt, and knocked on the door.

The details of what followed remain among the most chilling ever documented in American crime. Rader entered under false pretenses, telling the Oteros that he was a fugitive who needed their car and some money. He spoke softly, reassuring them that no one would be hurt if they cooperated. They believed him, at least for a moment. He ordered them to lie on the floor, binding their hands and feet one by one. He moved methodically, switching between husband, wife, and children, tightening the ropes with careful precision. His calmness was terrifying, he never shouted, never cursed. He spoke in measured tones, the way a parent might instruct a child.

But Rader had never intended to leave them alive. When Joseph Otero began to struggle, Rader tightened the cord around his neck. The man gasped and fought, but the bindings held. Rader watched the life leave him, studying his reactions with the detachment of a man observing an experiment. Julie begged him to stop, but her pleas only fed his sense of control. He strangled her next, then the children, first eleven-year-old Joseph Jr., then eleven-year-old Josephine. Each killing took time, each one less efficient than he expected. Later, in his confession, he would recall these moments not with remorse, but with technical critique, how the ligatures slipped, how the victims moved, how he might improve next time. He referred to them as "errors."

When it was done, the house was silent. Four bodies lay bound and lifeless, positioned as though sleep had overtaken them mid-movement. Rader moved through the rooms calmly, adjusting details, checking for missed evidence. He lingered, not in fear but in fascination. He took a few small items, a watch, a radio, and then paused before Josephine's body. Something about the child's death disturbed even his warped sense of control. In a later confession, he admitted to returning briefly to the basement where she hung from a pipe, taking a final, chilling moment to absorb the scene. To him, it was not horror; it was satisfaction.

He left through the back door and drove home. On the way, he stopped for a snack. That was the measure of his calm, four murders behind him, and he could still eat. When he walked through his front door, Paula was in the kitchen, unaware. He smiled, hung up his coat, and became her husband again.

The discovery came that afternoon when the Oteros' teenage son, Charlie, returned from school. The boy's screams carried down the street, summoning neighbors and police. The first responding officers found a scene that defied understanding. The bindings, the positioning of the bodies, the cold deliberation, it was unlike anything Wichita had seen. Investigators initially believed it was a robbery gone wrong or a personal vendetta. They cataloged evidence, took photographs, and searched for prints, but the crime made no sense. Nothing valuable was missing. There were no signs of forced entry beyond what the killer created himself. The violence seemed deliberate yet detached.

The coroner's report confirmed strangulation as the cause of death for all four victims. But even as the evidence mounted, it offered no explanation. The brutality was surgical, not impulsive. Whoever had done this had taken his time. Detectives theorized about multiple suspects, possibly a gang, possibly someone with military training. They could not imagine that it was the work of one man who had driven home to a quiet dinner that same night.

Rader followed the coverage obsessively. He clipped every article, listening to radio reports, watching television updates. He was elated by the confusion. They didn't know. They couldn't know. He replayed the scene in his mind over and over, polishing the memory until it became a story he told himself, a story in which he was the architect of fear and chaos, a man too intelligent to be caught. In his journals, he described the rush as "electric." The act of killing was not enough; the aftermath completed it. Seeing his name, well, not his name yet, but his handiwork, on the front page was proof of his superiority.

He had chosen the Oteros carefully. They represented what he envied most: order, structure, family unity. Killing them was not random; it was symbolic. They were everything he appeared to be but was not. By destroying them, he confirmed his secret power, asserting dominance over the life he could only mimic. In the years to come, he would seek similar victims, women and families that reflected stability, normalcy, or independence. Each was a mirror he longed to shatter.

Rader's arrogance began to grow in the days after the murders. He could feel it swelling inside him, a sense of invincibility that bordered on divine. He had done something monumental, and yet no one suspected him. He saw police cars on his street and felt only pride. He passed neighbors discussing the murders and nodded gravely, pretending to share their shock. At church, he bowed his head in prayer, pretending to mourn the tragedy that he himself had orchestrated. Every gesture of sympathy deepened the pleasure of his deception.

The trophies he took became sacred relics. The radio, the watch, and other items he pocketed were not valuable in any material sense. They were physical proof that the power he felt that morning had been real. Late at night, he would take them out, hold them, and feel again the surge of dominance that came with taking a life. These small rituals anchored him, giving form to his fantasies between killings. He was already planning his next one before the city had even buried the Oteros.

Wichita, meanwhile, was in mourning. Families locked their doors. Churches held vigils. Newspapers described the crime as "satanic," "unthinkable," "an act of pure evil." The words did little to ease the fear. For months afterward, the Otero house stood as a symbol of the unknown horror that had invaded the heart of the city. It was the day innocence ended, the day Wichita learned that evil did not always come from strangers in the night, it could live down the street, smiling politely as it passed.

Rader watched it all unfold, unseen, untouched. The city's panic was his masterpiece. It was what he had wanted from the beginning: not merely to kill, but to be remembered, to be feared. In the silence of his basement, surrounded by his notes and trophies, he smiled to himself. BTK had been born.

In the days that followed the Otero murders, Wichita was a city without sleep. Patrol cars prowled neighborhoods that had never seen real crime before. Parents checked locks twice, some three times, before going to bed. The Otero home, once an ordinary suburban house, became a haunted landmark. Police tape fluttered in the cold wind like a warning banner. The words "massacre" and "butchery" filled headlines across Kansas. For the first time in living memory, Wichita no longer felt safe.

Dennis Rader moved among the frightened with the composure of a man attending his own funeral and hearing everyone eulogize a stranger. He walked past people in grocery stores whispering about the killer. He sat in church pews while parishioners prayed for the victims. He listened to radio reports about the "madman" who must surely be from out of town.

Every word was nourishment. They were afraid, and they didn't know who to fear. That, to him, was power in its purest form.

Each evening, he sat in his easy chair and read every newspaper article he could find. He clipped them, highlighted them, annotated them in the margins. It was as though he was collecting reviews of his performance. He studied the reporters' descriptions, the detectives' theories, the community's speculation. He was fascinated by how wrong they all were. They called the killer a psychopath, a monster, maybe even a group of men working together. No one considered the possibility that the murderer was a married father, a church leader, a man who installed home alarms for a living.

Rader savored the irony. At work, customers begged him to install security systems after the Otero killings. They wanted protection, reassurance. And he, the man they feared without knowing, sold them safety one alarm at a time. "People are so predictable," he would later write in his journals. "They believe the danger is out there, never here."

Investigators worked tirelessly but were quickly overwhelmed by the senselessness of the crime. The lead detective, Lieutenant Bernie Drowatzky, said it felt like "a murder with no motive and no meaning." The Oteros had no enemies, no debts, no scandal. Their house hadn't been ransacked. Nothing fit the pattern of burglary or revenge. Detectives scoured pawn shops, interviewed co-workers, and followed dead-end leads. Every clue pointed to someone who seemed to have vanished into the air.

Rader followed the investigation's progress obsessively. When police described the killer as "methodical but careless," he bristled with pride and anger at once. They didn't understand. He wanted them to understand. His ego demanded acknowledgment. Killing had given him a taste of godhood, but anonymity left him starving. He wanted to be recognized, not as Dennis Rader, of course, but as something larger, something mythical. BTK.

That name came to him like an artist signing his work. Bind. Torture. Kill. It was not just what he did; it was who he was. The simplicity of it appealed to his need for order. It was a formula, a process, a ritual. He saw himself as the engineer of suffering, the conductor of pain. Every word of the acronym was deliberate, each a piece of the identity he was constructing.

Before he could give the name to the world, he rehearsed how he would reveal it. He wanted the police to know that Wichita had a new kind of killer, one who could think, plan, and strike without leaving a trace. He studied crime stories in magazines, noting how other killers had communicated with the press. The Zodiac Killer in California had written letters, and Rader admired his flair for publicity. But he wanted to go further. He wanted precision, structure, almost literary formality. When he finally put pen to paper, his handwriting was careful, his grammar oddly stiff, his tone coldly professional.

He began with the words, "Those three items you have listed in your paper are very correct. I did it myself." The letter, addressed to a local television station and later delivered to The Wichita Eagle, contained details that only the killer could have known, the bindings, the positions of the bodies, the sequence of deaths. He described his crimes clinically, as though he were reporting a completed assignment. "It's hard to control myself," he wrote, "you probably call me psychotic with sexual perversion hang-up." And then, almost proudly, he declared, "The code words for me will be... Bind them, Torture them, Kill them, BTK."

When the letter arrived, it detonated like a bomb. The media immediately grasped its implications: the killer was still out there, watching, reading. The city, already on edge, descended into panic. Wichita's quiet neighborhoods became fortresses overnight. People changed their routines, avoided walking alone, and looked twice at every stranger. Women reported being followed by cars, men claimed to see shadows near their homes. Some of it was hysteria. Some of it wasn't.

Rader reveled in the chaos he had created. Each headline was a mirror held up to his ego. "BTK WRITES POLICE." "MURDERER TAUNTS CITY." "KILLER DEMANDS RECOGNITION." These were the words he had longed for. He clipped every article, labeling and filing them meticulously in a private folder he titled "My Projects." He read them before bed, savoring each sentence like a prayer.

He was not content with fame; he wanted mythology. He began crafting his own narrative, telling himself that he was a new breed of killer, a man guided by unseen forces, driven by something beyond ordinary evil. Factor X became his mantra, his justification. "There's something dark in me," he later said. "It's been with me since I was young. I can't get rid of it." It was a lie he told himself to avoid confronting the simpler truth: he killed because he wanted to, because it made him feel powerful, because he enjoyed it.

The Otero murders had awakened something that could never sleep again. He found himself revisiting the neighborhood, driving past the house late at night, staring at the windows now covered with plywood. He knew the police still watched the site occasionally, hoping the killer might return. He smiled at the thought. He had already returned, many times, hidden behind his windshield, watching his own legend from the dark.

Investigators pored over his letter for clues. They studied the typeface, the syntax, the phrases that seemed oddly formal. Linguistic experts said the writer sounded educated, perhaps middle-class, maybe religious. They were right, but that profile only widened the field, it could have described half of Wichita. Police questioned hundreds of suspects, from factory workers to military men. None matched. BTK became a phantom.

As weeks turned into months, Rader began to enjoy the idea that he was untouchable. He had killed an entire family in daylight, left his calling card, and walked away unscathed. He believed he was destined for something larger, a game between himself and the world. His arrogance grew in proportion to his invisibility. He even joked about the killings with colleagues, disguised as idle chatter. When a co-worker remarked that the killer must have been insane, Rader smiled faintly and said, "Maybe he just liked control." No one thought anything of it.

The Otero investigation stretched into the summer without results. Leads dried up, and detectives grew exhausted. The city's fear settled into uneasy routine. People wanted to move on. They needed to believe the killer had fled. But Dennis Rader knew better. He knew he was still there, living among them, installing alarms, shaking hands, attending services. He was already planning again, already seeking his next "project."

The Otero case changed Wichita forever. Before that day, it was a city of unlocked doors and small kindnesses. Afterward, suspicion became a part of life. The name BTK had entered the public lexicon, a shadow at the edge of every conversation. Parents whispered it to their children as a warning. Police officers felt it every time they approached a darkened house. It was more than fear; it was transformation. And behind it all, in his quiet home on Independence Street, Dennis Rader sat reading his own myth, smiling at the world that had made him invisible.

The letter had done exactly what Dennis Rader intended, it had given life to the name BTK. The initials were simple, brutal, unforgettable. Newspapers printed them in bold black type; anchors said them in hushed tones on the evening news. Each mention sent a thrill through him. The name was no longer just an idea in his mind; it was public, alive, and feared. BTK had become a character in Wichita's imagination, and Rader relished playing him.

He collected every scrap of coverage, filing it away in the tidy boxes that lined his basement shelves. He titled one box "BTK Files," another "Projects." Inside were clippings, sketches, maps, and photographs, his own private museum of terror. The boxes were labeled in careful handwriting, organized like police evidence, though the evidence pointed only to him. He was meticulous, obsessed with documentation. Even his fantasies were cataloged like case files.

When he reread his first letter, he analyzed it like a craftsman judging his own work. The tone, the word choice, the structure, all were just right, he thought, but perhaps too restrained. Next time, he told himself, he would be bolder. He wanted to be understood, even admired, for his precision. The Zodiac Killer had written in riddles; Jack the Ripper had teased London with his mystery. Rader wanted to outdo them both. He saw himself as a man of intellect, a killer with order and method. What others called evil, he called art.

In truth, there was nothing artistic about what he did. His crimes were messy, cruel, clumsy. But the myth he built around them gave him meaning. The mask he wore in public, the husband, the Scout leader, the church councilman, had always been his disguise. Now, BTK became his truer identity, the one that existed when no one else was watching. The murders were not only acts of violence; they were performances for an audience he could control. And the audience, now terrified and captive, was the entire city of Wichita.

While investigators combed through dead-end leads, Rader returned to his routines with unsettling ease. At work, he measured grass lengths and wrote citations. At home, he watched television with his wife and children. On weekends, he attended Scout events and church meetings. All the while, he thought about the Oteros, the ropes, the sounds, the way their bodies had gone still. The memories weren't nightmares; they were trophies he replayed for pleasure. Sometimes, late at night, he would stage reenactments in his basement, binding himself, dressing in women's underwear, photographing his own fantasy. He called these "projects," too. Each session was both a rehearsal and a reminder.

The city's fear gave him power. Every police patrol, every whispered rumor, every frightened headline was an acknowledgment of his presence. He watched people double-lock their doors and install alarms, many of which he personally set up through his job at ADT. He took satisfaction in the irony. They were hiring BTK to protect them from BTK. It was almost divine, he thought, a perfect circle of control.

As the weeks passed, his confidence became arrogance. He began to believe he could do anything and remain unseen. The police were intelligent, yes, but he was smarter. They searched for patterns he intentionally distorted. He left clues designed to mislead, phrases meant to confuse. When he read articles about the investigation's failures, he grinned. "They'll never figure it out," he wrote in one of his journals. "They're not thinking the way I think."

He also began studying his own psychology, describing in his notes the emotions he felt before, during, and after a killing. He dissected his impulses like a scientist. He wrote about the "build-up phase," when his fantasies consumed him; the "act-out phase," when he committed the crime; and the "cooling phase," when he relived it through memory and ritual. He understood his compulsions not as madness, but as a system, a cycle he could control, manage, and perfect. It was delusion, but it gave him structure. He began referring to this process as "the Factor X Cycle."

The name Factor X had become his private theology. In interviews years later, Rader described it as "the dark side of me, something that makes me do what I do." But Factor X was not an external force; it was a story he told himself to justify his cravings. It allowed him to feel both chosen and blameless. He wrote, "Factor X is like the devil. It's part of me. God created it, and I must serve it." The language was grandiose, self-pitying, almost religious. In truth, it was just another layer of the mask, this time one he wore for himself.

In the spring of 1974, Rader began stalking again. His next "project," as he called it, was a young woman named Kathryn Bright, a college student who lived with her brother. He watched her from a distance for weeks, noting her schedule, studying her home. He planned another perfect attack, another moment of domination. But when he finally acted in April, things went wrong. Kathryn's brother, Kevin, was home that day. When Rader broke in, the encounter turned chaotic. Kevin fought back, struggling fiercely despite being shot and stabbed. Rader panicked, losing control of the scene. Kathryn was bound and stabbed multiple times, but Kevin managed to escape, staggering into the street, bleeding but alive.

It was the first time Rader failed. The news humiliated him. A survivor meant imperfection, a flaw in his system. He read the reports with anger and self-recrimination, analyzing what he had done wrong. He blamed luck, timing, and what he called "the human element." But deep down, he knew he had lost control. His arrogance had nearly exposed him. The fact that Kevin Bright survived should have led to his capture, but it didn't. The police never connected the attack conclusively to the Otero case. BTK remained a ghost.

That close call should have frightened him. Instead, it inflated his ego further. He believed he was untouchable, chosen, protected. He told himself that God, or Factor X, had spared him for greater acts. He returned to his routines, tightening the mask once more. The city was still in panic, still speaking his name, and he was still invisible. It was intoxicating.

Wichita's fear by now had become ritualized. Residents changed the way they lived. Hardware stores sold out of locks and chains. Gun sales rose. Churches preached about vigilance and morality. Local newspapers ran editorials about the city's "lost innocence." BTK had become not just a killer, but a symbol, an unseen force haunting the edges of daily life. Mothers warned daughters not to answer the door. Men left lights on all night. Every knock, every unfamiliar car, sent ripples of anxiety through neighborhoods.

And through it all, Dennis Rader walked among them. He installed alarm systems for fearful families. He joined neighborhood watch meetings to discuss safety. He volunteered for church security patrols. He even took part in conversations about BTK, offering theories about the killer's motives. "He probably gets off on control," he once said to a co-worker, barely suppressing a smile. The pleasure of deception was greater than the pleasure of killing. Each time he fooled someone, it reaffirmed his superiority.

Yet beneath the thrill, something else was growing, a dependency. The attention, the fear, the coverage, it all fed him like oxygen. When the headlines began to fade, he felt restless, irritable. The world was moving on, and he couldn't allow that. BTK, he believed, was too important to be forgotten. If fear was his currency, he needed to keep spending it. He began writing again, drafting new letters, new communications, new taunts. The need to be remembered was stronger than the need to kill. He didn't just want to commit crimes; he wanted to be a story.

The legend of BTK was spreading beyond Wichita now. Newspapers across Kansas and neighboring states ran features about the "mystery strangler." Television crews filmed outside the Otero home, broadcasting images of the yellowed siding and broken blinds. True crime magazines speculated about his psychology. Some compared him to Jack the Ripper. Others warned he might never be caught. Each comparison was a victory for Rader. The more they mythologized BTK, the more powerful he felt. He wasn't just a man anymore, he was an idea.

He began to think about his crimes the way artists think about legacy. He wanted to leave behind something permanent, something undeniable. He fantasized about future generations studying him, analyzing him, admiring his "discipline." In his private writings, he described his killings as "projects of perfection." He didn't see victims; he saw blueprints. He didn't see suffering; he saw symmetry. It was the ultimate delusion of a man who mistook murder for mastery.

But behind the arrogance, a shadow of paranoia began to stir. He knew that the police were still collecting evidence. He imagined detectives poring over his letters, tracing his words back to him. He began altering his habits, changing his stationery, varying his handwriting, watching his neighbors more closely. He even attended community safety meetings to listen to police briefings. It was part performance, part self-preservation. The mask had to hold.

And it did.

For now.

By the summer of 1974, the Otero killings and the Bright attack had left Wichita paralyzed. There had been no arrests, no confessions, no clear suspects, only a name: BTK. Those three letters hung over the city like a storm cloud. The police held press conferences, but they had nothing new to say. The public demanded answers, and the media filled the silence with speculation. Talk shows debated whether BTK was still in Wichita or had fled. Some said he would never strike again. Others said he was watching, waiting. Everyone agreed on one thing, fear had taken up permanent residence.

For Dennis Rader, that fear was victory. He fed on it quietly, like a parasite drawing strength from the panic of others. Each time he saw a frightened face in a store, each time he overheard someone whisper the letters "B-T-K," he felt a pulse of satisfaction. He didn't need to kill again right away. The fear itself was enough. He had achieved what every predator desires, not just domination of individuals, but of an entire community. Wichita was his captive audience.

The police task force, meanwhile, was drowning in dead ends. Every clue led nowhere. Fingerprints at the Otero house didn't match anyone in the database. The knots used on the victims were too common to trace. The bullets from the Bright attack were unremarkable. Even the letter, which Rader saw as his masterpiece, offered little forensic value. It had been typed on an ordinary machine using words cut from newspapers, a tactic he thought clever, though in hindsight it only revealed his obsession with theatrics. The detectives felt like they were chasing a ghost who could appear anywhere and vanish at will.

Rader followed their frustration like an avid reader following a serialized story. He read police statements line by line, circling phrases, noting inconsistencies, and taking pride in their confusion. It was as if he were grading their work. He had become both the author and the critic of his own legend. When he saw detectives described as "baffled" or "haunted," he smiled. He wanted them haunted. He wanted them to go home at night thinking about him, dreaming about him. That was his immortality.

But even as his arrogance swelled, his life above ground remained eerily normal. He went to work, raised his children, attended services, and mowed his lawn. Wichita's panic became background noise, and he thrived in the normalcy that others found unbearable. While his neighbors double-locked their doors, he walked confidently under the same streetlights they feared. He felt invisible, protected by the plainness of his life. The disguise was perfect precisely because it wasn't a disguise, it was routine.

He began to think of the city as his canvas. Every newspaper headline was a brushstroke, every patrol car another line in his masterpiece of control. He didn't need to act to maintain power; he only needed to exist. His silence became a weapon. Months passed with no new murders, and still his name dominated conversations. The absence of violence became its own kind of terror. People wondered if he had died, been arrested, or simply gone dormant. The uncertainty kept them awake at night. Rader found the power intoxicating. He could do nothing and still make the world tremble.

But silence was also a test. He was addicted to attention, and like all addictions, it demanded more. When the headlines began to fade, he felt an emptiness that frightened him. The city was starting to breathe again. Locks still clicked at night, but laughter had returned to playgrounds. He could feel his grip loosening. The power he had tasted was slipping away.

He turned inward, retreating to his secret rituals. In the basement, surrounded by his boxes of clippings and trophies, he recreated the fear he missed. He read old news articles aloud, whispering them like prayers. He arranged photographs of his victims, lighting them with a single lamp as if conducting a ceremony. Sometimes he bound himself again, posing for self-portraits that captured his fantasies of control and surrender. These sessions weren't about pleasure anymore, they were about preservation. They kept BTK alive when the world began to forget.

His journals from this time are disturbing in their calmness. He wrote about "the quiet between projects" as though describing weather patterns. "Like a storm system," he noted, "it passes and returns." He spoke of his need to "recharge the battery," of "building up energy for the next project." He described fear as something tangible, almost chemical, that he could sense in the air. "It's like static," he wrote. "I can feel it before a strike."

He viewed his crimes not as acts of emotion, but as natural phenomena, inevitable, cyclical, beyond his control.

Meanwhile, Wichita tried to reclaim its sense of normalcy. The police department formed a dedicated task force nicknamed "The Ghostbusters," assigned solely to track BTK. Hundreds of tips poured in, most of them useless. A psychic claimed the killer lived near a park. A neighbor reported seeing a suspicious man carrying rope in his car. A child insisted that BTK was hiding in their attic. The city's paranoia became absurd, but it was also understandable. When evil is invisible, it multiplies in imagination.

Rader watched it all unfold from the safety of his living room. He read about the psychic with amusement, about the police theories with contempt. He felt superior to everyone involved, victims, detectives, reporters, even the public itself. "They all think they're in control," he later said. "They're not." To him, the investigation was another theater, another stage for his performance. The more effort they wasted, the greater his victory.

His wife Paula noticed none of his detachment. He smiled, he worked, he prayed. On the surface, he was the same man he had always been. Yet something about him had changed, even if she couldn't articulate it. He was colder now, more rigid, less human. The things that used to animate him, family outings, Scout trips, Sunday dinners, seemed to bore him. When he wasn't working or attending church, he often disappeared into the basement for hours. She assumed he was tinkering with tools or writing church notes. She never looked too closely.

That blindness was his greatest protection. No one suspected Dennis Rader because no one wanted to. The thought that a family man, a husband, a father, a fellow parishioner, could be the monster that had terrorized Wichita was unthinkable. People preferred to believe in an outsider, a drifter, someone who didn't belong. Rader belonged too well. His very normalcy was his camouflage. He had built it perfectly, and the world rewarded him for it.

As the months turned into years, the investigation lost momentum. Detectives retired, leads dried up, the task force disbanded. The files were boxed, labeled, and shelved. BTK became another unsolved case, a ghost of the 1970s. Wichita tried to move on, convincing itself that the killer had died or moved away. The city's wounds began to scar over, but the fear never truly left. It lingered in small ways, the way people hesitated before opening a door, the way parents checked windows before bed, the way a shadow in the yard could still make a heart race.

Rader noticed that fear, still faint but alive, and he smiled. He had changed Wichita forever, and he knew it. Every act of caution, every whisper of unease, was a monument to him. He didn't need statues or headlines. The city itself was his memorial.

In his own mind, Dennis Rader was not a criminal but a creator. He had built something enduring, an invisible empire of fear that stretched through every neighborhood. His silence was the mortar that held it together. While the police archived their case files, he archived his trophies. While the city exhaled relief, he inhaled satisfaction. He had written himself into Wichita's history, not as a man of flesh and blood, but as a name, three letters, sharp as a blade: BTK.

And for nearly a decade, that name would vanish from headlines but not from memory. The mask would harden, the routine would deepen, and the city would forget just enough for him to strike again.

Chapter Four

Letters to the Police
The BTK Persona

When Dennis Rader sat down to type his first letter, he was not trembling with guilt or fear. He was excited. The Otero killings had made him a secret legend in his own mind, but the anonymity gnawed at him. The papers had printed the story of the murders again and again, but they had gotten it wrong. They had called it "a random home invasion," "a senseless act of brutality." To Rader, those words were insults. His crimes were not random. They were carefully planned, deliberate, precise. He wanted the world to know that there was a method behind the horror, a craftsman behind the chaos.

In his small, tidy home on Independence Street, he prepared his letter the way another man might prepare a sermon. The typewriter sat on a desk surrounded by notes and newspaper clippings. He chose his words with care, speaking in the detached, almost bureaucratic tone that would later become his hallmark. There was no rage, no remorse, only pride. "Those three items you have listed in your paper are very correct," he typed, "I did it myself with my hands."

He did not sign his name. He signed an idea. "The code words for me will be… Bind them, Torture them, Kill them, BTK."

When that letter arrived at *The Wichita Eagle* in October 1974, the newsroom fell silent. The editor, a veteran of crime reporting, read it twice before calling the police. The details inside were too precise to dismiss: the bindings, the order of deaths, the position of Josephine's body. Only the killer could have known them. There was no doubt now, he was alive, and he wanted to talk.

For Rader, this was the moment he had been waiting for. The city had feared the Otero killer, but it had not known him. Now, through his words, he could shape the fear, give it a name, control its narrative. In that single act of communication, he ceased to be a faceless murderer and became something far more powerful: an author of his own legend.

His need for recognition bordered on religious. He saw fame not as vanity, but as validation, a way to prove his superiority. Other men built careers or families; Rader built myth. In his mind, notoriety was immortality. He had studied the cases of other killers who had written to the press, the Zodiac, Jack the Ripper, the Black Dahlia Avenger, and decided that BTK would outshine them all. They killed for chaos. He killed for order. They taunted for attention. He would taunt for control.

The first article to publish excerpts of his letter exploded like a bomb in Wichita's collective psyche. For months, people had tried to believe that the Otero murders were a one-time horror. The letter destroyed that illusion. It proved that the killer was still out there, watching, intelligent, confident. His self-naming was especially terrifying. "Bind. Torture. Kill." The words themselves were a blueprint of suffering, simple, brutal, unforgettable. The city finally had a name for its nightmare, and that name was everywhere.

The media coverage was relentless. Reporters dissected every word of the letter, searching for clues in grammar, phrasing, and spelling. Experts speculated about the killer's background, suggesting he was educated, perhaps with military or law enforcement experience. They were partly right, and Rader loved it. He cut out each article and stored it in a folder labeled "BTK News." He reread them obsessively, savoring the way his words were analyzed by strangers who had no idea that the man they sought was reading their every theory over breakfast.

He was particularly proud of his writing style, though it betrayed him more than he knew. His letters were filled with awkward phrasing and misspellings, words like "advis" instead of "advise," "choosen" instead of "chosen." They were the linguistic fingerprints of a man trying too hard to sound formal, mimicking the tone of authority he so desperately craved. To the public, the errors made him sound unhinged. To Rader, they made him sound official, as if BTK were not merely a man but a force of nature with bureaucratic precision.

The police understood the danger of his correspondence, but they also recognized its value. The letters were evidence, breadcrumbs left by a man too proud to remain silent. Linguists, psychologists, and handwriting experts were brought in to analyze them. They noted the killer's grandiosity, his obsession with structure, his need for validation. He wrote not like a madman, but like a man desperate to be understood. That made him more dangerous.

Rader watched the investigation unfold from his living room with quiet amusement. He felt like a puppeteer, pulling strings that made the city dance. Each time the police held a press conference, he scrutinized their faces, their words, their tone. If they looked confident, he would plan another letter to remind them who was in control. If they looked frustrated, he savored it like wine. The fear he created was not spontaneous, it was orchestrated, measured, almost scientific.

What fascinated him most was how easily the media became his accomplice. Every article, every broadcast fed his ego. They called him "elusive," "methodical," "brilliant." Even their warnings glorified him. "Lock your doors," they said, "BTK is watching." That was exactly what he wanted, to be omnipresent, a phantom who existed in every locked room and every dark corner. Wichita wasn't just afraid of him; it was obsessed with him.

The more the city feared BTK, the more Rader feared being forgotten. The paradox defined him. Each letter was a desperate attempt to stay relevant, to keep his myth alive. He once wrote, "I'm waiting on a call from the media… I want recognition for my work." To him, the killings were work, projects completed, assignments fulfilled. Murder was not a crime in his mind; it was an achievement.

Detectives, meanwhile, walked a tightrope between secrecy and disclosure. If they released too much of his writing, they risked encouraging him. If they released too little, he might grow restless and strike again. The police chief called him "a narcissist with a typewriter," and he wasn't wrong. Rader's hunger for attention was insatiable. His letters grew longer, more elaborate, filled with self-analysis and invented terminology. He called his crimes "projects," his victims "subjects." He referred to himself as "a serial killer in the making." The self-awareness was chilling. He didn't just know what he was, he reveled in it.

His relationship with the police became a kind of correspondence game, a dialogue between hunter and hunted, though Rader always saw himself as the hunter. He wanted to prove that he could manipulate them, control their reactions, dictate their movements. Each letter was a test of power: could he make them look where he wanted, think what he wanted, fear what he wanted? And time after time, he could.

But what Rader failed to see was that the very thing he believed made him invincible, his need for recognition, was also his weakness. The more he wrote, the more he revealed. His phrasing, his rhythm, even his typewriter model became clues. Detectives noticed that his writing mirrored the tone of certain church documents and community notices. They speculated that the killer might be someone involved in civic life, perhaps even a man of faith. They were closer than they realized.

Still, for the moment, BTK reigned unchallenged. His words had turned him into a specter that stalked Wichita's imagination. Children whispered his name in schoolyards; adults avoided speaking it aloud. He was both real and mythic, everywhere and nowhere. The letters were more than confessions, they were performances. And like all performers, Dennis Rader craved applause.

He got it.

Every headline was a standing ovation.

By 1978, the city of Wichita had learned to flinch at the sight of an unmarked envelope. Every new letter that arrived at a newsroom or police station carried the same dread: another message from the unseen phantom who called himself BTK. The handwriting changed, sometimes typed, sometimes scrawled, but the tone was unmistakable, cold, self-congratulatory, obsessed with control. The envelopes were postmarked from within the city, taunting the investigators who still had no face to attach to the name.

Rader had discovered the intoxicating power of communication. Murder had given him control over individuals; the letters gave him control over an entire city. With a few paragraphs, he could send detectives scrambling, journalists into frenzy, and citizens into sleepless paranoia. Words became his new weapon, cleaner, safer, and far more theatrical.

Each letter was composed with ceremony. He would type or handwrite in his quiet home, often late at night after his family was asleep. His desk would be neat, his materials arranged with military precision: scissors, tape, envelopes, stamps, and the same deliberate sense of ritual that marked his killings. He thought of the letters as "packages," not unlike his "projects." Every word, every comma, every oddly capitalized phrase was chosen to project authority. He wanted to sound educated but also mysterious, a criminal mastermind who enjoyed watching the police struggle to understand him.

In truth, his writing revealed as much insecurity as intellect. He often misspelled common words, "torture" as "tortuer," "advice" as "advis," "choose" as "choosen." He wrote in a stilted, almost mechanical cadence, overusing semicolons and capital letters as though grammar could give weight to his delusions. He referred to himself in the third person, sometimes even in the plural, as if BTK were an organization rather than a man. Psychologists who studied his letters later noted how desperate he seemed to elevate himself into something larger than life. The errors, they said, weren't merely accidents; they were attempts to sound official, to cloak insanity in formality.

The police at first believed the killer might be trying to disguise his education level. Some detectives thought the mistakes were deliberate, an attempt to confuse investigators about his background. Others believed they revealed genuine limitations, that BTK was not as intelligent as he believed himself to be. In truth, both theories were partly correct. Dennis Rader was intelligent enough to plan, but not wise enough to hide his vanity. His need to be seen always outweighed his instinct for survival.

The tone of his correspondence grew darker and more theatrical with each message. In one letter, he wrote, "How many do I have to kill before I get some fame?" In another, he demanded that the media give him "credit" for crimes he claimed but had not even committed, including the murders of two women later proven to be unrelated. He wanted his name, his brand, to expand, to absorb every unsolved killing in Kansas. Fame was not enough; he wanted monopoly.

When the newspapers printed excerpts of his letters, they unintentionally gave him exactly what he wanted: immortality in ink. He clipped the articles, underlined his favorite lines, and stored them in binders. "I like the name BTK," he wrote. "It's got a nice ring to it." The ego in those words was chilling. He had turned murder into marketing.

The detectives assigned to the case faced a dilemma. They needed the letters for evidence, but they despised how much power the killer derived from them. Every public release risked feeding his vanity, yet total silence might provoke him to act again. They debated endlessly: ignore him and risk another killing, or respond and risk encouraging more correspondence? There was no good answer. Rader had forced them into his rhythm. Every move they made was reactive; he dictated the tempo.

Behind the scenes, linguistic analysts tried to decipher the hidden patterns in his writing. They studied his peculiar syntax, his fondness for formal address ("Gentlemen," "To whom it may concern"), and his occasional use of obscure biblical phrases. One expert suggested the writer might be active in a church, possibly even in a leadership role. The detectives dismissed it. The idea that a killer so depraved could also be a respected church member seemed absurd. Yet that single clue, had it been pursued more aggressively, might have exposed him years earlier.

Rader read those linguistic analyses with glee when they appeared in the papers. He imagined himself sitting across from the experts, smiling as they dissected his every word, unaware that he was reading along at his own kitchen table. He liked to imagine the police working late into the night, their desks covered in photographs, their eyes red from exhaustion, all because of him. The cat-and-mouse game had become his favorite pastime, his intellectual sport.

To further mystify investigators, he began including puzzles and coded messages in his letters. One contained a grid of numbers and symbols, another a crude map with the cryptic caption "the final resting place." Detectives spent weeks trying to decode them, convinced they contained vital clues. In reality, most were meaningless, designed purely to waste time and reinforce his illusion of genius. Rader derived deep pleasure from the thought of teams of professionals analyzing nonsense he had scribbled in minutes. To him, it was proof that he could make them dance to his music.

Even his envelopes carried a strange consistency. He folded each letter with exact symmetry, sealed them with minimal moisture, and placed the stamps in the upper-right corner with near mathematical precision. He believed that his tidiness separated him from ordinary criminals. He often bragged to himself about leaving "clean scenes" and "professional packages." To him, murder and communication were extensions of the same craft: domination through detail.

The media, for their part, began to recognize the pattern. Journalists nicknamed him "The Correspondent Killer," while columnists wrote op-eds debating whether publishing his words made them complicit. Some newspapers refused to print his full letters, while others argued that suppressing them would only inflame him further. Television anchors read excerpts on air in grave tones, their voices trembling between fear and fascination. Wichita had become a stage, and Rader was its self-appointed playwright.

The public's reaction was a mixture of horror and dark curiosity. People began collecting clippings, as if owning a piece of BTK's story could somehow contain the fear. Bookstores sold out of crime magazines featuring him. For Rader, it was intoxicating. He was no longer just a killer, he was a phenomenon. The city's obsession proved his importance. He was not forgotten. He was famous.

But the more he wrote, the more the mask of intelligence began to slip. Investigators noticed inconsistencies, contradictions in timelines, exaggerations about his crimes, even factual errors. Some detectives began to wonder if BTK was lying, if he was inflating his legend to maintain relevance. Others worried that his letters were bait, meant to divert attention from new crimes. They were both right. Rader's ego demanded constant feeding, and when reality offered too little, he manufactured his own mythology.

Every word he sent out into the world was both a confession and a shield. He needed to boast, but he also needed to mislead. The paradox drove him to keep writing even when silence would have kept him safe. His pride was louder than his caution. He taunted police with lines like, "How about some name recognition, gentlemen?" and "It's hard to control myself when I think of what I've done." The phrasing was theatrical, almost self-parodying. He wrote not to communicate, but to perform.

What he never realized was that the performance was turning against him. His letters were not just expressions of control, they were clues. Each one exposed a little more of his vocabulary, his habits, his psychology. Every envelope was a fingerprint in words. But for the moment, he was untouchable. His audience still feared him, the police still hunted him, and the newspapers still printed his name.

In his mind, BTK was not just alive, he was immortal. The killings had made him a monster. The letters made him a myth.

And for a man like Dennis Rader, myth was the only truth he ever wanted to live in.

By the late 1970s, the BTK letters had become part of Wichita's routine horror. Each new envelope that arrived at a newsroom or police precinct carried an eerie familiarity, an object that looked ordinary, yet felt like an artifact of evil. Reporters handled them with latex gloves; detectives opened them as if expecting something to leap out. Inside were Rader's latest performances: his taunts, his delusions, his twisted need to remind the world that he still existed.

Every word was an act of control. He didn't write because he had to, he wrote because he wanted to feel the city twitch under his fingertips. The murders had been physical domination; the letters were psychological. Both were about power, and power was the one thing he couldn't live without.

But even control can become an addiction. The more Rader wrote, the more he needed to outdo himself. He began to feel that each letter had to be bigger, more theatrical, more audacious than the last. The killings had stopped for now, but his craving for attention had not. To fill the void, he turned to language, each paragraph another substitute for the physical thrill he could no longer risk.

In one letter, he enclosed poems written about his victims. He titled one "Oh! Death to Nancy" and another "Shirleylocks." The words were grotesque imitations of nursery rhymes, written in the rhythm of children's verses but dripping with sadism. He described strangulation as if it were a courtship. "She squirmed and choked," one line read, "and I watched her eyes." The police were appalled by the cruelty, but the tone of the poems also revealed something else: the desperation of a man trying too hard to sound like a genius. The writing was adolescent, clumsy, and repetitive. Yet to Rader, it was art. He read and reread his poems in the privacy of his basement, reciting them aloud to himself, imagining audiences gasping at his brilliance.

Each new communication further exposed the fragile ego beneath the façade. He couldn't bear the thought of being forgotten. When newspaper coverage of BTK slowed, he grew angry. He believed the world owed him attention. In one letter, he scolded the police for not giving him enough publicity: "How many people do I have to kill before I get a name in the paper or some national recognition?" He complained as if he were an artist whose work had been ignored. The narcissism was staggering, but so was the neediness.

Detectives, meanwhile, debated whether the letters represented real danger or mere posturing. Some believed BTK had grown bored, that the correspondence was a way to relive old glories without risking exposure. Others warned that his writing was a prelude to another killing spree. They knew enough about serial offenders to understand that communication often preceded action. The more he wrote, the closer he might be to striking again.

Linguistic experts poured over the letters line by line. They noted Rader's fascination with order and lists, his formal structure, his compulsion to categorize everything. He titled his paragraphs as if they were official memos. He referred to murders as "projects" and victims as "subjects." He wrote of "phases" and "cycles," reducing human suffering to procedural language. One psychologist described it as "bureaucratic sadism", the mind of a man who turned killing into administration.

Yet there was something else in the letters that haunted investigators: the glimpses of domesticity. He mentioned "sitting at the kitchen table," "watching TV," "writing while the wife's asleep." These offhand details were easy to miss, but they painted a portrait that contradicted the myth of the lone, deranged predator. Whoever BTK was, he wasn't living in the shadows. He was one of them, an ordinary man hiding behind suburban walls.

That thought terrified the detectives. It also narrowed the scope of their search, but not enough. Wichita had thousands of men who fit the vague profile: married, middle-aged, religious, meticulous. Rader's mask of normalcy was working perfectly.

As the years passed, Rader's communication style became increasingly self-referential. He wrote about himself in the third person, as though describing a character in a novel. "BTK is like a monster in a cage," he wrote once. "He wants out, but the man inside won't let him." He seemed to believe that "Dennis" and "BTK" were separate beings, locked in a moral struggle. It was another layer of his self-mythology, a narrative that allowed him to kill without guilt. In his mind, BTK was destiny, and Dennis was merely its host.

The detectives saw through the act but couldn't pierce it. Every new letter contained just enough truth to prove authenticity, and just enough fabrication to send them down blind alleys. He loved watching them chase phantoms of his own creation. Each investigation that ended in failure was proof of his superiority. "They'll never find me," he wrote. "I'm too smart for them. They think I'm some kind of lunatic, but I'm organized. They can't see that."

In a way, he was right. They couldn't see it, not because they lacked intelligence, but because their imaginations couldn't stretch that far. They couldn't picture a killer who went home after strangling a woman, kissed his wife goodnight, and read scripture the next morning. The duality was unthinkable.

The taunting continued for years. Each time he felt forgotten, he sent another message, sometimes to the media, sometimes directly to the police. He was addicted to the response. He studied every public reaction, watching how reporters phrased their stories, how detectives answered questions. If a headline described him as clever, he clipped it and underlined it. If they mocked him as insane, he fumed and planned his next letter to "correct the record." He wanted control even over his reputation.

His correspondence began to include lists, compilations of his "projects," with cryptic notes about locations, dates, and methods. Some of the names were real, others imagined. He blurred fact and fiction intentionally, creating a mythology so dense that even he sometimes lost track of what was real. When police tried to cross-reference the names with actual missing persons, most led nowhere. He had turned murder into a kind of literature, half true, half invention, all meant to maintain power.

It wasn't lost on investigators that BTK's arrogance had a pattern. His letters often came after periods of silence, as though boredom were his true enemy. One profiler suggested that "BTK is most dangerous when ignored." The observation was prophetic. Each time Rader felt the city's fear fading, he considered killing again, not out of necessity, but to remind everyone that he was still there.

Wichita became a prisoner of its own memory. The name BTK was invoked like a curse. Children grew up hearing about him the way other cities whispered about urban legends. He had achieved what he wanted: ubiquity. He was the ghost everyone feared but no one could see.

The cat-and-mouse game reached its peak when Rader began inserting false clues into his letters, references to foreign films, archaic phrases, biblical verses. Some detectives believed these hints pointed to his identity; others saw them as deliberate misdirection. Both were true. He enjoyed the idea of sending investigators in circles, of forcing them to decode messages that meant nothing. Each wasted hour was a small act of dominance.

The media, by now, had turned him into a spectacle. Talk shows debated his psychology. Crime magazines ran speculative cover stories. National outlets compared him to Ted Bundy and the Zodiac Killer. Wichita, once an anonymous Midwestern city, had become synonymous with BTK. Rader couldn't have asked for more. The monster he had invented had eclipsed the man completely.

But beneath the triumph, cracks were beginning to show. Rader was aging. His family obligations grew heavier, his work more demanding. He found less time for his rituals, less energy for writing. The letters took longer to compose. His thrill was fading, and with it, his sense of control.

Silence began to feel like suffocation. He needed another outlet, another reminder that the world still belonged to him.

He told himself that BTK could never die, that the name was eternal. But names live only when people remember them. And soon, he feared, Wichita would forget.

That fear, the fear of being forgotten, was more powerful than any law enforcement strategy, more dangerous than any police trap. It would drive him, years later, to make the one mistake that ended everything.

But for now, BTK was still winning. His words were his kingdom, and the city of Wichita, terrified, confused, and enthralled, was still listening.

By the early 1980s, Wichita had lived with the name BTK for nearly a decade. It no longer felt like the name of a man, it had become a ghost story, a shadow whispered about in darkened kitchens and late-night news segments. "BTK'll get you," children said on playgrounds, half joking, half afraid. The city had learned to coexist with terror, to fold it into daily life like a permanent scar.

For Dennis Rader, that was the ultimate triumph. He had achieved something no ordinary killer ever could: he had become folklore. He didn't have to kill to be feared. He didn't have to act to be seen. His words alone carried weight. Every time a neighbor double-locked a door, every time a mother called her children in at dusk, he felt the echo of his power. "They still think of me," he wrote in his notes. "I am still here."

But fame, especially the kind built on fear, comes with decay. Once myth becomes routine, it begins to lose its edge. Rader could sense it. The letters that had once electrified the city now barely stirred it. Reporters still mentioned BTK occasionally, but the coverage had cooled. New crimes, new scandals, new stories filled the papers. Time was erasing him, as time always does. And that thought terrified him more than capture ever could.

To the public, BTK was dormant. To Rader, BTK was suffocating.

He reread his old letters obsessively, tracing each word with a finger as though reacquainting himself with an old lover. He studied the phrasing, the spelling, the rhythms. He still admired his own theatricality, but he also began to sense something missing, a lack of grandeur. "The public forgot too easy," he wrote in one private note. "Maybe they need a reminder of what I am capable of."

That need for recognition became his quiet obsession. He no longer sought thrills through violence; he sought validation through memory. He wanted to be remembered, not just as a killer, but as a figure of intellect, a man whose crimes were "orderly, planned, and artistic." It was absurd, even grotesque, but to Rader, the killings were his legacy, and the letters were his literature.

When he wrote, he imagined himself as a misunderstood genius communicating with lesser minds. "The police think they know me," he once typed. "They don't understand. This is all about Factor X." He used that term again and again, Factor X, the dark force he claimed drove him to kill. It was his mythology, a way to transform himself from a pervert with rope and fantasy into a vessel of destiny. In his mind, BTK wasn't evil; BTK was chosen.

Detectives reading his letters saw the same delusions but also something more fragile beneath them. The confidence had cracks. The sentences rambled. The tone swung between arrogance and anxiety. It was as though two people were fighting over the typewriter, one desperate to appear powerful, the other terrified of fading into irrelevance. The man who once commanded fear now begged for attention.

The police understood that his communication style revealed more than his words ever could. They noted his craving for acknowledgment, his compulsion to respond to silence. One behavioral analyst remarked, "BTK writes because he can't stand being ignored. He's addicted to the echo of his own name." That insight became key to understanding his psychology, and years later, it would become the lever that broke him.

In the meantime, the city adjusted to his silence. Detectives were reassigned. The task force disbanded. The files were boxed, sealed, and stored in evidence rooms. For the first time in years, Wichita exhaled. The murders faded into history, the letters into archives. Children who had grown up hearing about BTK became adults who spoke of him the way one speaks of local legends, real once, maybe, but long gone.

Rader watched this from afar with quiet fury. He had worked too hard to be forgotten. His entire life, his routines, his rituals, his secrecy, had been devoted to crafting the perfect mask and the monster behind it. Now that mask risked becoming meaningless. He wanted the world to remember his precision, his intellect, his "projects." He even imagined one day publishing his own memoirs, an autobiography of BTK, written by the killer himself. In his fantasy, he would tell his story in the calm, bureaucratic tone he loved so much, showing the world the genius they never recognized.

Of course, he couldn't publish. He couldn't even speak about it. So he wrote for himself. In private journals, he documented his crimes, his methods, his "achievements." He described his victims clinically, his fantasies in disturbing detail. The writing was meant to preserve the legend until the day it could be rediscovered. He called it his "future record." These were his letters to the world after death.

But even those writings couldn't fill the void that attention once had. The newspapers no longer printed his name. The police no longer mentioned him. BTK had become a ghost haunting a city that had moved on. The silence pressed on him like a weight. He began to feel invisible again, and invisibility to Dennis Rader was unbearable.

He sought small ways to remind himself of his power. When he read about other killers in the news, he scoffed at their mistakes. "Amateurs," he muttered, cutting out the articles and adding them to his growing scrapbook. "They don't know how to control it." He compared their crimes to his own, always concluding that BTK was smarter, cleaner, superior. The irony was cruel: the only audience for his comparisons was himself.

Meanwhile, law enforcement quietly evolved. Advances in forensic analysis, particularly in DNA collection, changed how detectives investigated unsolved crimes. Old evidence from the Otero house was reexamined. Fibers, hair samples, fingerprints, all stored carefully decades earlier, were tested again. The process was slow, but the net was tightening, though Rader couldn't see it yet.

He believed his methods had been perfect, his control absolute. He didn't know that technology was advancing faster than his myth. The same precision that had once protected him, his neat bindings, his careful planning, had preserved the microscopic traces that would one day expose him.

Still, for nearly two decades, Dennis Rader remained what he always wanted to be: invisible and immortal. He lived as a church leader, Scoutmaster, and husband. His children grew up, left home. He aged quietly into middle life. To everyone who knew him, he was the picture of normalcy. But beneath that mask, the letters, the persona he had built, were still whispering. He reread them occasionally, caressing the pages as if they were scripture. The words "Bind, Torture, Kill" still thrilled him, even after all those years.

He didn't realize that those very words would become his undoing. The letters that had made him a legend would one day betray him. His pride would lead him, years later, to reach out again, to send one final message to the police after decades of silence, desperate to feel relevant. That letter would not make him famous again. It would put handcuffs on his wrists.

But that was still far in the future. For now, the legend stood unbroken. The cat had stopped writing, the mice had stopped chasing, and the myth of BTK settled into uneasy slumber. The city moved forward. The man did not.

For Dennis Rader, the quiet wasn't peace. It was starvation.

Chapter Five
Blueprints of Depravity
The Secret Rituals That Sustained Him

In the dim light of his suburban basement, surrounded by the hum of a dehumidifier and the smell of paper and dust, Dennis Rader became someone else. Above ground, he was the dutiful husband and father, the church council president, the man who fixed fences and led Scout meetings. But below ground, in that private room of concrete and shadow, he returned to the one identity that made him feel alive. Down there, he was BTK again.

For Rader, the murders were only one chapter of a much longer story. The real narrative was written in secret, across binders, photographs, drawings, and boxes of clippings that chronicled his fantasies in obsessive detail. It was his private museum, a shrine to control. He called the collection "My Projects," but it was more than that. It was his memory, his theology, his pornography, and his confession all at once.

In that basement, he cataloged his life not as a man, but as a predator. The shelves held stacks of folders, each carefully labeled in neat handwriting: *Otero Family, Bright, Vian, Fox, Wegert*. Each name belonged to a person he had watched, stalked, or fantasized about, some real victims, some imagined. Inside the folders were photographs, newspaper clippings, sketches, maps, and written notes describing his observations. He treated each like a case study, analyzing their habits, schedules, and vulnerabilities. It wasn't enough to kill; he had to understand the geometry of his victims' lives.

His drawings were especially revealing. They were crude yet meticulous, done in pen or pencil, often on lined notebook paper. Many depicted women bound and gagged, sometimes suspended from ropes, sometimes trapped in boxes or coffins. Others were even more grotesque, scenes that mirrored his real crimes but with exaggerated theatricality. He often drew himself into the scenes, masked or hooded, standing proudly beside his victims. The art was less about violence than about staging, a performance of domination frozen on paper.

Next to the sketches, he kept a vast stash of magazine clippings. He collected images of women, models, actresses, even local advertisements, and altered them with scissors and tape. He drew ropes around their wrists, blindfolds over their eyes, or added captions like *"Captured"* or *"Subject Secured."* The images were trophies of imagination. They allowed him to relive his crimes without leaving the safety of his home.

One of his most disturbing rituals involved dolls. In moments of solitude, he staged elaborate mock crime scenes using dolls or mannequins. He would dress them in women's clothing, tie them with rope, and pose them in grotesque positions that mirrored his murders. Sometimes he photographed the scenes, carefully adjusting lighting and angles to heighten the realism. The photographs were stored in binders labeled *Doll Projects* or *Fantasy Sessions*. These pictures weren't just recreations, they were rehearsals for new fantasies. Each one was a simulation of control, a way to feed the hunger without drawing blood.

He also experimented on himself. In private, Rader turned his fantasies inward, binding himself with ropes and chains, dressing in women's lingerie or clothing stolen from victims. He took photographs using a timer, capturing himself in positions of mock captivity, sometimes with a mask, sometimes with a plastic bag over his head. In these photos, he was both victim and killer, prisoner and god. The duality fascinated him. In one of his notes, he wrote, "When I tie myself, I feel both sides, control and surrender. That's when I understand BTK."

To anyone else, the images would have been proof of a deranged mind. To Rader, they were spiritual. They represented what he called "the balance." He believed his fantasies were a necessary outlet, a way to "satisfy Factor X" without harming anyone. In his private logic, this made him disciplined, even moral. He told himself that his control over his urges was a sign of mastery, not madness. He never saw that the rituals themselves were madness incarnate.

The scope of his obsession was staggering. Investigators would later describe his stash as a labyrinth of depravity, thousands of pages of notes, drawings, and photos spanning decades. He organized it like a professional archivist, with indexes, categories, and cross-references. There were maps of neighborhoods, timelines of stalking routines, and lists of potential victims labeled "PJs", short for "Projects." He even wrote mock police reports describing his own crimes, as if investigating himself. In these reports, he would grade his performance, noting what went well and what needed improvement. He was his own detective, his own critic, his own god.

Every entry in his journals revealed the language of dehumanization. His victims were never people, they were "subjects," "entries," "targets," or "possessions." He described them with mechanical precision: height, weight, hair color, address, window placement, lock type. The details were so minute that the humanity of the person vanished entirely. Killing, for Rader, had always been about control, and control began with language.

To strip a person of their name and replace it with a category was his first act of dominance.

He often wrote of his "trolling sessions", nights spent driving through neighborhoods, watching women through windows, noting routines. He logged these activities like a scientist conducting fieldwork: time of day, lighting conditions, potential entry points. Voyeurism became an addiction. He described it as "hunting." Even when he didn't act, he was studying, planning, collecting. It wasn't the act of killing that sustained him, it was the anticipation, the mapping of control.

His stalking notes were chillingly precise. "Female, approx. 25, lives alone," one entry read. "Leaves for work 7:45, returns 5:25. Curtains open at 8 p.m. Sleeps with light on near bed." He made sketches of their homes, noting fences, trees, streetlights, and escape routes. Each page was a plan waiting for execution. Some of these women would never know how close they had come to death.

Photography became the bridge between fantasy and reality. He photographed potential victims from his car, sometimes using long lenses to capture them from a distance. Later, he would photograph himself reenacting the imagined attack, merging their image with his own. The photos weren't trophies of victory, they were blueprints of imagination. They allowed him to live inside his fantasy world without leaving evidence behind.

What made this private world even more chilling was its normalcy. Everything was labeled, dated, and stored with care. There was no chaos, no frenzy. The darkness was orderly. Rader's obsession wasn't wild, it was methodical. His basement didn't look like a madman's den; it looked like an office. Binders were stacked neatly, folders alphabetized, photographs sleeved in plastic. It was bureaucracy as pathology, the paperwork of evil.

And through it all, he believed he was controlling himself. The rituals, the writing, the drawings, they were, in his mind, safety valves. "Better this than acting out," he once wrote. "It keeps BTK satisfied." But every ritual only deepened the addiction. The fantasies didn't release the urge; they reinforced it. They kept the hunger alive. Each photograph, each note, each staged doll was another spark in the fire he could never extinguish.

He convinced himself that this private world was harmless. He was wrong. The archive wasn't a containment, it was incubation. It was where BTK grew stronger, waiting for the day when fantasy would no longer be enough.

The next time he killed, he would do so with the precision of a man who had rehearsed it a thousand times in the dark.

Dennis Rader lived two lives, but as time went on, the barrier between them grew dangerously thin. To the people around him, he was the same steady, predictable man, punctual, courteous, responsible. He waved to neighbors, helped fix fences, gave safety talks at the church. But beneath the routine, his mind was always elsewhere. The world he presented was a mask; the real Rader lived in the constant orbit of his private obsessions.

Even at work, he thought in terms of hunting. His job as a compliance officer in Park City required him to inspect homes, issue citations, and enforce ordinances. Most saw it as tedious government work, but for Rader, it was reconnaissance. He noticed doors, locks, window placements, details that most people never thought twice about. Every assignment was potential research. Every complaint that brought him into someone's home was an opportunity to study how people lived, where they were vulnerable, how easily they could be entered.

He kept these observations tucked away like treasures. Sometimes, after returning home, he would write them down in his notebooks, turning a simple inspection into a psychological case study. "Female tenant alone," he might note. "Backdoor loose. Sliding window lock defective. Good candidate." He would then fold the paper and file it in his growing archive. The city was his hunting ground, and his government badge was his camouflage.

But it wasn't just work that fed his secret life. Rader's obsessions followed him everywhere, on drives, errands, walks with his children. He could never stop scanning, never stop noticing. His eyes were trained to read windows the way others read words. Curtains open meant invitation. A lighted room after dark was an accidental confession. Every woman who crossed his path became, in his mind, a potential "project."

He called it trolling. The term, borrowed from fishing, meant cruising slowly through neighborhoods, watching, waiting, cataloging. He would drive aimlessly at night, his headlights off, coasting in silence as he studied houses, driveways, parked cars. He looked for patterns, when lights went on, when curtains closed, when people came and went. He preferred women who lived alone or with children. He wanted to know their routines better than they did.

The thrill wasn't in the violence, it was in the surveillance. Rader experienced an almost physical pleasure from knowing he could see without being seen. It was the essence of control, the same intoxicating feeling that his crimes had given him, distilled into its purest form. He once wrote in a journal, "To watch is to own. They don't even know they are mine."

At first, the trolling was enough. It gave him a rush of power that carried him through the monotony of daily life. But as with every addiction, tolerance built over time. Watching wasn't enough. He needed to capture, to preserve. That's when the camera returned.

Photography had always been Rader's chosen medium of memory. He photographed everything, family vacations, Scout trips, neighborhood events, but beneath those wholesome albums was another, secret set of rolls. On those, the subjects were women he followed from a distance, houses he planned as potential "projects," or himself in poses that replayed his fantasies. He developed the film at small photo shops across Wichita, always careful to stagger his visits so no one would notice a pattern.

Many of his photos were clinical, even architectural, shots of windows, fences, doorways, shadows across curtains. To anyone else, they would seem meaningless. To Rader, they were maps. Each image represented possibility, each house a stage for the performance that never ended in his head. He would annotate the photos later, scribbling notes in the margins: "Two kids. Husband gone evenings. Dog barks but stays inside." He built an entire geography of fantasy, and he knew it by heart.

But some photographs crossed into pure depravity. Using tripods and self-timers, he staged elaborate self-portraits in the privacy of his home or secluded woods. He dressed in women's clothing, bras, panties, stockings, and sometimes dresses stolen from his victims' homes or from laundry lines in the neighborhoods he patrolled. He bound himself with ropes or belts, sometimes gagging himself, sometimes slipping a plastic bag over his head, reenacting the suffocation of his victims.

In these photographs, he wasn't just playing the role of killer, he was becoming the victim too. The contradiction fascinated him. He wanted to feel both dominance and helplessness, the dual pleasure of power and surrender. It was, in his mind, a kind of spiritual symmetry, a ritual of control and confession. "BTK can't live without the balance," he wrote in one of his notes. "To control, one must also feel what it is to be controlled."

He took hundreds of these photographs. Some were crude, others strikingly composed, with deliberate attention to light and framing. He positioned himself hanging from pipes or kneeling before mirrors, eyes wide behind plastic, face twisted in mock terror. He kept these images hidden in folders labeled "Self-Projects" or "Experiment Sessions." They were both trophies and tools, visual proof that he could contain BTK within the ritual, at least for a time.

Of course, this containment was an illusion. Each ritual only deepened the obsession, feeding the hunger instead of sating it. The photographs became like prayers, repeated endlessly, each one a plea to a god that never answered. They didn't calm him; they conditioned him.

Rader justified everything with the same cold logic. He told himself he wasn't hurting anyone. His fantasies, his games, his photography, they were private. "It's all in my head," he once wrote. "Better this than going out." But even as he typed those words, he knew the boundary between imagination and reality had already dissolved. His fantasies weren't confined to his head. They lived in his hands, his camera, his paper. They were real enough to have gravity, to pull him closer and closer to acting again.

The voyeurism became more reckless. Sometimes, he parked outside women's homes for hours, watching through binoculars. He began entering unlocked houses when the owners weren't home, just to look around, to feel the thrill of crossing the threshold. He called these "practice runs." He rarely stole anything, sometimes only a small piece of clothing, a photograph, or an object that could be easily hidden. He described these moments later as "samples," little fragments of possession that tied him to his targets.

Each intrusion, each stolen item, became a physical link to his private archive. A lock of hair, a bra, a Polaroid, each went into the growing collection that filled his basement drawers. To him, they weren't trophies of crimes; they were research materials for the ongoing "BTK Project."

What's most chilling about this phase of his life is how ordinary everything seemed on the surface. Rader was active in his church, teaching Sunday school lessons about morality and self-control. He lectured children in the Boy Scouts about discipline and responsibility. He volunteered for neighborhood watch programs, patrolling the same streets where he'd spent nights stalking. The mask had become second nature, so seamless that even those closest to him saw nothing amiss.

In many ways, the ritual of normalcy was part of the obsession. The contrast thrilled him. Each time he shook a hand or smiled at a neighbor, he felt a secret superiority. "They have no idea," he wrote. "I could take them anytime." The mask wasn't protection, it was part of the pleasure. Living in plain sight, invisible yet omnipotent, made him feel like a god disguised as a man.

His fantasies grew more elaborate. He began writing stories in which he fictionalized his murders, casting himself as a character called "Bill Thomas Killman", an obvious play on his own alias, BTK. In these stories, he described kidnappings, tortures, and executions in painstaking detail. He wrote as both narrator and participant, alternating between confession and instruction. He even graded his fictional murders as if scoring performance reviews. "Good bind," he noted beside one paragraph. "Too quick on choke. Work on control."

The writings reveal the extent of his delusion. He saw killing as a craft, a discipline that could be studied and perfected. Each victim was not a person, but a problem to be solved. Each "project" was an opportunity to improve. The coldness of the language is what makes it so horrifying, it's not rage that drives him, but calculation.

Rader's basement was not simply a hiding place for evidence. It was a workshop of evil, where imagination and reality fused until they were indistinguishable. Every photograph, every story, every object reinforced the same narrative: BTK was real, eternal, beyond judgment.

What Rader could never grasp was that his secret world, so carefully ordered and controlled, was also his greatest vulnerability. The obsession that kept him alive as BTK was the same one that would eventually betray him. The need to document everything, to preserve every fantasy, would become a paper trail of his own destruction.

But for now, in the quiet of his basement, surrounded by boxes labeled in his precise hand, Dennis Rader believed he was untouchable. He believed he had mastered the darkness inside him. He believed that the archive made him immortal.

He couldn't yet see that it was writing his epitaph.

By the late 1980s, Dennis Rader's secret rituals had evolved from obsession into routine. They were no longer acts of indulgence; they were maintenance. The fantasy world he had built in his basement needed constant feeding, and Rader, ever the creature of habit, obeyed the ritual with the same discipline he brought to his job or church duties. Every photograph, every note, every self-binding session was part of what he considered "keeping order."

He liked that phrase, *keeping order.* It was how he justified everything he did, whether it was issuing a citation to a neighbor for overgrown grass or spending hours in the basement photographing himself in stolen lingerie. Order was his creed. Control was his religion. And nothing was more sacred to him than the illusion that he was in control of BTK.

But the illusion was slipping.

The more Rader sought to contain his urges through fantasy, the more those fantasies demanded reality. His self-binding sessions grew longer, more elaborate. He experimented with new methods, handcuffs, pulleys, chains. He drew diagrams of "improved setups," designing harnesses that would allow him to simulate strangulation while keeping him safe from actual harm. He even built contraptions in his basement, using ropes and counterweights to create the perfect balance between pain and survival. He called these setups "Field Experiments," as if he were conducting scientific research instead of ritualized perversion.

He photographed everything. Dozens of rolls of film captured him in these sessions, sometimes masked, sometimes wearing wigs, sometimes in full disguise. He created entire narratives in front of the camera, staging his own mock kidnappings and murders with himself as both victim and captor. In one photo, he knelt before a mirror, bound and gagged, staring into his own eyes through a nylon hood. In another, he lay inside a makeshift coffin made of plywood, his hands tied to his chest, a camera timer flashing before the lid closed.

Each photo was a performance, a form of theater that blurred the line between guilt and gratification. Rader once wrote, "I am the director and the subject. The play never ends."

His writing during this period became more introspective, almost philosophical. He referred to his compulsions as "The Dark Side" and described them as an eternal battle with "Factor X." He wrote that his crimes were "the manifestation of a program running in the background." He even compared himself to biblical figures, claiming that his urges were his "cross to bear." In one entry, he wrote, "God allows demons in men. Mine just happens to like knots."

The self-awareness was eerie, but it wasn't true understanding. Rader didn't see himself as evil, he saw himself as exceptional. He believed his urges made him unique, even chosen. He admired his own restraint, convincing himself that his fantasies, not his killings, defined his genius. "Most men just dream," he wrote. "I *record*."

Still, he couldn't escape the escalation. His voyeurism intensified. He prowled neighborhoods with a camera hidden in a briefcase, snapping photos through windows, car windows, and fences. He returned to old hunting grounds, including the homes of previous victims, driving past slowly, revisiting the memories like sacred sites. He would sometimes park for hours near playgrounds or parks, watching women jog or walk their dogs, mapping their routes in his head.

The risk thrilled him. He loved the idea that the world above was blind to the world below. He could sit in a car with his camera, only feet away from his prey, and no one would suspect. "They think I'm just another guy eating a sandwich," he once wrote. "They don't know what's in my head."

At home, Paula noticed little changes but couldn't articulate them. Dennis seemed distracted, preoccupied. He still fulfilled his duties, he cooked, cleaned, attended services, but there was a distance in him, an unspoken absence. He was there, but not present. When she asked if he was all right, he smiled the practiced smile that had fooled detectives, neighbors, and priests alike. "Just tired," he'd say. "Too much paperwork."

The truth was that Rader was more active than ever, just not in ways anyone could see. His private hours were consumed by documenting, organizing, and refining his fantasies. He started using code systems to categorize his files, letters, numbers, and symbols that corresponded to different "projects." His collection had become so vast that he worried about losing track of it. "It must be catalogued," he wrote. "Future reference will require accuracy."

"Future reference." The phrase was telling. Rader wasn't just archiving his life, he was curating it for posterity. In his mind, BTK was a historical figure, and Dennis Rader was merely his biographer. He believed that one day, long after his death, someone would find his journals and finally "understand" him. He fantasized about being studied by criminologists, written about in books, remembered as a man of intellect and discipline rather than perversion. "They will see the order," he wrote. "They will see the genius in the plan."

But while he imagined immortality, his control in the present began to fracture. The rituals that once satisfied him now left him empty. The photographs, the drawings, the stalking, they weren't enough. He needed the rush of real fear again, the trembling of a living victim, the sound of breathing under a gag, the moment of absolute power.

He started selecting new "projects." Quietly, methodically, he built a fresh list of potential targets, revisiting the steps that had defined his earlier crimes: surveillance, entry routes, escape plans. He drove through neighborhoods at dawn, memorizing the sound of dogs, the rhythm of lights. He began leaving his house late at night again, under the pretext of "security patrols."

The internal dialogue returned, the conversation between Dennis and BTK. In his notes, he wrote of the voice in his head as though it were an old friend. "BTK wants to play again," he wrote. "I tell him no, not now. But he doesn't like to be told no."

He wrote of dreams where he was hunting again, dreams where the rope was in his hands and the world was silent except for his breathing. He described waking up in a cold sweat, heart racing, the smell of nylon and dust in his nose. "It's still there," he wrote. "The need. The plan. The program."

He began visiting hardware stores again, buying rope, tape, gloves, one item at a time, never too much from one place. He stored them in small, labeled containers in his garage, hidden among old Scout gear. To Paula, they were just supplies. To Rader, they were instruments of worship.

The most disturbing part of this escalation was how calmly he managed it. There was no frenzy, no panic, no remorse. He didn't see it as losing control. He saw it as returning to form. BTK, after all, had never left. He had just been dormant.

And so, while his neighbors waved to him on quiet streets and his church congregation trusted him to keep watch over their children, Dennis Rader's mind slipped deeper into its labyrinth. The fantasies were no longer rehearsals, they were invitations. The letters and photographs weren't enough. The hunger was back, stronger than ever, whispering from the dark corners of his basement archive.

The man who believed he had mastered his darkness was about to find out that darkness was the master all along.

By the time the 1990s arrived, Dennis Rader had convinced himself that he had mastered the hunger. The years of silence since his last known murder had become his proof of control. He was older now, a husband with grown children, a church leader with a reputation for decency. The city of Wichita had moved on, and so, he believed, had he.

But control for Dennis Rader was never peace, it was repression. And repression, for him, was simply the prelude to relapse.

In the quiet corners of his home, his rituals continued, as constant as breathing. The photographs, the journals, the drawings, they were still there, still growing, still whispering to him in the dark. The basement was no longer just a place; it was a state of mind, a private temple built to sustain BTK. The binders filled shelves, each labeled with dates and "project numbers." The neatness of it all gave him a strange pride. "My life," he wrote once, "is well documented."

That was his fatal truth. He was documenting himself into damnation.

At night, when his wife was asleep, he would descend into that basement like a pilgrim entering a sacred space. He'd turn on a single light bulb and sit at his desk surrounded by the trophies of his private world, maps, Polaroids, sketches, ropes, clippings, bits of stolen clothing sealed in plastic bags. He'd leaf through them slowly, reliving moments he'd long since sterilized into memory. He never saw blood or suffering, only form, order, accomplishment. Each page was another reminder that he had once been powerful, and that he could be again.

The fantasies returned stronger than ever. They had matured with him, becoming colder, more deliberate, less impulsive. The self-binding resumed, but now it carried a new purpose. He saw it as a renewal of identity. He would photograph himself in ritual poses, marking anniversaries of his crimes. He dressed himself as his victims again, bound and gagged, photographed in the same positions they had died. The ritual gave him a sense of continuity, a way to keep BTK alive while maintaining the illusion of normalcy above ground.

But the rituals also reawakened the hunger for control. It was no longer enough to revisit the past; he needed new experiences to catalog. The act of documentation, the writing, the labeling, the categorizing, had become inseparable from the act of killing. Each fed the other. The archive demanded more material.

Rader began trolling again. Slowly at first, then habitually. He cruised the same neighborhoods he'd once haunted, but the city had changed. There were new homes, new families, new women behind the windows. The sight of them filled him with the same electric tension he'd felt decades earlier. He started keeping new logs, sketching new houses, writing down names and addresses. The language was always the same, clinical, detached, as if he were conducting a civic survey rather than planning another murder.

He told himself he was only observing. But observation was the first step to possession, and possession always led to action.

He began entering homes again when no one was there, just to feel the silence of intrusion. The smell of another person's bedroom, the creak of a floorboard under his shoe, the sight of photographs on nightstands, it all reignited the old thrill. He would sometimes take small objects: a scarf, a glove, a piece of jewelry. He told himself these were harmless mementos. In reality, they were preludes to violence.

Every stolen item was added to the archive. He would tag it, bag it, photograph it, and file it. His organization was impeccable. Each object was paired with a note describing where it was found, when it was taken, and what he imagined doing with its owner. The collection had evolved into something far more than a secret, it was a blueprint of his mind, a map of every impulse and deviation.

The archive was his mirror. It showed him the person he truly was, but instead of recoiling, he worshiped it.

It was around this time that his writing took a darker turn. He began composing letters again, not to send, but to keep. They were addressed to the police, to journalists, even to imagined readers. He wrote as BTK, narrating his life in a detached, almost smug tone. "I'm still out here," one letter began. "You've forgotten, but I haven't." He signed them the same way as before, *BTK, Yours Truly.*

He never mailed these early drafts, but the act of writing them was enough to rekindle the old intoxication. The letters gave him the same rush of omnipotence he had once felt in the 1970s. The cat-and-mouse game had defined his identity; without it, he felt invisible. Writing to the police, even in secret, restored that sense of drama. He was once again the unseen director of fear, if only in his imagination.

But imagination wasn't enough for long. His hands began to itch for real control. He revisited his old crime scenes, walking the perimeters at night like a pilgrim retracing sacred ground. He stood outside the Otero home, now occupied by another family, and stared at the windows where it had all begun. The memories weren't ghosts to him, they were blueprints.

The fantasies took on a new tone, one tinged with nostalgia. He began to see himself as a man in decline, yearning for one last "project" to prove that BTK still lived. His notes from this period contain phrases like "last hurrah," "final act," and "retirement project." He was planning a comeback, not for pleasure, but for legacy. He didn't want to fade quietly into old age. He wanted to be remembered, feared, studied.

In his mind, BTK was not finished, he was merely waiting for an encore.

And so the line between fantasy and reality dissolved completely. The trolling became active surveillance. The maps became plans. The dreams became directives. By the time he killed again, after years of silence, it was almost mechanical, as if he were fulfilling an old contract with himself. The murder of Marine Hedge in 1985, followed by that of Dolores Davis in 1991, bore the same precision as his earlier crimes. The rituals were identical. The photographs were new. The archive, once dormant, was alive again.

Rader documented every step of these later murders with obsessive care. He photographed the victims, their bindings, the rooms. He even recorded the aftermath, cleaning up, writing notes, labeling items. The murders were no longer impulsive acts of domination; they were exercises in preservation. He wasn't just killing, he was curating.

In one of his journals, he compared himself to an artist restoring an old masterpiece. "The project continues," he wrote. "BTK lives through the record."

That sentence reveals everything. For Rader, murder had always been less about death than documentation. The act of killing was the creation of material. The photographs, the trophies, the writings, those were the true end products. The victims were means to a psychological archive that only he could understand.

He believed the archive would make him eternal. He never understood that it would make him visible.

Years later, when investigators finally uncovered his collection after his arrest, they were stunned by the completeness of it. It was as if he had written a step-by-step manual for his own capture. Every fantasy, every murder, every trophy, catalogued, dated, and described in his own hand. The precision that had protected him for so long was the same precision that destroyed him.

But in those years before his fall, Rader couldn't imagine that possibility. In his mind, BTK would live forever in the dark, untouched, admired, feared. He believed that when he died, his archive would be discovered and studied like ancient scripture, a testament to his "discipline."

The truth was far simpler, and far sadder. The archive wasn't a monument. It was a confession. Every photograph was evidence. Every page was proof. Every label was a signature.

He had written his own indictment in the same careful handwriting that once made him feel invincible.

And above that basement, the quiet house on Independence Street sat in perfect order, windows clean, lawn trimmed, lights off by ten. The neighbors never knew that beneath the floorboards, surrounded by binders and rope, the BTK killer was still at work, recording his darkness one page at a time.

Chapter Six
Beyond the Body Count
The Lost Victims of BTK's Hidden Hunts

When the public thinks of BTK, the story tends to revolve around the canonical murders, the Oteros, Marine Hedge, Shirley Vian, Nancy Fox, Dolores Davis. But the official record is only a fraction of the truth. Beneath the headlines and the grisly crime-scene photographs lies a darker, less visible reality: the attacks that failed, the stalkings that never escalated, and the people who survived without ever knowing how narrowly they escaped. In those shadows, the full portrait of Dennis Rader emerges, not just as a killer, but as a compulsive hunter whose appetite extended far beyond his confirmed victims.

The most glaring example is Kathryn Bright. On April 4, 1974, only three months after the Otero murders, Rader broke into the small house she shared with her brother Kevin. He had stalked her for weeks, memorizing her schedule and preparing another "project" designed to replicate the thrill of his first success. He came armed with a gun, knife, and his standard assortment of ropes and cords. His plan was to bind, control, and kill Kathryn in the same coldly ritualized manner he had used on the Oteros. But almost immediately, things went wrong.

Kevin Bright was home that afternoon, an unanticipated obstacle in Rader's carefully scripted plan. As Rader tried to subdue them, Kevin fought back ferociously. The scene turned chaotic. Rader shot Kevin twice at close range and then stabbed Kathryn repeatedly as she struggled against her bindings. Convinced he had killed them both, Rader fled. Kevin, however, managed to survive and stumbled bleeding into the street, where neighbors called for help. Kathryn Bright, only 21 years old, died from her wounds, but Kevin lived to describe the attack to police.

This should have been the moment BTK was unmasked. A living witness, a surviving brother, a clear physical encounter, all the elements that usually lead to an arrest. Yet Kevin, traumatized and gravely injured, could only describe a vague white male in his 20s or 30s, with no distinguishing features beyond glasses. The evidence at the scene was messy, contaminated by emergency responders, and the bullets and ligatures yielded no immediate forensic breakthroughs. Wichita police did not connect the Bright case conclusively to the Otero murders. For Dennis Rader, it was a near miss, a catastrophic failure that somehow left him unscathed.

The Kathryn Bright case shows something essential about Rader's pathology. Killing was not improvisation; it was choreography. When the script broke, he faltered. The "BTK system" only worked when he controlled every variable, entry point, timing, victim profile. When chaos intruded, his mask slipped. Kevin Bright's survival marked the first and only time Rader left a living witness to one of his attacks, and it terrified him. In later interviews, he admitted he had been "sloppy" that day, "not fully prepared." It was the closest he came to losing his anonymity in his early career.

But the Bright case also suggests something larger: how many times had Rader stalked someone, entered a home, or attempted an attack that was aborted midstream? His journals, recovered decades later, contain chilling lists of "missed projects", women he had targeted but never attacked, or plans he had drawn up but never executed. In his coded language, these are "PJs" with lines through them, dates scribbled but crossed out, as if erasing a dream. Each one represents a life spared by chance, a phone call that arrived at the right time, a visitor knocking at the door, a husband home unexpectedly.

Some of these women would later learn, after his arrest, that they had been watched. They came forward with stories of strange cars idling near their homes, silent phone calls in the night, or missing items from their laundry lines. They had chalked these incidents up to random creepiness, never imagining that BTK himself had been outside their windows. One woman remembered finding her back door unlocked multiple times, assuming it was her own forgetfulness. Another recalled a figure in a parked car watching her walk to her front door every night after work. Years later, those fragments of memory took on a horrifying new clarity.

Rader's own notes confirm the breadth of his hunting. He created detailed dossiers on women who never appeared in any police file. He logged their daily routines, drew maps of their homes, and wrote disturbing fantasies about their deaths. Some of these entries are clearly preparatory work for murders he eventually committed. Others remain mysteries, "projects" never acted upon, perhaps because circumstances changed or his courage faltered. In his notes, he sometimes wrote "cold feet" or "too risky" beside a name, as if grading himself on restraint.

The voyeurism behind these near misses was as deliberate as any of his murders. Rader derived enormous satisfaction from simply watching, from knowing he could strike at any moment. It was a form of psychological ownership. "They don't know it," he wrote once, "but they're mine already." That sense of invisible possession became a substitute for actual violence when killing wasn't feasible. But it also kept the hunger alive, priming him for future attacks.

Law enforcement in the 1970s lacked the framework to understand this pattern. The idea of a "serial killer" was still relatively new, and the concept of a stalker who maintained extensive files on potential victims without acting on them seemed almost implausible. Detectives working the Otero and Bright cases focused on immediate evidence, not long-term behavioral patterns. This gap allowed Rader's second life to continue unchallenged for decades.

The chilling reality is that the official BTK victim count, ten murders, may be only part of the story. His notes and the inconsistencies in his letters hint at more. He boasted of "many" projects, of "dozens" of targets, of plans spanning years. Some of these claims were self-aggrandizing, but others line up eerily with unsolved cases in Kansas from the same period. Investigators continue to examine cold cases, looking for the telltale signatures of Rader's method: bindings, sexual humiliation, careful staging. Whether more victims will ever be conclusively linked to him remains an open question.

Equally disturbing are the survivors who never knew they were survivors. Many of the women he stalked only learned of his interest after his arrest, when police showed them his logs. Some of them recognized the times and places; others were horrified to see their lives mapped out in a killer's handwriting. One described it as "finding out a ghost had been living in your house all along."

The terror that went unseen may be the most unsettling aspect of the BTK case. The murders were horrific, but at least they were visible, documented, and acknowledged. The near misses, the aborted attempts, the silent stalking, these left no headlines, no obituaries, no crime scenes. They were acts of predation that existed entirely in the shadows, crimes of intent rather than execution. Yet for Rader, they were as real as any murder. He invested the same energy, the same planning, the same rituals into these "projects" as he did into actual killings.

This hidden side of BTK also underscores the limitations of law enforcement at the time. Without digital surveillance, DNA databases, or unified case management, the patterns remained invisible. Police departments were siloed, cases went cold, and unsolved incidents were forgotten. Rader exploited this fragmentation expertly. He counted on the city's inability to connect the dots, and for decades, he was right.

But his own notes betray him. They show a man whose life was far more consumed by hunting than even his murders reveal. They show a compulsive archivist of terror, someone who measured his existence not in years or milestones, but in projects completed and projects aborted. The Kathryn Bright case and the other missed projects reveal the true scope of BTK's hidden hunts: a shadow world of victims who never knew they were prey, of near-murders that left no trace but a line in a notebook, of terror so quiet it went unrecorded for decades.

And in that silence, Dennis Rader thrived. He could be BTK without killing. He could be the hunter without firing a shot. He could live in two worlds at once, family man above ground, predator below. For him, the almost-victims were as satisfying as the victims themselves, because they proved his power extended beyond death.

Yet the same compulsion to record, to map, to log would one day expose him. The archive that sustained him was also his Achilles heel. Every crossed-out name, every sketch, every coded note would become a breadcrumb for investigators. Years later, when they opened his boxes, they would discover not only the murders he had confessed to but also the ghosts of the ones he hadn't.

For now, in the 1970s and early 1980s, those ghosts walked unseen. Kathryn Bright's brother Kevin lived with the memory of that day, carrying survivor's guilt and trauma. Other women went about their lives unaware of the danger that had passed them by. Wichita itself slept under the illusion that the nightmare had ended.

But the nightmare hadn't ended. It had simply gone underground, into notebooks, photographs, and the mind of a man who believed he was writing a private epic. The city saw only the body count. The rest, the stalking, the attempts, the forgotten victims, remained hidden in plain sight, waiting decades for the truth to surface.

When investigators opened Dennis Rader's meticulously labeled binders after his arrest, they expected to find evidence of the ten known murders. What they did not expect was the extent of his planning, the maps, sketches, and handwritten "Project Logs" for attacks that had never happened. Each entry read like a grim case file. A woman's name, her address, a list of routines. Notes about pets, curtains, and work hours. Sometimes a crude floor plan, arrows showing where he might enter or exit, and in the margins, small comments: "Good opportunity, alone Fridays," or "husband home weekends, too risky."

There were dozens of them.

To law enforcement, this was the most disturbing revelation: BTK's obsession had not faded between murders, it had only gone underground. He had continued to stalk, to watch, to plan, even during his long silences. Some of the women in those notes had no idea their lives had ever intersected with his. Others had always suspected something was wrong.

One woman remembered waking in the middle of the night to the sound of her back door creaking. She found it unlocked, though she was sure she'd secured it. She dismissed it as forgetfulness, but weeks later, her house key vanished from the hook near the kitchen. It reappeared days later on her counter. She changed the locks, told herself it was nothing. Only after Rader's arrest did she learn her name appeared in his logs under the title *PJ-22: Access Confirmed*.

Another woman recalled being followed home from a grocery store, the same sedan showing up behind her on multiple trips. The driver wore glasses, his face unremarkable. She told a friend she felt watched, but it stopped after a few weeks. Rader had likely lost interest or decided the conditions weren't right. She lived, but the file in his archive remained. Her address, her car make, her schedule, all preserved in his neat, looping handwriting.

Rader treated these aborted projects like fieldwork. In his journals, he sometimes wrote about "testing entry points" or "trial observations." He would park blocks away, approach houses quietly at night, and note the sounds, barking dogs, the hum of a television, the flicker of a security light. Each failed approach became data for future success. He called it "homework."

The chilling part was how ordinary these notes looked. They read like property assessments or neighborhood watch logs. "Curtains closed by 10:30. Porch light out by 11. No car in drive after 7:15." There was no emotion in them, no anger, no thrill, just observation. Rader didn't write as a man obsessed with violence; he wrote as a bureaucrat recording a process. The horror was in the precision.

When he did mention emotion, it was in strange, detached language. "Good prospect," he'd write after a week of stalking. "Factor X strong." The term "Factor X" appeared frequently in his writings. He described it as a kind of force, the dark current that drove him, the "thing that makes the hunt necessary." For him, these "missed projects" weren't failures; they were sacrifices to his own restraint. Each one proved that he could stop himself if he wanted to.

But that restraint was an illusion. The logs show that Rader often returned to old "projects," sometimes years after abandoning them. He would circle a name in red ink and write "Revisit, new opportunity?" In a few cases, the same names appear multiple times over decades. Women who had moved, married, or aged out of his fantasy parameters reappeared when circumstances changed. The idea that he could resume a "project" after years away shows how patient he was, and how permanent his obsession became.

Some of these aborted missions almost became murders. Police now believe that in at least three cases during the 1980s, Rader entered homes while the intended victims were away or asleep, only to retreat when conditions weren't perfect. He left behind small traces, a moved curtain, a cigarette butt near a window, an open door that should have been locked. Investigators later matched his notes to these incidents. In each case, he wrote afterward, "aborted, risk too high."

That phrase, "risk too high," appears over and over. It was his way of giving himself credit for caution, as if self-control made him disciplined rather than dangerous. "Discipline" was a word he used often, and it was central to his self-image. In his mind, the perfect project wasn't necessarily one completed with violence, it was one executed with control. To walk away undetected gave him almost as much pleasure as completing the act. It was proof that he could dictate not only who lived and died, but when.

The surviving witnesses from these attempts remember fragments, the sound of footsteps outside, missing underwear from clotheslines, the sensation of being watched. One woman who lived near Park City recalled finding her basement light on after work one night. She turned it off, only to find it on again the next morning. "It didn't feel like a prank," she said years later. "It felt like someone was rehearsing."

Rehearsing was exactly what Rader was doing. His aborted attempts were not failures; they were dry runs. He studied locks, routines, and responses. He once wrote that "each project, successful or not, increases the knowledge base." He thought of himself as a scientist of control.

The Kathryn Bright attack had taught him a lesson: chaos was unacceptable. Every project afterward was refined to eliminate unpredictability. He targeted women who lived alone, with no pets, no male partners. He avoided households with children after the Otero murders because the crying and noise had shaken him. He learned to cut phone lines, to disable lights, to choose nights with bad weather when neighbors were less likely to look outside. Each "missed project" refined the next.

What investigators realized only later was that his patterns of stalking overlapped with unsolved break-ins and peeping incidents that had been dismissed as petty crimes. He had a habit of lingering on the periphery , lurking behind houses, observing from parks, testing backdoors. Residents often reported these incidents, but they were too scattered across jurisdictions for anyone to connect them. Wichita, Park City, and surrounding counties each had their own police departments, none of which were sharing data effectively in the 1970s and 1980s. Rader exploited that fragmentation the way a spider exploits cracks in a wall.

The chilling implication of his notes is that the known ten murders might represent only the tip of a much larger landscape of terror , a hidden world of attempts, rehearsals, and unfinished hunts. For every confirmed victim, there may have been half a dozen women who were followed, photographed, or mapped. In some cases, Rader left behind physical reminders , a rope found coiled behind a shed, a cigarette butt left near a window, a glove in the grass. Each one, in hindsight, looks like a fingerprint of intent.

In the margins of his notebooks, he often drew small sketches , stick-figure outlines of rooms, furniture, windows. The crude simplicity of these drawings makes them even more disturbing. They're not art; they're tools. He drew the distance from the front door to the bedroom, the placement of light switches, the angle of hallways. Each line represents someone's home, someone's sanctuary, dissected into a schematic of vulnerability.

When asked years later why he didn't go through with these aborted attacks, Rader gave a chillingly banal answer: "Timing wasn't right." He spoke of them as logistical failures, not moral choices. He didn't spare lives out of compassion; he simply waited for better circumstances.

This cold arithmetic is what separates Rader from other killers. He didn't live in chaos , he engineered it. Every near-miss was another data point, every restraint a temporary delay. The missed projects weren't mercy. They were maintenance.

And as much as the public imagines Rader disappearing during his "quiet years," these logs prove otherwise. He never stopped. He was always watching, always recording. The city simply stopped looking.

For decades, those who survived unknowingly carried pieces of his story , fragments of encounters that never coalesced into a pattern. A door left ajar. A car that followed too long. A shadow outside a window. Each one seemed small at the time. Together, they form the invisible half of BTK's legacy: the lives not taken, but forever brushed by his presence.

In those quiet close calls, his true horror reveals itself. Murder was only one outcome of his obsession. The stalking, the observation, the intrusion , those were the acts that defined him. The killings were simply the moments when his patience ran out.

When detectives opened Dennis Rader's binders in 2005, the first impression was almost absurd in its neatness. The pages were clean, organized, and obsessively detailed, more like an accountant's ledgers than a serial killer's diary. But as they turned the pages, the horror deepened. There were addresses, directions, hand-drawn maps, and lists of women labeled as "projects," some marked with checkmarks, others with question marks or X's.

It was the X's that chilled investigators the most.

Each X indicated an aborted attempt, women who had been chosen, watched, sometimes even approached, but who remained alive because of chance, timing, or sheer luck. In Rader's handwriting, the X symbol didn't mean "safe." It meant "incomplete."

Detective Ken Landwehr, who led the task force that ultimately brought Rader down, later said that reading those notes was "like walking through the city's memories in the dark." Names and addresses from neighborhoods long changed or demolished reappeared like ghosts. Many belonged to women who had moved away or died years earlier, never knowing they'd been targeted. Others were still alive, their lives quietly intersecting with a predator they'd never met.

The investigation into these forgotten victims became its own kind of excavation. Detectives began comparing Rader's notes against old police records: reports of prowlers, burglaries, and "peeping tom" complaints filed in the Wichita area throughout the 1970s and 1980s. What they found was staggering.

The pattern matched almost perfectly.

Dozens of reports, dismissed as isolated incidents, now aligned with Rader's stalking logs. Some victims had described a man in a tan sedan, or footprints outside their windows, or mysterious cut phone lines. Others mentioned small thefts: underwear missing from laundry lines, photos gone from albums, a broken lock. Each of these fragments, meaningless in isolation, became proof of the vast shadow Rader cast over the city.

The more detectives matched reports to his notes, the more they realized how close he had come to expanding his known body count. Some near-misses were separated from actual murders by mere days or blocks.

In one instance, Rader had logged two separate women living in the same neighborhood, one became a confirmed victim; the other was crossed out with a single note: "Too many people around that day."

It was luck, not foresight, that kept the second woman alive.

Investigators began contacting the women named in his files, an agonizing process that reopened decades of buried fear. Many had no idea who BTK was until they received the call. When detectives told them their names had appeared in his handwriting, the responses ranged from disbelief to collapse. One woman broke down sobbing and said, "I knew something was wrong back then. I could feel it." Another said quietly, "He was in my house, wasn't he?"

In some cases, yes, he had been.

Rader's notes referenced interior details that could only have come from direct observation: "Blue wallpaper in hallway. Dog food by kitchen door. Two photos on piano." Investigators confirmed those details with the women, many of whom recalled strange signs from decades earlier, a window left open, a misplaced object, the subtle sense that something in the room had changed.

These confirmations made the BTK case even more horrifying than before. The murders were visible horrors, but these unfulfilled "projects" represented something more insidious: a psychological occupation of his victims' lives. For Rader, the act of watching, recording, and intruding was itself a form of domination. He didn't need to kill to feel control; he only needed to know he could.

And he wanted that knowledge preserved.

The recovered materials included hundreds of photographs, houses, mailboxes, driveways, and occasionally blurred figures of women unaware they were being watched. There were sketches of interiors, and index cards summarizing routines: "Tues , work 8–5, returns home 5:30. Thurs , friend visits 7 p.m." In some cases, investigators found more than one set of notes for the same person, written years apart. Rader had updated them like a census.

It became clear that his fantasy life and his real-world surveillance had fused into one continuous system of control. His "archives" weren't passive keepsakes; they were living documents he revisited, refined, and expanded. They were how he maintained his secret identity when he wasn't killing.

Even the language he used in his notes was telling. He never wrote "victim." He wrote "subject." He didn't write "house." He wrote "scene." His private lexicon stripped away humanity, reducing people to locations, opportunities, and patterns. When detectives read phrases like "observe again next week" or "plan B: alternate entry route," they weren't reading plans, they were reading a psychology of ownership.

Years later, when questioned about these logs, Rader was disturbingly matter-of-fact. "I had a lot of projects," he said. "Some just didn't work out."

He said it the way a carpenter might talk about unfinished jobs.

The scale of those "projects" remains uncertain even today. The FBI has reviewed hundreds of unsolved assaults and homicides in Kansas and neighboring states that share similarities to BTK's known methods. While no definitive new murders have been linked, the pattern of stalking incidents and intrusions suggests that Rader's active predation was far broader than his confessions revealed. The ten murders were simply the moments where his self-control failed to keep pace with his fantasies.

What haunted investigators most was how casually he integrated his predatory work into the rhythm of his normal life. Many of the addresses in his notebooks were along routes he drove daily for his job as a city compliance officer. He weaponized familiarity. The same neighborhoods he inspected for weeds and broken fences were the same ones he mapped for potential victims. His government job gave him legitimate access to private property, and he used it to feed BTK's database.

The irony was devastating. Rader spent his career enforcing rules, city ordinances, building codes, safety laws. His entire life was about control, about making sure others followed order. Yet beneath that veneer of civic duty, he was building a secret empire of disorder. Each "project" was a private rebellion against the conformity he publicly demanded.

The people of Park City had trusted him implicitly. They waved when his white city truck drove by. They let him into their homes for inspections. They told him about their schedules, their families, their routines. They handed him the keys to their safety without ever suspecting what he really was.

And when investigators later matched some of those inspection records to the names in his BTK files, they realized that the line between his two worlds had never been as separate as he pretended. BTK and Dennis Rader were never masks switching back and forth, they were a single organism feeding on both lives at once.

The discovery of his "missed projects" changed the public understanding of the case forever. It proved that BTK's terror extended beyond the ten confirmed murders into a vast network of surveillance, intrusion, and near-violence that spanned decades. It forced Wichita to confront an even more terrifying truth: that the monster hadn't only killed in the dark, he had lived in the light, unnoticed, unchallenged, and often welcomed.

Detectives who worked the case often described the emotional toll of interviewing survivors. Some felt guilt for not reporting strange events more forcefully decades earlier. Others struggled with the knowledge that they had lived through something they couldn't remember. But the most painful realization came from those who discovered that Rader had used their trust, inspectors, neighbors, fellow church members, as a shield for his stalking.

The contrast between his meticulous organization and his moral emptiness made the evidence feel almost inhuman. Every line of his writing was clean, legible, and calm. There was no madness in the script, no chaos in the handwriting. That, more than anything, terrified the investigators. The orderliness of evil.

When the last of the binders was catalogued, one detective reportedly closed the final folder and said quietly, "This isn't the story of ten murders. It's the story of a city that never saw the rest."

And that is the true meaning of BTK's hidden hunts, not the lives he took, but the countless lives he entered and cataloged without ever touching, the people whose safety existed only because he decided not to act. His victims were not just those who died; they were all those who lived in the illusion of safety while being watched by a man who saw them as entries in a ledger.

The forgotten victims of BTK are not just ghosts of failed attacks. They are proof that evil can exist as paperwork, that horror can be logged in tidy handwriting, and that the most terrifying predators are not those who strike, but those who wait.

In the years following Dennis Rader's arrest, Wichita began the painful process of revisiting its past. The official number of victims remained ten, but investigators and journalists quickly realized that the psychological scope of his crimes was far wider. For every name engraved in the public record, there were dozens of others, unnamed, uncounted, but forever touched by his obsession. These were the forgotten victims: the survivors who never knew they had survived, the neighbors who lived beside evil without recognizing it, and the families who had brushed against the shadow of BTK without ever feeling its full weight.

As detectives continued combing through Rader's archive, they reached out to the people whose names appeared in his "missed projects." Some of them had long since moved out of Kansas. Others had changed their names, started new lives, built families. When they learned that BTK had written about them , described their homes, drawn their floor plans, logged their schedules , many felt their pasts collapse under the weight of a new, retroactive fear.

It is one thing to survive danger; it is another to discover, decades later, that the danger was inches away.

One woman, identified only by her initials in court documents, had been listed in Rader's notes as "PJ-17: good subject, fair access." She remembered nothing unusual from that time except a single night when her back door was found open. Her husband had dismissed it as wind. After the arrest, she was shown Rader's entry: *"Unlocked backdoor 02/15. Watched from park, clear view of bedroom light. Interrupted by car at 9:45 , aborted."* She stared at the handwriting for several minutes before saying softly, "I guess I wasn't crazy after all."

For the detectives who delivered these revelations, the work was emotionally grueling. They were not informing families of death , they were informing them of near-death, of survival through sheer chance. The survivors described the experience as haunting. They had lived full lives under a shadow they never saw, only to realize, years later, that their names had been written into a killer's script. "It makes you look back at your own history differently," one said. "You start to wonder how many ordinary moments weren't ordinary at all."

Psychologists who later studied the case coined a term for what these individuals experienced: **retroactive victimization** , the trauma of realizing, after the fact, that one had been in mortal danger without knowing it. For many, it shattered their sense of control over their own memories.

Some described nightmares and anxiety years after learning the truth. One woman refused to enter her basement again after reading that Rader had once written "possible entry point through basement window."

Even investigators weren't immune. Detectives who spent months reading Rader's notes developed what they called "BTK fatigue", a numbing dread that crept into daily life. They reported driving home and checking their own doors twice, staring at curtains from the outside to see how visible they were from the street. The precision of Rader's stalking had infected their routines. As one officer said, "You can't read his words and ever feel unseen again."

What made this phase of the investigation especially painful was how ordinary the lives of these forgotten victims were. Teachers, nurses, mothers, students, all going about their days while unknowingly being catalogued by a man who saw them as pieces in a private game. They were proof that Rader's terror was not just a series of murders but a prolonged campaign of surveillance. He had turned an entire community into his hunting ground, and the community never noticed.

The media, eager to sensationalize the story, focused largely on the known murders and the "monster next door" narrative. But beneath the headlines, the stories of the unseen victims carried a quieter, deeper horror. These were the lives he didn't destroy but had nonetheless contaminated, people who would forever see their homes and memories differently. A woman who discovered her name in his notes sold her house immediately, unable to sleep there another night. Another replaced every door and window in her home, even though Rader had been imprisoned for years. "You can lock the doors now," she told a reporter, "but you can't lock out what already happened."

For criminologists, the discovery of these aborted projects offered a crucial insight into Rader's psychology. They revealed that killing was only one manifestation of his pathology. His true addiction was control , the ability to dominate lives from a distance, to shape fear even without bloodshed. The stalking, the observing, the note-taking , these were acts of ownership. Murder was simply the moment when ownership became irreversible.

FBI profilers later used the BTK case as a study in what they called **"cognitive predation."** Unlike impulsive killers driven by rage or psychosis, Rader engaged in long-term planning that treated human life as a problem to be solved. He experienced satisfaction not only from the act of violence but from the preparation and recollection that surrounded it. His notes about "missed projects" showed that the anticipation and aftermath were as gratifying to him as the killing itself. In effect, his crimes never ended. They existed in an endless loop of planning, acting, and remembering.

The forgotten victims were part of that loop. They were the proof that his control extended even to lives untouched by physical harm. When he revisited their homes in his notes, years after abandoning the "projects," it wasn't nostalgia , it was proof that he still possessed them in his mind. The power of memory was his ultimate weapon.

In his later prison interviews, Rader acknowledged these aborted hunts without remorse. When asked if he regretted stalking so many women who had never been harmed, he replied flatly, "They were part of the study." To him, their survival wasn't mercy. It was data.

The paradox of Dennis Rader's story is that the same compulsive documentation that enabled his long secrecy also ensured his exposure. He believed that recording his fantasies gave him power , that by cataloguing everything, he was preserving BTK's legacy for future generations. He was right, in a sense. His notes did preserve BTK's story, but not the one he imagined. They revealed a man enslaved by his own delusion of control, whose empire of paper and photographs ultimately became a roadmap to his own undoing.

For the people of Wichita, the revelation of his "hidden hunts" altered the city's relationship with its own past. It wasn't just about revisiting crime scenes or reading old headlines. It was about realizing that BTK had been everywhere, in churches, schools, city offices, and neighborhood streets. He had lived not only among them but *within* them, shaping their fear even before they knew his name.

To this day, when residents of Park City describe their memories of the BTK years, they speak not only of the murders but of the *feeling* that lingered afterward, the sense that someone could be watching. The legacy of his unseen victims became part of the collective memory of the place, a silent acknowledgment that safety had always been an illusion.

In the end, the "forgotten victims" may be the ones who best define who Dennis Rader truly was. Not the man who killed ten, but the man who watched a hundred, stalked fifty, and frightened thousands. His power was never in the body count. It was in the idea that he could have done more, that control itself was the point.

When the last of his boxes was sealed into evidence storage, one detective wrote in the margin of his report, "He never stopped hunting; he just ran out of time."

That line has stayed with everyone who's studied him since. Because in truth, Rader's crimes were not only against his victims, they were against the very concept of ordinary life. He turned routine into ritual, familiarity into exposure, safety into performance. Every open window, every dark street, every quiet house became a potential stage for his fantasies.

The forgotten victims remind us of that terrifying truth: that evil doesn't always announce itself with violence. Sometimes, it lives next door, patient, invisible, taking notes.

Chapter Seven
The Codes in the Sermons
How BTK Turned Faith Into a Language of Control

Every monster needs a mask, and Dennis Rader's favorite one was holiness.

In the small, quiet community of Park City, Kansas, the Christ Lutheran Church was not only a house of worship but a social hub, the kind of place where trust was automatic, where neighbors prayed together and never imagined that evil could kneel beside them. Within those walls, Rader rose through the ranks, first as a member of the congregation, then as a council president, and eventually as a man so embedded in church life that his presence seemed indistinguishable from virtue itself.

To understand the depth of his deception, one must understand what Rader found in the church: structure, hierarchy, ritual, obedience. These were the pillars of his personality long before they became tools of domination. The liturgy's cadence, its repetition, its emphasis on confession, power, and submission, spoke directly to the architecture of his mind.

In faith, he saw not contradiction to his darkness but validation of it. The church gave him language for his obsession with order.

He volunteered for nearly everything: maintenance work, security, planning committees, usher duties. He knew the rhythms of the church's schedule better than anyone. Sunday services, Wednesday meetings, choir practices, all of it documented in his tidy notebooks, as if religion were another system to be managed. He thrived in predictability. Predictability meant control.

The congregation saw him as a model of diligence and integrity. He was the man who remembered birthdays, organized bake sales, delivered announcements with formal precision. He quoted scripture fluently and spoke often about discipline and morality. Parents trusted him with their children; pastors trusted him with keys. The irony was blinding in retrospect: Dennis Rader had more access to the church's private spaces than anyone else.

He used that access not for violence, not there, not directly, but for concealment. The church was the perfect mask, the ideal stage for his act of duality. On Sundays, he was the servant of Christ. On weeknights, alone in his basement, he was BTK cataloguing his darkness. The contrast was not hypocrisy to him. It was balance.

In interviews years later, Rader would describe this duality with disturbing calm. "I compartmentalized," he said. "There was Dennis the church man, and there was BTK. They didn't mix. I could be one on Sunday and the other on Monday."

But the truth is, they did mix, in language, in thought, and eventually, in the very sermons he helped write.

As council president, Rader occasionally assisted with composing devotional materials, announcements, and newsletters. His writing had the formal, almost bureaucratic tone of someone who prized order above warmth. Yet within that order were traces of the same vocabulary he used in his BTK communications: "obedience," "submission," "calling," "the struggle within," "the need to discipline the self." They were words that carried dual meanings, innocent in the pulpit, sinister in the basement.

To the congregation, they were the language of moral instruction. To Rader, they were echoes of the private commandments he wrote to himself in his journals. The pulpit became another form of expression, another place where he could encode his worldview under the guise of faith.

He saw himself, in some perverse sense, as both sinner and shepherd. In his mind, his actions did not disprove God's order, they confirmed it. His murders were not rebellion; they were distorted imitations of divine authority. Just as scripture described the separation of light from darkness, Rader divided his own life into sacred and profane halves. The church gave him a vocabulary to justify that division.

During one Bible study session, a fellow parishioner remembered Rader leading a discussion on the Book of Romans, emphasizing the verse about man's sinful nature and the need for discipline. He spoke passionately about the "battle within every man to master his impulses." At the time, it sounded like the reflection of a devout man. Years later, that same verse would appear, almost word-for-word, in one of the letters Rader sent to the police, describing how BTK had to "control Factor X, the demon inside."

The duality was complete. He was using scripture to explain himself to God and the police in the same breath.

To Rader, religion wasn't just camouflage. It was structure, ritual, and metaphor. He saw confession, sin, and punishment as transactional, the way a bureaucrat sees forms and filings. Confession could reset the slate; penance could justify transgression. It was the same logic he used to rationalize his murders: if he acknowledged his sins privately, he believed he was maintaining internal order. He once wrote in his notes, "God knows I am not perfect, but He made me what I am. I just follow the nature He gave me."

He wasn't mocking God, he was misusing Him.

That perversion extended to how he viewed his victims. Rader believed in a warped form of divine hierarchy: those who submitted to control were "in their rightful place." His favorite biblical passages often dealt with authority and obedience, verses from Ephesians about wives submitting to husbands, or Proverbs about the discipline of the righteous. He quoted them often, sometimes too often.

One former member of Christ Lutheran recalled that Rader's tone when reading scripture was always precise, but detached, almost mechanical. "He read it like an engineer," she said. "No feeling, just accuracy." It was the same precision that defined his crimes. Every verse, every word, measured and deliberate.

His fascination with control extended into church leadership. He thrived on order, meeting minutes, attendance lists, scheduling rosters. If something was misplaced, he took it personally. Once, when the church bulletin was printed with a misspelling, he sent a long memo correcting it line by line, quoting scripture about "doing all things decently and in order." To his fellow council members, it was quirky. To Rader, it was sacred law.

The parallels between his church life and his crimes were not coincidence. Both revolved around ritualized control. In the sanctuary, he orchestrated the small world of order and obedience; in his crimes, he imposed that same order through domination. Both required silence, submission, and ceremony. The difference was only in outcome.

Even his methods of writing to police carried the imprint of faith. His letters often borrowed biblical phrasing, "Thou shalt not let BTK fade away" or "There is a time to kill and a time to reap." It wasn't parody. It was a self-styled theology of control, a belief that his crimes fit into some cosmic order he alone understood. He wasn't mocking religion; he was reciting it in his own corrupted language.

In his later confessions, Rader described feeling "closer to God" after his murders. He said the calm he felt afterward was "like when the church goes silent before communion." That statement revealed more than he realized. He didn't see killing as rebellion against morality, he saw it as ceremony. He had turned faith itself into a ritual of control, just as he had turned his victims into objects of worship through domination.

For years, the community saw nothing but goodness in him. He showed up early to services, helped set out hymnals, read from the lectern, organized potlucks. When the police finally arrested him, his pastor wept. The man who had opened and closed the church doors every Sunday was the same man who had locked people in their own homes to die.

And yet, even after his arrest, some members of the congregation struggled to reconcile the two images. "He was one of us," one woman said quietly to a reporter. "He was the church."

That may be the most chilling truth of all, that Rader didn't hide from the church. He hid *within* it.

He didn't wear his mask only on Sundays; he built it into the fabric of his faith. Every hymn, every sermon, every act of service reinforced the illusion of righteousness. The sanctuary that should have been a refuge became his cover, and the scripture that should have condemned him became his code.

Rader once wrote in a personal note later found by investigators: "The Lord knows all things. He knows me too. He understands BTK."

Whether he believed that or used it as justification hardly matters. In his mind, there was no contradiction between the God he served and the demon he became. The church gave him both the vocabulary and the permission to exist in pieces.

To the outside world, Dennis Rader's devotion seemed genuine. His attendance was flawless. His speech precise. He could quote scripture from memory, never fumbling over a verse. In the pews, he appeared humble, even reverent, the kind of man who bowed his head with conviction when the pastor prayed. But Rader's faith wasn't submission. It was disguise.

He understood religion the way an engineer understands a structure, not through belief, but through function. It provided a framework, a vocabulary, and most importantly, a hierarchy. He liked that God sat above, commanding order and obedience. In that system, he saw a reflection of his own need to dominate. His church life became both practice and theater, a stage for his need to appear righteous while privately worshipping control itself.

Investigators later found that many of his BTK writings were steeped in religious phrasing. He often borrowed the cadence and syntax of the Bible, embedding it in his letters to the police. In one note sent to the *Wichita Eagle*, he quoted Ecclesiastes: "There is a time for everything under heaven." Then, beneath it, he wrote, "And this is the time for me to be heard again." The message was clear, he was not confessing. He was proclaiming.

That blend of scripture and arrogance ran through all his communications. He spoke of "judgment," of "reckoning," of "sins against BTK." He wasn't mocking religion, he was trying to *appropriate* it. The killer saw himself not as an enemy of God, but as an instrument of His structure. "I am what He made me," Rader wrote in one of his private diaries. "Each has his purpose. Some build. Some destroy. Both serve."

To him, divine order was not moral; it was mechanical. In his worldview, every creature played its part, and his part was to enact domination. His crimes became ritual reenactments of biblical imagery, not in theology, but in symbolism. The power to bind, to control, to decide the fate of another person was, in his eyes, a reflection of God's own dominion over life and death.

He saw no contradiction between kneeling in prayer on Sunday and reliving his murders in private the next night. To Rader, both were acts of ritual, one public, one secret, both about mastery, both about submission and control. "Discipline," he once told a fellow church member, "is what separates us from chaos." He meant it as moral advice. In his own mind, it was doctrine.

The police and FBI analysts who studied his writings noted a peculiar consistency between his spiritual and predatory language. In both, he cast himself as the "shepherd." His victims, like the congregation, were his "flock." The metaphor was not accidental. In one chilling letter, he referred to "culling the herd," a phrase drawn directly from a sermon he had once helped write about moral corruption in society. His church vocabulary had fused completely with his identity as BTK.

Rader's duality didn't stop at language. It shaped his entire sense of identity. At church, he was meticulous about protocol, how meetings should be opened, how notes should be archived, how the sanctuary should be cleaned. He kept rules because rules gave him shape. And in his crimes, he followed the same principle. Every murder followed a "procedure." Every act, documented. Every message, structured. His theology and his pathology were twins.

For years, his faith insulated him from suspicion. Church life provided credibility and cover. It gave him an alibi for his stability. When the BTK letters stopped after 1991, some parishioners joked that the killer must have "found Jesus." In a way, he had, not as savior, but as shield. He wrapped himself in piety so tightly that no one could imagine the evil beneath it.

He relished that invisibility. During his later police interrogations, he spoke with pride about being "trusted." He said, "They never looked at me , they thought I was one of the good guys. The church man." He smiled when he said it. It wasn't remorse; it was satisfaction. His faith hadn't failed him. It had succeeded exactly as he designed it to.

There's a photograph from the late 1990s, Rader standing at the front of Christ Lutheran, wearing a beige suit, glasses slightly slipping down his nose, holding a Bible at his chest. Behind him, a banner reads *"Serve the Lord with gladness."* To his congregation, it captured a man of faith in service. To history, it captures the calm face of duplicity. He served , but never the Lord.

The coded connections between his church life and his crimes extended even further. When investigators compared his letters to church bulletins and newsletters, they noticed repeating words and phrasing. The same scripture he quoted in his communications with police appeared, often within days, in church programs he had helped draft. Psalm 23 , "He maketh me to lie down…" , had been highlighted in one bulletin just a week before he used it in a BTK message describing a "restful" victim.

That discovery sent chills through the task force. He wasn't quoting scripture randomly , he was embedding private signals within public words, blending his worlds so completely that even those who read his words aloud in church unknowingly echoed his language of domination.

In later prison interviews, Rader admitted to what he called "cross-referencing." He said he liked to "borrow" from his faith life when constructing BTK communications because it made the words "sound right." Asked whether it gave him a sense of safety or control, he shrugged. "I liked the symmetry," he said. "It made me feel balanced."

That word , *balanced* , appeared repeatedly in his writings. He saw his existence as a moral equation, his good deeds balancing his crimes. In his logic, service in church offset the darkness he kept hidden. "God likes order," he once wrote. "I am both sides of His creation."

There's something almost liturgical in that line, a blasphemous echo of the Book of Job. Rader didn't reject God; he redefined Him in his own image. He wasn't interested in redemption, he was interested in justification. He believed his intelligence, his restraint, and his devotion to form set him apart from "ordinary sinners." The arrogance was theological as much as psychological.

His sermons reflected this duality. Parishioners remembered that he often emphasized personal discipline and self-control over forgiveness or compassion. His version of faith was about rules, not grace. "Dennis didn't talk about love," one church member recalled. "He talked about structure, obedience, and duty." It was a gospel of order, one that mirrored the same cold precision that defined his killings.

Even in his later years, long after his crimes had ceased, Rader continued to use religious imagery to describe BTK. He called his alter ego "the dark angel," a term that conflated the demonic with the divine. He viewed his murders not as random acts but as rituals, ceremonies that brought him closer to his own conception of perfection. "BTK was my ministry," he wrote in one notebook. "It's what I was meant to do."

He wasn't boasting. He was rationalizing.

In his mind, sin without structure was chaos, but sin with purpose was art. That distinction allowed him to coexist with himself, to sit in church every Sunday surrounded by families and children and never once feel out of place. To him, the sanctuary wasn't sacred ground, it was neutral territory between two selves.

For the congregation, Rader's arrest was a kind of theological earthquake. Their faith had taught them to see goodness in service, to equate piety with morality. The revelation that their council president, the man who read scripture from the lectern, had spent thirty years murdering and writing to the police shattered that link. "We trusted the wrong kind of order," one parishioner said later. "We thought obedience meant safety. He knew that."

Indeed, Rader had built his entire life around exploiting that assumption. In both church and crime, he used the same principles: appear disciplined, follow procedure, demand control. He never had to hide behind faith; faith was the hiding place.

The more investigators studied his communications, the more they saw how scripture functioned not as redemption, but as encryption. The words of peace became the language of his power. The psalms, the verses, the cadence of sermons, all of it had been twisted into a private code of authority.

He didn't just believe in God. He believed he shared God's job.

By the time Dennis Rader entered his fifties, his faith had become something far more personal, and far more dangerous. What had begun as camouflage for his darker life evolved into a private theology, a framework that not only excused his actions but gave them meaning. Rader didn't hide behind religion anymore. He lived inside it, reshaping it around himself like a reflection warped in a mirror.

To his congregation, he was still the reliable servant of Christ Lutheran Church, punctual, polite, and pedantic. But beneath that façade, his faith had become infected by his need for control. He had turned religion into an equation, a system that mirrored his view of the universe: hierarchies, submission, consequence, and balance.

In his later writings, recovered after his arrest, Rader often quoted scripture not to confess, but to *explain* himself. His diary entries read like the sermons of a man preaching to a congregation of one. He referenced Job, Proverbs, and Ecclesiastes repeatedly, using each as justification for his internal "struggle." The verses he chose weren't about love or forgiveness. They were about order, power, and the subjugation of the will.

One passage he copied multiple times came from Romans 13: "For there is no authority except that which God has established. The authorities that exist have been established by God." To most believers, it is a call for obedience to lawful order. To Rader, it was evidence that his authority, his control over others, was not evil but ordained. In one margin, he scribbled: "BTK follows His design. Discipline is creation."

He had built a theology of control.

When he spoke about faith with others, he framed obedience as the highest virtue. "We're all servants of something," he once told a friend after a church meeting. "The question is: who's really in charge?" The friend assumed he meant God. In truth, Rader was speaking about himself.

The shift from camouflage to conviction can be traced through the tone of his writings. Early BTK letters were mocking, arrogant, and performative, a killer taunting the world. But as the years went on, his private notes adopted a solemn, almost devotional tone. He began writing about his crimes as "sacred duties," about his victims as "offerings of control." He saw himself as both sinner and priest, the hand that sinned and the hand that sanctified.

That blending of roles, executioner and confessor, defined his later years. When he stopped killing, he didn't stop ritualizing. His self-binding sessions became ceremonies of repentance and reaffirmation. He photographed himself kneeling in mock prayer, bound and gagged, sometimes surrounded by Bibles or religious imagery. He labeled some of these photos "Communion," as if they were acts of worship. The rituals satisfied the same need the murders once did, control, containment, and renewal.

He wrote about these experiences as "spiritual maintenance." To him, control was cleansing. Submission, even self-inflicted, was purification.

He didn't understand sin as transgression; he understood it as imbalance. When he bound himself, he believed he was restoring symmetry between his two halves. "When the ropes are tight," he wrote in one note, "there is peace again. The world is ordered."

That was his religion: order through bondage.

Even his use of language reflected his belief that power and holiness were intertwined. He described his victims not as people, but as "souls under authority." The terminology is theological, but the intent is monstrous. To Rader, domination was not cruelty, it was divine order made flesh. The strong rule the weak; the disciplined rule the chaotic. He once wrote, "If God is Lord of all, then BTK is Lord of his chosen few."

He saw no contradiction in worshipping both.

The pastors who had once worked with Rader struggled deeply after his arrest to reconcile the man they knew with the man they read about. One of them, in an interview years later, said, "I think he honestly believed he had a relationship with God, it's just that he thought he *was* God."

It's not hard to see why. His obsession with control mirrored the language of scripture he admired most. "Thy will be done." "I am the shepherd." "The fear of the Lord is the beginning of wisdom." For Rader, fear *was* wisdom, and will was power. He inverted the meaning of faith until it served only him.

Investigators later discovered that he had inserted biblical references into his personal communications with police, not as mockery, but as coded affirmations. When he wrote, "BTK will rise again," he paired it with verses about resurrection. When he described his need to "complete the work," he paralleled it with the words of Christ on the cross: "It is finished." To him, scripture was a universal language, one he could bend to his private mythology.

And yet, his use of religion wasn't random. It followed a pattern, control, confession, absolution, repeat. Every murder, every ritual, every letter, and every prayer fit into that cycle. His church provided the framework; his crimes gave it meaning. The hymns about obedience and surrender echoed his fantasies of domination. The act of kneeling before God mirrored his victims kneeling before him. In every way that mattered to him, the two worlds were reflections of each other.

His own family absorbed this duality without ever seeing it. He led them in prayer before dinner, quoted verses to his children, and carried a Bible in his car. To his wife, Paula, it was one of his better traits, the mark of a man grounded in faith. She later told investigators that she believed "church kept him steady." It did, just not in the way she imagined.

Rader's theology became his scaffolding. Without it, the illusion of order would have collapsed. His rituals, both spiritual and homicidal, existed to reinforce that illusion. In one chilling entry, he wrote, "BTK is the sin that proves my faith." He believed that by acknowledging his darkness privately, he was living truthfully, that others were hypocrites because they hid their own sins, while he, in his mind, lived honestly with his.

The delusion was total.

Even in prison, after his arrest, that duality remained unbroken. He attended Bible studies, quoted scripture to guards, and told interviewers that he believed God had forgiven him. When asked if he prayed for his victims, he said, "I pray for understanding." Then, without irony, he added, "He used me for His purpose."

That statement sent shivers through everyone who heard it. Rader had never stopped believing he was chosen, only that his mission had changed. Now, he said, his purpose was to "teach others about the dangers of living a double life." He saw his downfall not as punishment, but as divine instruction. "God got my attention," he said. "He had to stop me to save me."

The self-pity in that sentiment reveals how deeply his theology of control remained intact. Even stripped of freedom, he still saw himself as part of a grand order, a man so important that God Himself had intervened to correct his path. His faith never broke. It simply folded itself around his guilt.

The strange consistency between his crimes, his church work, and his belief system is what makes Dennis Rader unique among serial killers. He didn't simply pretend to be religious. He *was* religious, but his religion served him, not God. He took the bones of Christianity, confession, redemption, judgment, and built a dark mirror image of them. Every verse about obedience became justification for power. Every sermon about order became a blueprint for control.

And in that mirror, he found comfort. The church pews, the Bibles, the hymns, all of them were part of his camouflage, but they were also his home. They allowed him to believe that he wasn't a monster, only a man fulfilling his "role" in God's creation.

That belief made him untouchable for decades, because no one suspects the man quoting scripture. No one suspects the shepherd.

No one suspects the man holding the Bible in one hand and the rope in the other.

When the news broke in February 2005 that the BTK killer had finally been caught, and that he was Dennis Rader, the council president of Christ Lutheran Church, disbelief swept through Park City like a storm that would never pass. The name alone seemed incompatible with evil. People had trusted him with their homes, their children, their prayers. He had organized church picnics, stood at the altar during baptisms, read aloud from Psalms about mercy and truth. Now the man with the Bible had been unmasked as the man with the cord.

The first Sunday after his arrest, the pews were silent. No one knew what to say. Some wept openly. Others stared ahead, motionless, as if their very memories had turned against them. The pastor tried to speak about forgiveness and grace, but the words fell flat. It was too soon. Forgiveness felt like betrayal. Grace felt like complicity.

For the congregation, the wound was existential. Their church, their sanctuary, had been the very stage upon which Rader performed his deception for decades. Every meeting he'd chaired, every sermon he'd helped write, every smile he'd offered was now contaminated by revelation. The sanctuary that had once represented safety now felt like a crime scene.

Some members couldn't bring themselves to return. They left quietly, unable to pray in the same building where Rader had bowed his head. Others stayed, determined to reclaim what he'd taken. One woman said later, "He stole our church for years. We weren't going to let him have it forever."

The Lutheran hierarchy sent counselors and clergy from neighboring states to help the congregation process what had happened. What they found wasn't just grief, it was shame. Shame that they hadn't seen it. Shame that the man they'd trusted to uphold moral order had been using that very trust as camouflage. The congregation's guilt was misplaced, but understandable. Rader had weaponized their faith against them.

Investigators who searched the church in the aftermath found nothing incriminating, no physical evidence, no hidden trophies. But spiritually, the building bore his fingerprints. In meeting rooms, his notes still sat in drawers, written in his neat, deliberate handwriting: attendance counts, sermon drafts, scheduling reminders. On one yellowing piece of paper, he had written a verse from Proverbs: "The wicked flee when no man pursueth, but the righteous are bold as a lion." He had underlined *righteous*.

That single word captured everything about his duplicity. Rader had convinced himself, and everyone else, that righteousness was a matter of order, not morality. As long as he appeared disciplined, he was safe. As long as the ritual of faith was maintained, the content didn't matter.

For the pastors and theologians who later studied his writings, this distortion of faith was the most haunting aspect of the case. Many serial killers hide behind religion. Rader lived inside it. He didn't use God as a shield, he used God as scaffolding. His belief system wasn't false; it was infected. He took the shape of faith and filled it with control.

One minister who reviewed his writings for a criminal psychology symposium described it as "a theology of tyranny." Rader's interpretation of scripture wasn't accidental; it was systematic. He selected verses about obedience, subjugation, and divine authority because they reflected his worldview. He ignored the ones about humility, compassion, and love. His version of Christianity had no Christ, only hierarchy.

When Rader was brought to court, he carried that same false calm. He stood before the judge and spoke in a tone that might have belonged to a deacon explaining church protocol. His confessions were procedural, not emotional. He detailed each murder with the same clarity he once used to summarize council meetings. When asked if he understood the gravity of his actions, he replied, "Yes, Your Honor. I've confessed my sins. I've talked to God."

The courtroom fell silent. The arrogance in his composure, the implied righteousness, left even seasoned investigators unsettled. He wasn't defiant; he was devout.

After his sentencing, his pastor issued a statement to the press that became emblematic of the church's collective grief:

"We must separate the man from the faith. Dennis Rader does not define God. He is proof of how belief can be twisted when the need for control replaces the call to serve."

It was a simple truth, and yet a profound warning.

In the weeks that followed, reporters camped outside Christ Lutheran. They photographed the brick building, the white cross rising above the entrance, the empty parking lot where Rader's car had once sat every Sunday. To outsiders, the church was a symbol of misplaced trust. To those inside, it was now a test of endurance.

The community held a candlelight vigil not for the killer, but for the idea of faith itself, a quiet reclaiming of what had been stolen. Parishioners read aloud from scripture, choosing verses about light, compassion, and discernment. One woman read from John 1:5: *"The light shineth in darkness, and the darkness comprehended it not."* For a long moment afterward, no one spoke. The silence wasn't emptiness. It was defiance.

Even years later, the echoes of Rader's deceit lingered. Members spoke about how the sermons he'd helped write now sounded different when reread, colder, more mechanical, heavy with words like "obedience" and "discipline." They began to recognize the hidden fingerprints of a man who had used religious language as a cipher for power. The words hadn't changed; their meanings had.

Criminal psychologists later identified this linguistic duality as part of Rader's pathology. He didn't lie in the usual sense. He *repurposed*. He took truth and redefined it to suit his structure. Scripture wasn't false to him; it was functional. It gave him vocabulary. It lent gravity to his fantasies. In his letters, "judgment" didn't mean God's reckoning. It meant his own.

One FBI profiler described his religious self-perception as "a bureaucrat of damnation", a man who believed he could systematize sin, log it, and file it away like church minutes. The metaphor was chilling because it was accurate. Rader's sins were documented, categorized, archived, and in that documentation, he believed, controlled. His faith was never about absolution; it was about management.

The theological aftermath of the BTK revelation rippled far beyond Park City. Scholars began writing about what they called *"the Rader paradox"*, the way a devout life can mask moral emptiness. How ritual without empathy becomes performance. How structure without compassion becomes tyranny. Rader was its perfect embodiment: the orderly killer, the faithful predator, the man who could bow his head in prayer hours after binding a victim.

In the years since his arrest, the church has rebuilt itself quietly. The building remains the same, but its spirit changed. There are fewer decorations, fewer banners proclaiming cheerful verses. The sermons speak more about discernment, about the danger of confusing appearance with goodness. The congregation that once trusted structure above all else now listens differently.

The pastor who leads the church today keeps one of Rader's old council memos locked in a drawer, not as relic, but as reminder. "Evil doesn't always shout," he once told a journalist. "Sometimes it reads from scripture in a calm voice."

For Dennis Rader, faith was never about redemption. It was architecture. A design of control. His pew became his pulpit; his pulpit became his mask. The codes in his sermons were not confessions, but commandments, a language of order twisted into worship of himself.

When he looked up at the cross each Sunday, he didn't see salvation. He saw structure. A shape of power, symmetry, and authority. In its shadow, he felt safe , because it reminded him of his own rules, his own dominion, his own belief that control, not compassion, was divine.

And so, for thirty years, the man who called himself BTK prayed beneath the symbol of mercy while serving only the god of domination. He never hid from the light. He stood directly beneath it , knowing no one would ever think to look for darkness there.

Chapter Eight

The Boy Scout Leader's Dark Side

The Oath and the Rope; How BTK Twisted Trust Into Control

On paper, Dennis Rader was the perfect Boy Scout leader. A father, a churchgoing man, a reliable neighbor with a steady job, the kind of adult every parent hoped would guide their sons toward discipline and integrity. In the 1970s and '80s, he led troop meetings with precision, planned camping trips with enthusiasm, and carried himself like a man who believed deeply in the Scout Law: trustworthy, loyal, helpful, obedient.

To those around him, he embodied that code. To himself, he was its master manipulator.

Rader's fascination with the Boy Scouts wasn't merely civic duty; it was structural. The organization appealed to everything he valued, order, uniformity, rules, and ritual. The Scout Oath demanded obedience; the Scout Handbook outlined hierarchy. It was a world of commands and consequences, of badges earned through discipline, of lessons in tying, binding, and control. To most, those were innocent skills. To Rader, they were tools of affirmation.

He volunteered not out of altruism, but because it gave him access, access to trust, to community, and to the perception of moral purity. Every camping trip, every meeting, every knot demonstration reinforced his image as a man devoted to mentorship. Parents admired his patience. Other leaders praised his dedication. His son thought he was a hero. And that image of heroism gave Rader a kind of psychological immunity. No one questions the Scoutmaster.

Behind that smile, however, was a man who understood how easily structure could be turned into control. The same rules that governed discipline could be inverted into domination. The same knots that symbolized preparedness could be used to simulate restraint. The same oaths that bound boys to virtue reinforced his private belief that order was power.

He once wrote in a diary entry recovered after his arrest: "The Scouts are the perfect system. Discipline and reward. I feel calm there."

That word, *calm*, appears repeatedly in his writings when he describes places of control. The church, his home, the Scouts, all of them provided order. Each gave him a role where he could assert authority while appearing virtuous. The uniform, the badges, the salute, they were props in the performance of righteousness.

During troop meetings, he was exacting but not harsh. He demanded punctuality and precision. He praised tidiness and obedience. When a Scout made a mistake during knot practice, Rader would correct him with careful hands, showing exactly how to loop and cinch. To the boys, it was instruction. To Rader, it was rehearsal. The physicality of ropework, the friction, the pull, the tightening, stirred something familiar inside him, something dark and disciplined that he kept perfectly hidden behind the mask of mentorship.

On weekend camping trips, Rader often volunteered for logistics, tents, supplies, safety checks. He liked control. He liked lists, protocols, order. Other Scoutmasters appreciated his efficiency. Parents admired his dedication. No one ever noticed that his attention to detail wasn't about safety; it was about surveillance. He observed constantly. He noted behaviors, vulnerabilities, opportunities. It was the same instinct that guided his stalking in Wichita, the quiet, methodical cataloguing of lives.

His own son, Brian, was often present on those trips, which deepened the disguise. To the outside world, Rader was the model father, active, involved, invested. To Rader, the presence of his child made his mask unbreakable. "Who would suspect the man who camps with his son?" he once wrote. That rhetorical question captures the essence of his camouflage. His evil thrived in ordinary settings.

Former Scouts remembered him as strict but fair. "He ran things like a small army," one recalled years later. "Everything had to be just so, the tents lined up, the ropes coiled, the fires built exactly right. He made us recite the Oath like it was law." That intensity seemed admirable then. In hindsight, it was chilling. The Oath was sacred to Rader not because of its moral message, but because it codified obedience.

The Boy Scout Law became another scripture for him. "A Scout is trustworthy, loyal, helpful, courteous, kind, obedient, cheerful, thrifty, brave, clean, and reverent." He recited it often, emphasizing *obedient* and *reverent*. He spoke about them as if they were commandments. In his mind, they were, not divine laws, but personal affirmations of his worldview. Obedience and reverence: submission and order. The words resonated far beyond the campfire.

In one of his later interviews, Rader described the Scouts as "a great outlet for my structured side." He said it calmly, without irony, as if he were discussing a hobby. That phrase, *structured side*, was his euphemism for the compulsive need to control. The Scouts gave him a sanctioned environment to express that need, to enforce rules, to issue commands, and to be admired for it.

He didn't need to harm anyone there. The power itself was the satisfaction. The trust of parents, the respect of boys, the uniform that commanded deference, it all fed the same hunger. In that sense, the Scouts were both camouflage and therapy. The control he could not exert openly elsewhere, he found there in miniature, legitimate form.

But Rader's involvement with the Boy Scouts went beyond meetings and merit badges. He used the position as a vantage point. The outdoor settings, the isolated campsites, the long drives outside Wichita, all of them provided opportunities for observation. His diary entries mention "rural scouting trips" near areas later linked to his stalking activity. He kept records of trails, remote cabins, and unlit backroads, not as official logs, but as potential landscapes for his fantasies.

Nothing in those notes directly tied his crimes to Scouting events, but the proximity is unnerving. Investigators later concluded that his time as a Scout leader sharpened his skills, knot-tying, ropework, planning, and the calm required to maintain control under pressure. They were practical applications of the same discipline he applied to his murders.

He had mastered what the Scouts called *preparedness*. But for him, "Be Prepared" was not a motto, it was doctrine.

In the 1980s, Rader's reputation as a Scout leader deepened his credibility in the community. He earned awards for service, received letters of appreciation from parents, and was even photographed in local newspapers with his troop. Those images, smiling children, tents in the background, Rader standing tall in his uniform, would later haunt Wichita. They were symbols of innocence retroactively poisoned by revelation.

One photograph, in particular, struck investigators after his arrest. Rader is pictured kneeling beside a campfire, adjusting a coil of rope while two Scouts watch. The rope rests across his hands like a sacred object. The image, once ordinary, now seemed prophetic, a visual metaphor for his entire life: the rope, the trust, the watchful eyes, the mask of mentorship.

The diaries recovered from his home contained scattered references to Scouting activities. Some are mundane, notes about troop meetings, camping supply lists, schedules. Others are darker, veiled in euphemism. He wrote about "special feelings" during certain outings, about the "discipline of order," about the "purity of control." The language mirrors that of his crime journals. It is impossible to know where the Scout leader ended and BTK began, or if there was ever truly a boundary between them.

For Rader, the Scouts reinforced the illusion that his two worlds could coexist, the public man of rules and the private man of fantasies. Both operated by systems, both rewarded precision, both demanded obedience. And as long as the structure held, so did the mask.

At night around the campfire, he would lead the boys in prayer or reflection, his voice calm and steady. "A Scout's honor is his word," he'd remind them. "Never break your word." The irony is unbearable. He had built his entire life on broken oaths, to his church, to his family, to his victims, to God. But to the boys, he was a figure of certainty. They couldn't have known that their Scoutmaster's lessons on honor were spoken by a man who had none.

He understood the power of symbols, the handshake, the salute, the uniform. They provided structure, repetition, and belonging. To most, those were virtues. To Rader, they were containment. Every symbol was another mask, another way to blend in. The Boy Scout emblem, sewn neatly on his chest, became another shield in his collection, an icon of innocence hiding a mind addicted to control.

In his life, every world fed the other: the church gave him language, the Scouts gave him legitimacy, and his job in compliance gave him power. Each reinforced his identity as a man of order. Each reminded him that the best place to hide a monster was inside a man who seemed obsessed with rules.

And in the Boy Scouts, perhaps more than anywhere else, Dennis Rader found the perfect reflection of himself: a world that worshipped discipline, revered authority, and believed without question in the virtue of obedience.

The rope and the oath , bound together in his hands , were all the disguise he ever needed.

The Kansas wilderness at night can feel infinite , an ocean of trees, the silence broken only by the shifting wind and the slow burn of a campfire. For the boys in Troop 820, those moments were the highlight of every trip: the quiet under the stars, the laughter fading into tired murmurs, the comforting certainty that their Scoutmaster was keeping watch.

He was always watching.

Dennis Rader preferred the edge of the firelight, where his face was half-lit, half-shadowed. The darkness suited him. There, surrounded by obedience and ritual, he could play the role of protector while secretly reveling in control. He liked knowing that every boy trusted him implicitly , that the parents back home slept soundly because *he* was out there with their sons. It wasn't lust or cruelty that drove him in those moments. It was satisfaction , the quiet power of being the unchallenged authority in a world that worshipped structure.

He kept the Scout Oath pinned to the inside cover of his field notebook: "On my honor, I will do my best to do my duty to God and my country... to obey the Scout Law..." To Rader, those words had resonance beyond their surface meaning. Duty. Obedience. Law. They were the commandments of his private religion of control. When he recited them with his troop, he wasn't reaffirming morality; he was reaffirming himself.

He ruled the camp like a small kingdom. Every chore had a schedule. Every tent had a rule. He taught the boys how to tie bowlines, square knots, and clove hitches, demonstrating each with slow, deliberate precision. "A knot," he'd say, "isn't strong unless it's neat." It became a kind of mantra, one that mirrored his life. Everything had to appear neat, structured, perfect. Disorder was danger.

The irony, of course, was that the man preaching order was living in absolute deception. By day, he wore the khaki uniform of honor; by night, he still wore the invisible one of BTK. Between those two worlds, he walked a line so thin it should have snapped. But it didn't, because the world he inhabited rewarded precision and ritual.

In the Boy Scouts, Rader found ritual everywhere. The flag ceremonies, the salutes, the campfire pledges, all were small liturgies of obedience. They appealed to his sense of hierarchy. He wasn't content to be a participant; he needed to be the orchestrator. He planned every outing meticulously, timing the activities to the minute. He assigned tasks in quiet tones, expecting instant compliance. To the other leaders, it looked like discipline. To Rader, it was control perfected.

On one camping trip, a former Scout remembered, Rader spent nearly an hour instructing the boys on how to coil rope properly. When a few grew restless, he scolded them softly but firmly. "A good Scout respects the line," he said. "If you don't control it, it controls you." The boys laughed. Years later, that line would seem grotesquely prophetic.

Investigators later found several notebooks in Rader's home filled with references to Scouting trips. Most were routine: meal plans, tent arrangements, supply lists. But scattered between them were fragments that revealed something deeper, "remote clearing near pond, good isolation";

"route north, few houses"; "privacy after dark, no lights." Whether those were innocent observations or extensions of his private fantasies remains unknown. But the handwriting was the same as in his crime journals: neat, deliberate, emotionless.

He compartmentalized even in ink.

Parents saw nothing but dedication. He was the first to arrive at troop meetings, the last to leave. He drove the supply truck, fixed broken lanterns, cleaned up after everyone. He had the energy of a man who believed in purpose. His fellow Scout leaders described him as "strict but reliable." They liked that he kept the boys in line. "He made the kids listen," one recalled. "We could trust him to keep order."

That trust was his camouflage. It gave him freedom to move, to travel, to plan. No one questioned his absences or his solitude. When he lingered at the edge of the woods during night patrols, others assumed he was ensuring safety. In truth, those moments, the silence, the dark, the solitude, fed him. They gave him time to think, to replay fantasies, to write invisible scripts of control. The wilderness was his church, the campsite his altar.

The diary entries from those years reveal a man who saw meaning in small acts of dominance. "Guiding them," he wrote once, "gives me peace. They follow. They trust. They learn." The line could have been written by any proud mentor. But in Rader's lexicon, words like *follow* and *trust* were never innocent. They were proof of power.

He measured himself constantly, how well he played the part, how completely the world accepted it. The Boy Scouts gave him affirmation that his mask worked. Every parent handshake, every thank-you note, every smiling photograph was validation. Each was a reminder that he could be both: the man of rules and the man of ruin.

For Rader, the duality wasn't stress. It was equilibrium. "Balance," he called it in his notes. "Good on one side, dark on the other. Keeps me steady." He believed his good deeds, church service, Scout leadership, community work, offset the darkness of BTK. It was a personal theology of balance, a ledger of morality in which he was always even.

He once told an acquaintance, "I think everyone's got two sides. Some just manage it better." At the time, it sounded like wisdom. Later, it would read like confession.

In the late 1970s, as BTK's murders temporarily ceased, Rader's involvement with the Scouts deepened. He poured energy into it, organizing longer trips, earning commendations, teaching merit badge classes. It wasn't rehabilitation; it was substitution. The structure of Scouting replaced the structure of stalking. The camp became his containment. He could channel the same obsessive need for precision into harmless form, at least temporarily. It wasn't redemption. It was repression.

Investigators would later note how his "hibernation years" overlapped almost exactly with his most active period in Scouting. Between 1979 and 1985, there were no confirmed BTK murders, but dozens of detailed scouting records. The link was psychological, not logistical. The control he once expressed through violence was being fed through legitimate channels. He was still the same man; he had simply found another ritual.

Rader's wife, Paula, saw the Boy Scouts as a blessing. It kept him busy, gave him purpose, and, in her eyes, brought him closer to their son. She saw the photographs, her husband teaching, smiling, surrounded by boys in uniform, and felt pride. She could never have known that those same photographs would one day appear in case files labeled *evidence of dual identity*.

Rader's Scout materials became part of the investigation after his arrest, not because they contained direct proof of crime, but because they showed his obsession with control. Every entry was logged with precision, every trip documented like a military report. One investigator described reading his notes as "entering a mind that worshipped structure." Even his handwriting looked disciplined, as though emotion were an error he refused to allow.

It's easy to imagine him on those trips, standing just outside the glow of the fire, clipboard in hand, watching the boys laugh and roughhouse. He would smile faintly, correct a tent line, and remind them to be quiet after dark. To the Scouts, he was a guardian. To himself, he was something else entirely, a man quietly measuring the boundaries of trust, testing the perfection of his disguise.

One former troop member, interviewed decades later, said something that captures the quiet terror of hindsight: "He made us feel safe. That's what gets me now. I realize he probably liked that. The power of it."

That power was his lifeblood. Whether in the suburbs or the wilderness, Rader sought one thing above all else, control cloaked in virtue. The Boy Scouts gave him both. It was the perfect camouflage, the perfect laboratory for his rituals of obedience, and the perfect test of how fully a monster could live inside a man of order.

Every campfire was a rehearsal for control. Every knot was a sermon. Every oath recited in unison was a quiet echo of his favorite illusion: that the world would always trust the man who taught them how to tie the line.

By the mid-1980s, Dennis Rader's life had reached its most deceptive equilibrium. To everyone who knew him, he appeared balanced, a husband, father, church leader, Scoutmaster, and city compliance officer. Every corner of his existence was ordered, cataloged, and clean. But beneath that symmetry, something was beginning to fracture.

The same structure that had protected him for so long began to suffocate him. Control, once his refuge, became a cage of his own making. He had designed a life of perfect containment, but the walls were closing in.

The compulsion that had driven him since childhood, the hunger for dominance, the thrill of private power, had not vanished during the years of quiet. It had merely adapted, waiting for new ways to manifest.

In his diaries, later seized by police, the language began to shift. Early entries from his Boy Scout years were crisp and factual, lists, observations, reminders. But gradually, new words appeared: *urge, temptation, release.* They marked the reawakening of his internal conflict. He wrote of "testing discipline," of "keeping control," of "quiet urges near the woods." The tone was one of struggle, not guilt, a man measuring his own self-restraint as if it were a contest of will.

Camping gave him proximity to the sensation he missed most: surveillance. The act of watching had always been central to his psychology. Before he was BTK, he was a voyeur, a man who found power in invisibility. At the camps, in the solitude of night, surrounded by sleeping tents and the pulse of quiet wilderness, that old instinct stirred again.

He would sit at the edge of the clearing, the fire behind him reduced to embers, scanning the shadows beyond the campsite. It wasn't the boys he watched; it was the boundary between darkness and control. Every rustle of leaves, every shifting shadow fed the paradox that defined him, fear and mastery intertwined. In those moments, he was both the protector and the predator, the watcher and the watched.

He began recording details again, not of potential victims, but of sights, patterns, triggers. "Moonlight through tent fabric," one entry reads. "Sound of breathing in night air. Stillness after curfew." He was cataloguing sensation, not planning violence. But those sensations were the same ones that had once preceded it. His old language of control was returning, quietly, inevitably.

At home, his family saw little change. He was meticulous as ever. His wife noticed he sometimes stayed up late after Scout trips, sitting alone at the kitchen table, writing in his notebook. She assumed he was logging troop expenses or preparing reports. In reality, he was documenting what he called "discipline exercises." He described moments of temptation, then the calm that followed their suppression. Each entry ended the same way: *"Still in control."*

That phrase became his mantra. Control defined him. It was his proof of superiority, his shield against chaos. Yet the more he wrote it, the less it seemed true.

The Scouts had given him legitimate outlets for his structured mind, but they had also placed him in proximity to secrecy, isolation, and ritual. He thrived on the authority, but the ritual itself became intoxicating. Every rule he enforced, every rope he coiled, every curfew he imposed became part of a subconscious script, one that blurred the line between leadership and obsession.

Former Scouts remembered him as quietly intense during those years. "He didn't joke much," one said. "He was serious about everything, even folding flags. You couldn't tell if he was proud of us or inspecting us." That detachment, once mistaken for professionalism, was something darker, the same cold focus that had defined his earlier crimes. It wasn't cruelty; it was disconnection. He didn't see people as people. He saw them as parts of a system.

Psychologists later analyzing his case noted that this detachment was a critical stage in his unraveling. His compulsion didn't disappear during the quiet years, it sublimated. Denied the outlet of violence, it transformed into private ritual. He sought satisfaction in small acts of control: managing behavior, observing details, rehearsing the internal calm of domination. But repression isn't removal. It's postponement.

One entry from his notebooks reads: "Still dream. Still project. But family and Scouts keep BTK asleep." The wording is clinical, but the meaning is unmistakable. BTK had become, in his mind, a dormant presence, an alter ego restrained by duty and order. But to Rader, restraint was only meaningful if it could be tested.

During some Scout trips, he began sneaking away at night under the pretense of security patrols. He would walk the perimeter, flashlight in hand, listening to the hum of insects and the distant chorus of frogs. These were moments of solitude, and temptation. He later wrote that the silence "made the mind wander back to old times." That phrase, *old times*, was how he referred to his killings. He was reliving them in memory, through ritual, through control.

The Boy Scouts, in essence, became a behavioral substitute, a structured performance that allowed him to maintain the illusion of balance while privately feeding the same psychology that once drove him to murder. He wasn't healed; he was rehearsing.

At church and in the neighborhood, his reputation only strengthened. The longer he remained disciplined, the more people admired him. He took pride in that admiration. Each handshake, each compliment was proof that his system worked, that he could contain darkness behind the façade of decency indefinitely.

But that belief began to crack in small ways. His writing grew impatient. The word *calm* appeared less often; *need* began to replace it. He described dreams in which he was "testing the line," a metaphor that investigators later interpreted as both literal and symbolic, the line of the rope, the line of control. He was circling the edge again, feeling the pull of his hidden self.

At work, colleagues noticed minor shifts. He became more irritable, more insistent on authority. His reports as a compliance officer were increasingly punitive. He wrote citations for trivial infractions, overgrown lawns, misplaced trash bins, with a kind of bureaucratic zeal that bordered on obsession. It was another form of control, another way to reassert his dominion in a world that never questioned his motives.

Meanwhile, at home, he grew quieter. Paula assumed it was stress. Their children were teenagers; life was routine. But Rader's silence was not fatigue, it was tension. The equilibrium he'd built between the church, the Scouts, and his hidden fantasies was eroding. The more ordinary his life became, the louder BTK's silence grew.

During one particularly long Scout trip, he wrote about a "familiar surge of energy." The entry ends abruptly: *"Felt alive again. Not sure why."* That vague admission marked the reawakening of what investigators later called his "control cycle." It was the moment when the performance of discipline could no longer contain the impulse it was meant to suppress.

The wilderness that had once soothed him began to taunt him. The quiet nights no longer brought peace; they brought temptation. He began describing the woods as "pure space", empty, unjudging, free. The same language appears in his earliest writings about stalking. The environment of the Scout trips, isolation, silence, control, had rekindled his internal theater.

The cracks widened. He started referring to BTK again in third person. "He's patient," one note reads. "He's still there." The duality was back in full force. Rader was speaking of himself as two entities: the man of order and the man of hunger. He had kept them separate for years, but the wall was thinning.

To the public, nothing had changed. The Scout meetings continued. The camping trips went on. Parents still praised his commitment. But in his private notebooks, a different story was unfolding, one of restlessness and relapse. His mask of mentorship was holding, but just barely.

In psychological terms, Rader's hibernation years weren't a remission. They were pressure years. The longer he repressed his compulsions, the more they demanded expression. The Scouts had given him structure to contain them, but structure without empathy is brittle. It can hold only until the first fracture.

And by the late 1980s, that fracture was coming.

By the late 1980s, Dennis Rader had built his life into a fortress of discipline. Every wall was neatly aligned , the church, the Scouts, the job, the family. His calendars were immaculate, his routines unwavering. He believed the order he'd constructed was unbreakable. But inside that fortress, pressure was mounting.

He had spent nearly a decade living in the narrow space between two selves , the public man of duty and the private man of fantasy. For years, the mask had held, sealed by the predictability of suburban life. Yet the more ordinary his world became, the more fragile his equilibrium grew. The stillness he'd once prized had begun to echo.

He was forty-four now, heavier, grayer, but still sharp. His daughter was growing up. His son was nearly out of Scouts. The structures that had defined him , family, youth programs, nightly rituals of order , were shifting beneath him. The scaffolding of control that had kept his darker self at bay was eroding, and he felt it.

The diaries from those years read like a man arguing with himself. "The world is good," one entry begins. "Work steady, family fine, Scouts steady." Then, a few lines later: "Still dreams. Still the old stirrings." He ends the page with two words written hard into the paper: *"Don't wake him."*

BTK was never gone. He was only dormant , a mind folded inside another mind, patient and waiting.

At work, Rader's temperament changed. As the Park City compliance officer, he had authority over neighbors' lawns, pets, and property upkeep. It was minor power, but it fed him. Residents began describing him as "strict," "cold," even "cruel." He cited families for grass too long, dogs too loud, sheds too close to fences. He measured compliance like morality. The authority of rules replaced the thrill of the hunt, temporarily. But enforcement wasn't enough. It was passive control. He missed the intimacy of power.

That longing began to leak into his routine. He lingered longer on patrols. He noticed faces again, women hanging laundry, walking dogs, closing blinds. He began to catalog them, though now he told himself it was professional observation. In truth, it was the old rhythm returning, scanning, noting, projecting.

The dormant patterns were reforming, piece by piece.

In his notes, he began referring to "projects" again, though in vague terms. "Project thoughts creeping back," one entry says. "Test control. Keep balance." He described "watching routes" and "logging ideas." The words were cautious, almost clinical, but the intent was unmistakable. He was building scaffolds for the old impulses, quietly, deliberately, under the guise of curiosity.

At home, the tension surfaced in subtler ways. He became impatient with Paula, irritable about small mistakes, controlling in conversation. When she mentioned missing church one Sunday, he snapped. "We have obligations," he said flatly. "We don't get to choose discipline." She thought it was stress. It wasn't. It was the voice of a man whose internal order was slipping.

The Boy Scouts still provided him structure, but the satisfaction was waning. The boys were older now; the routines too familiar. He needed something new, something unpredictable to remind him of power. He began walking alone at night again, the same quiet neighborhood patrols that had once preceded his earliest murders. He told Paula he was "clearing his head." He was, but not of thought. Of restraint.

Rader's fantasies evolved with the times. He began collecting news clippings again, stories of crimes, missing women, police investigations. He analyzed them not as a citizen, but as a professional of deception. "They always make mistakes," he wrote in one note. "Patience is the key." That patience was the thread holding him together, but it was fraying.

In one entry from 1987, his tone shifts sharply:

> "BTK still sleeps. But sometimes I feel him move. Like a muscle I haven't used in a while. It feels good. It feels natural."

Investigators who later studied that line said it was one of the most chilling in his entire archive. The calmness of it, the ease with which he described awakening the darkness, revealed that Rader saw BTK not as a secret to hide, but as a faculty to manage.

The transformation was underway.

Around that time, he began visiting old locations, not the exact crime scenes, but familiar routes. He drove by former stalking areas, sometimes parking near intersections he had once watched from his car in the 1970s. He told himself it was nostalgia, a kind of private reflection. In reality, it was rehearsal. Each familiar street reactivated the old rhythm of surveillance.

He felt alive again.

During one spring Scout trip, Rader's internal balance nearly snapped. He wrote afterward about an overwhelming sense of agitation, "like too much energy inside." He described standing at the edge of camp, staring into the woods long after the others were asleep. The quiet made him restless, not peaceful. He wrote, "The darkness feels close again. I've been too still."

Too still, that was the key. For Rader, stillness was no longer safety; it was stagnation. The equilibrium he'd built through order, faith, and civic duty had turned against him. The same discipline that once suppressed BTK was now amplifying him. The killer's silence had become unbearable.

At church, he began quoting scripture about "awakening" and "restoration." His pastor found it inspiring. It wasn't. To Rader, those words had private meaning, resurrection, renewal, return. He saw his self-control not as virtue, but as imprisonment. BTK had become his hidden god, the source of order and meaning that gave his existence its shape. Without it, he was hollow.

He began testing boundaries in small ways, the way a prisoner tests the lock on his cell door. He reactivated his old surveillance habits, photographing random houses under the pretext of "code enforcement," taking notes on window coverings, backyard layouts, entry points. He wasn't planning yet; he was reacquainting himself with the language of control.

His wife never noticed the shift. To her, he was just busy again, focused, methodical, perhaps a bit cold. But she welcomed the predictability. Predictability had always been his greatest disguise.

By 1988, Rader's diary entries became shorter, sharper. The word *balance* disappeared entirely. In its place, a single recurring phrase: *"Project time soon."*

He started driving longer distances, sometimes claiming to be checking county ordinances. In truth, he was scouting again. He wrote about "testing lines of sight," "watching habits," "revisiting potential areas." He was back in motion, the same calm predator, now older, quieter, but no less meticulous.

The final entries before the killings resumed show a man fully awake to his old self. "I can manage both," he wrote. "The world needs both sides." It was the ultimate justification, his theology of duality restored. The Scout Oath, the church hymns, the compliance reports, all of it had been scaffolding. Now the real architecture returned.

In his mind, the long silence had been an act of discipline, not repentance. He hadn't retired BTK; he had perfected him.

In early 1989, he began assembling what he called "activity notes", sketches, plans, photographs. They were almost identical to his earliest murder preparations from the 1970s, down to the handwriting and numbering. He was back in ritual. The notebooks that had once recorded troop attendance and city inspections were now filled again with the language of predation.

On the surface, nothing changed. The same man still led Scout meetings, still attended church, still enforced ordinances. But behind that familiar composure, the old rhythm was building, methodical, inevitable, mechanical.

The final entry of that period reads simply:

"He's back."

That was all. No signature. No elaboration. Just two words written with the same deliberate precision as always.

For nearly a decade, BTK had been silent, lulled by family, masked by the Scout's uniform, restrained by order. But in the quiet suburbs of Wichita, beneath the steady hand of a man who seemed incapable of chaos, the killer had begun to breathe again.

The rope would tighten soon.

Chapter Nine
Polaroids of a Killer
The Photographs That Exposed BTK's Dual Reality

The box was unremarkable, plain, weathered, and tucked deep inside a storage cabinet in Dennis Rader's suburban home. It looked like the kind of container anyone might use for tax records or family photos. When investigators opened it, they didn't find family memories. They found the visual diary of a killer.

The discovery came during the exhaustive search of Rader's house after his arrest in 2005. Detectives expected to find written notes, they already knew he was meticulous. What they didn't expect were hundreds of photographs: Polaroids, slides, negatives, all catalogued with the same obsessive precision that marked every part of his life. Inside them lay the most disturbing confirmation of who BTK truly was.

The images weren't snapshots of violence. They were something stranger, more personal, a catalog of Dennis Rader *as* BTK. He had photographed himself in elaborate scenes of bondage, often wearing women's clothing, wigs, and masks. In many, he was bound and gagged, sometimes inside his own home, sometimes outdoors, sometimes in settings meant to recreate the positions and postures of his victims.

The photos weren't trophies of crime. They were *rituals of memory*.

Detectives laid them out on the evidence table one by one, and a grim silence filled the room. The pictures were staged with meticulous care, ropes tied with exact symmetry, props arranged with almost theatrical precision. In some, Rader had used mannequins or himself as stand-ins for victims, binding them with the same kinds of knots he had used in real life. He photographed these scenes not as an act of art, but as documentation. Each one was a performance of control, frozen in time.

For investigators, the shock wasn't only in what they saw, it was in what the images revealed. Rader hadn't just committed murders; he had built an alternate universe where he was both killer and victim, executioner and subject. Through the lens of his own camera, he was performing his duality, documenting the private rituals that kept BTK alive during the long years of silence.

One detective described it later: "It was like he was building a museum to himself. Every photo was evidence, but it was also self-worship."

The photographs spanned decades. Some were clearly taken in the 1970s, faded and discolored, while others were more recent, dated as late as 2004. They showed the evolution of his compulsion, how his fantasies matured and mutated as he aged. In the early photos, he appeared younger, thinner, wearing stolen women's lingerie, posed in carefully bound positions on a bed or basement floor. Later ones were darker, Rader older, heavier, still binding himself, still photographing every angle as though recording an experiment.

He wasn't capturing pleasure. He was preserving control.

What the investigators began to understand was that photography, for Rader, was more than a fetish. It was an act of engineering, a way to replicate and relive. Each photograph was a reconstruction, a frozen affirmation that BTK still existed, even when he wasn't killing. The lens was his confessional. The camera, his accomplice.

He labeled some of the photos with cryptic notes: "Project X," "Revisit," "Scenario B." The terminology mirrored the language in his writings, where he often referred to murders as "projects" and "hits." The photos were not random; they were organized like a portfolio. He had arranged them into themes , bondage, burial, confinement, re-creation , each representing a facet of the world he had built for himself in secret.

Detectives found not only Polaroids but also slides, negatives, and handwritten logs. He had recorded technical details: the type of rope used, the angle of light, the duration of the pose. The precision was almost scientific. It was the same mechanical detachment he brought to his killings, now redirected toward self-documentation.

The basement where many of the photos were taken became, in hindsight, his private stage. It wasn't merely a hiding place , it was a workshop of identity. The concrete floor, the bare walls, the faint smell of storage , all became the setting for his transformation. He didn't see it as sordid. He saw it as process.

In several photos, Rader's face is obscured by masks , crude, featureless, almost childlike. The anonymity was deliberate. He wanted to erase Dennis and become BTK entirely. In others, his expression is visible , calm, composed, eerily detached. His gaze meets the camera with clinical precision, as if he were both specimen and scientist.

When the evidence team presented the images to the psychological profilers working on the case, one of them described the collection as "a visual manifesto." Rader wasn't just recording perversion; he was expressing ideology. The photographs illustrated his belief that control was the highest form of existence , that by binding himself, he was mastering his own nature.

To the public, the revelation of these photos was almost incomprehensible. The same man who had read scripture at church, who had led Boy Scout trips, who had attended neighborhood barbecues, had also spent nights tying himself to pipes in his basement while photographing every angle with a timer. The contrast was more shocking than the acts themselves. It was the proof of total duality, the living embodiment of deception.

When the photos were shown, in limited form, to law enforcement briefings, the reaction was visceral. "We thought we knew what kind of man we were dealing with," one agent said. "But those pictures... they were the inside of his mind. You could see how he kept the fantasy alive all those years."

The collection also included props, mannequins, ropes, masks, pieces of clothing belonging to victims, and carefully folded women's undergarments labeled with initials. Some were confirmed as trophies; others were objects he used to recreate crimes. The mannequins were positioned in grotesque mimicry of his victims' final states. Yet, again, it wasn't sadism that dominated the imagery, it was control. Everything was ordered, symmetrical, methodical. There was no chaos, no blood, no frenzy. Just choreography.

Rader photographed his own body as though he were both artist and artifact. He adjusted lighting, arranged the frame, then recorded the result, sometimes dozens of images from slightly different angles. To most, they were disturbing. To him, they were documentation of achievement.

Even the choice of Polaroid film carried meaning. Instant, tangible, and private, the perfect medium for someone obsessed with control and secrecy. No negatives to process, no lab technicians to question. Every image stayed in his hands, literal proof that the memory belonged solely to him.

Forensic psychologists later described the collection as a "feedback loop of control." The acts, the photographs, the viewing, the storage, each step reinforced his self-image as BTK. The photos were not mementos of guilt; they were validation of power. By photographing himself, Rader ensured that BTK could never truly die.

When detectives asked him about the collection during interrogation, Rader's tone was disturbingly neutral. "Those were personal projects," he said. "Private time. I liked to document things." There was no shame in his voice, only precision, as though he were discussing inventory rather than confession.

Pressed further, he said something that chilled even veteran investigators: "They were part of the system. You have to record the system, or you lose the sequence."

The "system" was his word for BTK's methodology, the rules, rituals, and hierarchies he created to sustain his identity. In his mind, the photographs were maintenance records, proof that the system was still functioning even when he wasn't killing.

The photos bridged the gap between fantasy and reality, providing continuity where there might otherwise have been guilt or collapse. For Rader, the lens was not a barrier, it was a portal. Through it, he could become BTK again, if only for seconds, frozen in the frame of his own creation.

Investigators came to see those Polaroids not as curiosities, but as key evidence in understanding the man they had caught. They were not confessions, nor were they excuses. They were self-portraits of delusion, images of a man who had built an entire world of control, photographed it, catalogued it, and then returned to the surface to mow his lawn and wave to his neighbors.

Every image was proof of what he'd always believed, that he could live both lives indefinitely.

The photos made it clear he was wrong.

The evidence room at Wichita Police Headquarters filled quickly. Cardboard boxes, labeled in black marker, *Rader, D., Evidence Set 17 through 32*, lined the long metal table. Inside them were the photographs, carefully separated into categories by forensic technicians. Each image had been assigned an evidence number, cross-referenced with notes, and logged into a growing database that documented every trace of Dennis Rader's hidden world.

For weeks, analysts pored over them one by one, wearing gloves, masks, and the kind of quiet concentration usually reserved for archaeological digs. What they were excavating wasn't physical evidence; it was psychological.

The Polaroids were grouped according to content: self-bondage, re-creations, props, mannequins, trophy arrangements, and unidentified locations. Each group became a window into a different layer of Rader's mind. The photographs didn't follow a simple timeline. They were cyclical, recurring in patterns that mirrored the rhythm of his killings, planning, control, reflection, and renewal.

Detectives soon realized that the images could be mapped against his known crimes. Certain poses, angles, and settings echoed the details of individual murders. A photograph showing Rader bound near a tree line, for instance, matched descriptions he later gave of a victim's outdoor burial site. Another, taken in his basement, recreated the same bindings used in the Otero case. The parallels weren't coincidental, they were deliberate acts of reconstruction.

The forensic photographers called it "ritual re-entry." Rader had been returning to his own crimes through staged photography, revisiting them, controlling them, mastering them again and again.

But the analysis went deeper than correlation. The task-force psychologists saw in these images a blueprint of the killer's evolution. Early photos showed rough staging, simple bindings, poor lighting, no props. Later ones displayed elaborate composition: tripods, lighting rigs, precise angles. His compulsions had become more sophisticated, more ritualized. What began as crude documentation had transformed into ritual choreography.

The photographs also revealed something investigators hadn't fully grasped, the degree to which Rader's life revolved around process. Every image showed order, precision, and control. There was no chaos, no randomness. Even in self-bondage, the ropes were tight but clean, the knots deliberate, the frames symmetrical. One detective remarked, "He couldn't even let his madness be messy."

That obsession with order was the key to understanding BTK's duality. The photos weren't expressions of emotion. They were exercises in control, experiments in re-creating dominance without risk. The act of photographing himself bound, helpless, was not submission; it was ownership. He was directing both sides of the image, captor and captive, god and sinner, Dennis and BTK.

The FBI's Behavioral Analysis Unit (BAU) received copies of the photographs to aid in building a complete psychological profile. Their conclusion was chilling in its precision: Rader's photography was not merely sexual; it was structural. Each photo represented the codification of a compulsion, a moment in which fantasy replaced reality but achieved the same psychological result. The process, not the act, was his true addiction.

Dr. Katherine Ely, one of the forensic psychologists consulted during the review, described it this way:

> "He didn't photograph pain; he photographed control. Every image is a study in symmetry, emotional coldness turned

into visual design. The camera was his confessional, and the Polaroid was his absolution."

That symmetry extended beyond his body into his environment. In some photos, Rader's basement was spotless, tools aligned on the wall, ropes coiled neatly beside labeled containers. Investigators noticed that he staged his scenes the same way he organized his workspace at the church and the city office. The parallel was undeniable. His life's two halves, public order and private ritual, mirrored each other perfectly.

Even the choice of camera angle revealed his mindset. He often placed the lens low, shooting upward at himself. The resulting images gave him the stature of a figure in control, towering, central, framed by shadow and light. In other shots, he photographed himself from above, as if observing a subject. These shifting perspectives reflected the ongoing dialogue in his head: the man who commanded and the man who obeyed.

The BAU analysts coined a term for this pattern: *The Mirror Loop*. It described how Rader used photography to maintain his double life. By alternating between dominance and submission in his self-images, he sustained the illusion of balance between his two identities. It was self-reinforcement, psychological maintenance disguised as documentation.

Every photograph was an argument against chaos.

Detectives also noted the meticulous labeling. Each Polaroid was numbered and often cross-referenced with shorthand codes found in his notebooks, "MB2," "Ref-B," "XRevisit." These codes matched entries describing "sessions," "projects," and "memories." The photos, in essence, were the visual wing of his archive. Rader wasn't just reliving his past; he was archiving it like a historian of his own pathology.

The cataloguing was so detailed that investigators were able to reconstruct timelines of his secret activities. They noticed spikes in his photographic output that aligned with moments of external stress, job changes, family milestones, or public anniversaries of his crimes. The Polaroids weren't random indulgences; they were pressure releases. Whenever his façade of normalcy grew too tight, he returned to the ritual.

At one point, detectives even used the backgrounds of certain photographs to identify exact locations, sheds, tree lines, drainage ditches. Some matched areas he'd mentioned in his confessions. Others were new, places that might have served as what investigators called "psychological crime scenes", sites where he reenacted the feeling of control without physical victims.

The most disturbing revelation came when analysts compared the photographs with his writings. In his journals, Rader often described moments of "becoming the scene." The phrasing echoed his photographic practice. He wasn't content to remember. He had to *inhabit* the memory, to step back into the architecture of control he had built. The photographs were his way of doing that, reliving power through image.

Forensic teams also noted the calculated risk in keeping the collection. Rader, who understood law enforcement procedure, must have known that discovery would expose him completely. Yet he preserved the images meticulously. Psychologists concluded that the act of keeping them, of *risking* exposure, was part of the thrill. The possibility of discovery validated his belief that he was untouchable.

"Rader's arrogance," one FBI analyst wrote, "was not loud but structural. He believed that order itself would protect him, that as long as his boxes were labeled, his life would stay intact."

The photographs dismantled that illusion. They showed that his control was never about mastery, it was about fear. Fear of disorder, fear of himself, fear that if he didn't document every piece of the monster, it might consume him entirely. In binding himself, he was containing the chaos. In photographing himself, he was proving it was contained.

When prosecutors reviewed the collection, they understood that these images would never be shown in open court. They were too intimate, too revealing of the psychological sickness behind the crimes. But they also recognized their evidentiary value. Together with his journals, the Polaroids created a complete map of his internal world, every impulse, every rehearsal, every justification captured frame by frame.

In the end, what shocked investigators most was not the depravity of the images, but their clarity. There was no confusion in Rader's gaze, no madness in his expression. He looked calm, competent, deliberate. He wasn't documenting insanity. He was documenting belief, the belief that he could control the darkness within him forever.

And for nearly thirty years, he did.

The Polaroids were the proof. They were the threads that stitched together both halves of his existence, the man in the church pew and the man in the rope.

When one detective was asked what the photographs ultimately revealed, he said quietly, "They showed us that BTK never needed to kill every year. He only needed to *know* he could."

That was the essence of Dennis Rader's dual reality, not bloodlust, but the pursuit of perfect control, captured one Polaroid at a time.

When the formal analysis concluded, the photographs were no longer just evidence; they had become a psychological dossier. The BTK task force stored the original prints in temperature-controlled vaults, each image sealed in its own archival sleeve. But for months afterward, many of the people who handled them said they could still see the photographs when they closed their eyes.

Lieutenant Ken Landwehr, the veteran homicide commander who had pursued BTK for decades, described the moment the meaning finally crystallized. "It wasn't what he did in those photos that haunted me," he said later. "It was the order. He'd turned evil into paperwork."

That insight reframed everything the investigators thought they knew about Dennis Rader. The photographs, once deciphered, became the connective tissue linking his public life, his writings, and his crimes. Each image served as a node in a larger structure of control, and once the analysts mapped them, a pattern emerged, one that revealed not spontaneity, but long-term design.

The Behavioral Analysis Unit compiled a joint report titled *Visual Ritualization and Self-Documentation in Compulsive Offenders.* The document circulated quietly among law-enforcement psychologists. It argued that Rader's case demonstrated a new dimension of organized offenders: not simply the keeping of trophies, but the systematic creation of self-records meant to perpetuate identity. In their terminology, BTK was "a curator of himself."

Every photograph reinforced his self-mythology, and every act of cataloguing stabilized it. The analysts concluded that Rader's entire life had been a closed circuit of control, family, work, church, and fantasy all governed by rules of his own making. The images were the proof that the circuit existed and that he worshipped its perfection.

The discovery forced investigators to revisit earlier assumptions about the hiatus years. Before the Polaroids, many believed Rader had gone dormant because of fear or conscience. Afterward, the consensus shifted: he had paused only because he had found another method of satisfaction. The photographs were the bridge that carried BTK through the silence.

Forensic psychologists compared the structure of the photo sets to architectural blueprints. Each sequence began with a simple frame, Rader preparing the scene, and built toward a climax of complete immobilization, followed by a denouement in which he appeared relaxed or reflective. The arc repeated itself across decades. The photographs, they said, were "ritual architecture," proof that his compulsion was not chaos but design.

The Wichita detectives, most of them seasoned in homicide, found that realization more disturbing than the crimes themselves. They had seen violence before; they had not seen obsession rendered so clinically. "It was engineering, not mania," one officer said. "He planned his darkness the way an accountant plans taxes."

The BAU's psychological summary noted that Rader's images stripped away the romanticized notion of the serial killer as impulsive predator. He was deliberate, procedural, bureaucratic. His murders were not expressions of rage but experiments in total mastery. The photographs extended that mastery into permanence.

For weeks after the analysis, the task-force offices were unusually quiet. Investigators who had spent years chasing BTK now found themselves confronting the anatomy of his mind in freeze-frame. Several requested counseling, a rare admission in law enforcement. One analyst described the images as "a contagion of control," explaining that studying them too long made ordinary order feel suspect: lists, files, neat handwriting, all echoes of the same pathology.

The Kansas Bureau of Investigation began using the case in advanced training seminars, emphasizing how documentation itself could be evidence of compulsion. Detectives learned to look for micro-patterns, photographs, digital folders, labeled containers, as potential indicators of organized obsession. Rader's Polaroids had changed methodology.

In parallel, a team of forensic psychiatrists examined what the photographs revealed about his inner structure. Their conclusion was that Rader's identity depended on constant proof of existence. Without external validation, records, notes, images, his sense of self began to dissolve. The camera gave him that proof. Each shutter click reaffirmed that BTK was real, and that Dennis Rader controlled him.

One psychiatrist compared the behavior to a feedback loop in artificial intelligence: "He built a system that learned from itself. The more he documented, the more real the persona became, which required further documentation to sustain."

This insight explained why Rader had preserved the photos despite the risk of exposure. To destroy them would have been, in his mind, to erase part of himself. The photographs were not keepsakes; they were components of identity.

Investigators who interviewed him after his conviction confirmed that interpretation. When asked why he kept such incriminating material, Rader answered matter-of-factly, "They were records. I keep records of everything." His tone was the same he used when describing municipal inspections or Scout meetings. Record-keeping was morality; it meant order.

Landwehr recalled feeling a chill at that statement. "He said it like he was proud of it. Like we should respect the bookkeeping."

The photographs also clarified how deeply Rader compartmentalized his life. The BAU report identified distinct cognitive boundaries he had maintained: *Domestic Self* (husband, father, employee) and *Controlled Self* (BTK). The Polaroids belonged entirely to the latter. By capturing them on film, he could literally file his darkness away, store it, and return to his daily routine unburdened.

The analysts began calling this mechanism *externalized conscience*. Instead of feeling guilt, Rader stored it in images. Once recorded, the act no longer pressed on his mind; it existed in the archive, safely contained. The photographs were his moral quarantine.

That discovery unsettled even veteran profilers. If a person could neutralize guilt through documentation, how many others might be using similar rituals in the digital age? The BTK case became a cautionary reference for the coming era of online self-documentation, a warning that technology could serve pathology as easily as art.

Inside the task force, a quiet reverence grew around the photo boxes. Detectives treated them almost as sacred artifacts, not out of respect for Rader but because they represented the complete unveiling of deception. For thirty years, he had hidden behind sermons, Scout uniforms, and city ordinances. Now, through his own meticulous images, he had confessed without words.

One afternoon, as analysts prepared the final psychological summary, a young technician paused over a photograph showing Rader seated on the concrete floor, hands bound, eyes staring into the camera. She asked her supervisor, "Do you think he ever knew he was giving himself away?" The supervisor replied, "I think that was the point."

That exchange captured the paradox haunting everyone who studied the case. The photographs were both concealment and revelation. Rader had built them to preserve secrecy, yet they became the evidence that destroyed it. His need for documentation, his belief that order was protection, had led him to create the very archive that proved his guilt beyond doubt.

When the investigators finally sealed the boxes for long-term storage, the room was silent. No one wanted to look again. The lead crime-scene photographer turned off the lights and said quietly, "He wanted to be remembered. Now he will be, but not the way he planned."

For the profilers, the Polaroids became more than the record of one man's pathology. They were a lesson in the fragility of order itself: how a life built on perfect structure can conceal absolute disorder beneath. In every classroom, every lecture, that image endures, the man who photographed his own duality until the film ran out, believing control could save him from exposure, when in truth it was the thing that exposed him most.

When the last photograph was logged and filed, a strange silence settled over the task force. It wasn't relief; it was a kind of exhaustion that went deeper than work. For months, they had dissected the inner world of Dennis Rader frame by frame, looking into the eyes of a man who had meticulously preserved his own evil , not for memory, but for maintenance.

In the weeks that followed, many of the investigators described feeling changed. "You spend too much time in his order," one detective said. "It starts to feel like gravity." They meant the pull of structure , the seduction of neatness that Rader embodied. Everything in his world had boundaries, sequences, labels. And for a while, working through those boundaries, some began to feel a perverse respect for the craftsmanship of his deceit. It frightened them to realize how easy it was to admire precision without seeing what it concealed.

That was the lesson they carried away: evil, in the modern world, doesn't always look like chaos. Sometimes it looks like paperwork, calendars, Polaroids.

The BAU later codified those insights into training modules for future profilers. They began teaching the concept of *ritual continuity* , the idea that compulsive offenders maintain their identities through structured repetition rather than constant violence. Rader's Polaroids became the case study for this principle. His crimes were finite, but his rituals were infinite. The camera had allowed him to extend his compulsion across decades without detection.

Another lesson came from the emotional residue the photographs left behind. Unlike ordinary crime-scene photos, these images carried intimacy. They were self-directed, self-aware, the killer communicating only with himself. That intimacy was what lingered with the investigators. "He wasn't performing for us," a profiler said. "He was performing for the mirror."

The deeper the team studied those images, the more they began to see reflections of everyday normalcy inside them, the tidy surroundings, the domestic props, the calm demeanor. It wasn't the monstrousness that disturbed them; it was the familiarity. "He looked like a man at work," one agent recalled. "Focused. Composed. You could take the rope out of the picture and it would look like someone fixing a shelf."

The recognition haunted them. It blurred the boundary between the procedural and the personal. For the first time, many investigators questioned not only how Rader had lived undetected for so long, but how easily the same pattern could exist unnoticed anywhere else. His duality was not exotic; it was suburban. That realization was harder to face than the crimes themselves.

Several members of the unit later admitted they stopped taking photographs at family events for a while. The camera, once a tool of memory, now felt contaminated, a reminder of how easily the lens could lie. "It made me think about why we take pictures at all," one analyst said. "Rader took them to remember control. We take them to remember love. But the mechanics are the same, you frame something, freeze it, own it."

That awareness reshaped forensic training across agencies. Analysts were taught to look for psychological signatures in seemingly ordinary documentation, the need to record, to catalog, to preserve. "Every collection tells a story," became a quiet mantra in behavioral seminars. "Ask what the collection is protecting."

For the Kansas investigators, the Polaroids remained a wound and a warning. Some retired early, unwilling to immerse themselves again in what one called "the quiet kind of horror." Others continued teaching, using BTK's case as a study in duality. They learned to speak of him not as a monster, but as an engineer of identity, a man who built a system so tight it collapsed under its own perfection.

When Rader was transferred to the state penitentiary to begin serving his life sentence, a handful of detectives attended the transfer ceremony. They said nothing to him. He nodded politely, as though leaving a city meeting. To them, that gesture said everything, the bureaucracy of evil distilled into a single, meaningless courtesy.

Afterward, they returned to the evidence room one final time to oversee the permanent archiving of the photographs. The boxes were numbered, sealed, and stacked in chronological order. Each one was labeled with a code that meant nothing to outsiders, just numbers and letters. To those who had handled them, though, the codes represented chapters of a human mind dismantled and stored away.

One detective lingered as the archivist slid the last box into the storage vault. He looked at the gray metal shelves, row upon row of cardboard, and said softly, "He thought control would keep him safe. Now it's what keeps him locked up."

The vault door closed with a hydraulic hiss. The lock clicked. The temperature gauge blinked to green.

That sound, the final seal of containment, became the true ending of the BTK case. Not the courtroom confession, not the sentencing, but the quiet moment when the photographs were shut away, the light gone from them forever.

To the men and women who had spent months studying those images, that closing door meant more than justice. It meant reversal. The same order that Rader believed would protect him had become his prison. The structure that once hid his darkness now confined it, catalogued and forgotten behind layers of evidence tape.

In the years that followed, the photographs were viewed only by specialists and trainees. They became legend in criminology circles, not for their content, but for what they represented. They were the anatomy of deception, the map of how evil wears a uniform of normalcy. Professors displayed sanitized reproductions in lectures on forensic psychology, always with the same preface: "These are not pictures of violence. These are pictures of control."

And somewhere in a climate-controlled vault in Kansas, the originals remain. The color will fade, the paper will yellow, but the symmetry will endure, the ropes, the masks, the sterile angles that once held meaning for a man who thought perfection could replace conscience.

He believed he was preserving power.

In truth, he was documenting his own captivity.

Chapter Ten

The Vanishing BTK

The False Calm; How Dennis Rader Hid in Plain Sight for Thirteen Years

The body of Dolores Davis was found beneath a bridge on the outskirts of Park City, Kansas, in February 1991. She had been missing for days, her disappearance sparking local concern but little panic. By then, Wichita had learned to forget. The city hadn't seen a confirmed BTK killing in years, and though his name still lingered in whispered caution, most residents believed the nightmare was over.

In truth, the nightmare had simply changed shape.

For Dennis Rader, Davis's death marked both an ending and a test. It was his last known murder , a final act before he slipped into what would become a thirteen-year silence. But that silence was not peace. It was calculation. The same meticulous instinct that had allowed him to live a double life for decades now turned inward. He no longer needed to prove power through death. He could sustain it through control.

After the Davis murder, Rader returned home that night to the same quiet routine , washing his hands, eating, talking with his wife, checking the thermostat before bed. The contrast between what he had just done and the normalcy of the house around him only strengthened his sense of mastery. He had crossed the line again and returned without consequence. That was his ultimate thrill.

But the act also changed him. He was older now, slower, and more aware of the risks. The 1980s had ended with a technological shift in policing that unsettled him. DNA testing, computer databases, electronic evidence , these were tools he didn't fully understand. He read about them in magazines and technical journals, always with an anxious fascination. The world was modernizing around him, and he knew his old methods would not survive the new era.

So, he adapted.

He buried BTK beneath layers of ordinary life. The next morning, he went to church. By that weekend, he was attending Scout meetings. Within a month, he was back to work at his new position as a compliance officer for Park City. There, he found something unexpected: a new kind of control.

His job was to enforce city ordinances , inspecting yards, measuring fences, citing residents for violations. It was the perfect profession for a man obsessed with rules. He could knock on doors, issue warnings, and demand obedience. The power was small, but to him, it was pure. The badge, the clipboard, the authority to compel , all became substitutes for his old rituals.

Residents quickly learned to fear the man in the city truck. He was polite but cold, strict to the letter of every rule. If a dog barked too long, if grass grew too high, if trash bins lingered on the curb, Rader would appear. He would photograph the property, take notes, and issue citations in immaculate handwriting. He called it "keeping order." His neighbors called it something else: harassment.

In private, Rader considered his work civic duty. He believed discipline kept society intact. In reality, it was his outlet. The structure of law enforcement gave him permission to exert dominance without suspicion. He could enforce compliance and feel justified. It was, in his mind, the perfect camouflage, the same thrill of control now sanctioned by bureaucracy.

Wichita, meanwhile, settled into the quiet complacency of the 1990s. New families moved in. Old fears faded. The police department archived the BTK case, occasionally revisiting it when new tips arrived, but most officers had never worked the original murders. To a generation of residents, BTK was an urban legend, a cautionary tale told by parents who remembered the 1970s.

Rader liked that. Oblivion was power.

He began to study his own mythology, clipping old newspaper articles about himself and saving them in binders. He noted the mistakes reporters made, incorrect dates, misquoted details, errors in description, and took satisfaction in knowing the truth they'd missed. He was, in his own words, "the keeper of the real record."

His marriage to Paula Dietz provided the next layer of camouflage. To the community, they appeared steady, even admirable. She was quiet, kind, devoted to family. He was dependable, organized, involved in church. Their home was clean, their children well-mannered, their lives ordinary to the point of invisibility. Rader took pride in that invisibility. It was proof that his system worked.

In his private notes, later recovered from his computer and journals, he referred to this period as "Phase L" for "Life Mode." He described it like a military operation: "Objective, maintain cover, monitor urges, channel control through civic duty." The language was chillingly detached. Even in dormancy, he treated his life as procedure.

He replaced the thrill of stalking with the satisfaction of observation. He patrolled neighborhoods not for prey but for infractions. He wrote memos with the same care he once used to plan abductions. He photographed code violations as though documenting a crime scene. The methodical repetition kept him balanced, or so he believed.

At home, he was attentive but distant. His children remembered him as strict but predictable. He kept meticulous household records, finances, vehicle maintenance, even grocery inventories. His control extended to every aspect of domestic life. He measured time by tasks. Sundays were for church, Mondays for inspections, evenings for paperwork. Every deviation was recorded, corrected, or punished.

To outsiders, he appeared reformed. To himself, he was refining.

What no one knew was that the BTK persona still existed, alive in notebooks, sketches, and coded documents stored in his private files. He continued to write fantasy scenarios, describing "projects" he never executed, rehearsing imagined murders like stage plays performed only in his mind. These writings were never random. They were organized by theme, by method, by "type." Each one was another exercise in control.

In one entry dated 1995, he wrote: "BTK still rests but watches. Discipline strong. Must keep system intact." It was a journal of restraint, the language of a man who saw murder not as chaos but as structure to be managed.

Investigators would later see this period as crucial in understanding his psychology. The absence of killings did not indicate rehabilitation; it showed transformation. He had learned to replace action with order, violence with paperwork, chaos with hierarchy. His power no longer required blood, it required obedience.

As technology advanced, Rader remained trapped in an older world. He read about DNA breakthroughs, computer databases, and digital forensics with fascination but distance. He was curious, yet dismissive. "They only catch the sloppy ones," he once told a coworker, joking about television crime shows. His arrogance insulated him from fear.

That arrogance would prove fatal.

By the early 2000s, he believed he had outlasted the legend. The media had moved on. The BTK case was unsolved, but cold. He assumed the detectives who once hunted him were retired or dead. He viewed himself as an invisible success story, the man who had beaten the system.

He didn't realize the system had changed.

In quiet office buildings, new databases were being connected, DNA, fingerprint, property records, communication archives. The digital age was making anonymity impossible. Rader didn't know that his old letters, saved in police archives, were being scanned into searchable databases. He didn't know that new forensic linguistics could identify writing patterns.

He thought the world had stopped watching. In reality, it had learned to see differently.

During these years, the BTK investigation existed only as a ghost file , reopened occasionally, then returned to the shelf. But technology was creeping closer. When the case would finally reignite in 2004, it would do so because Dennis Rader himself reached out, unable to live without recognition.

For now, though, he remained hidden in plain sight: a man enforcing local ordinances, attending church, caring for his family , and quietly maintaining the illusion that he had conquered his darker self.

He hadn't. He had only taught it patience.

And patience, for BTK, was never peace. It was preparation.

By the mid-1990s, Dennis Rader had perfected his new identity, not as a killer, but as a man of rules. He wore his city-issued badge like a symbol of moral authority, a small emblem that gave structure to his days and permission to command others. The Park City truck he drove became his patrol car, his clipboard his weapon. For a man who once hunted in darkness, sunlight now served as his cover.

He liked that his authority was official. No more pretending, no more shadows. When residents defied him, he could knock on their doors and speak in the calm voice of government. "Sir, you're in violation of city code." The tone was bureaucratic, but the pleasure was familiar, the quiet rush of forcing compliance. Control, the heartbeat of his secret life, had simply found new form.

Rader thrived on confrontation cloaked in civility. He was polite, even deferential, but unyielding. A neighbor's untrimmed hedge, a dog without a leash, a car parked at the wrong angle, all became small moral battles he could win. He catalogued each citation meticulously, keeping duplicate records at home. To coworkers, he seemed efficient; to himself, he was conducting order like a symphony.

He spoke of his work as though it were sacred. "People need structure," he would say. "If you don't enforce it, chaos spreads." In truth, the chaos he feared most was internal. Every warning he wrote, every ordinance he enforced, was another layer of defense against the disorder that lived inside him.

Paula, his wife, saw the change but didn't question it. Her husband had always been methodical. Now he was simply more serious, more focused. He spent evenings updating inspection logs, typing reports long after dinner. He filed everything alphabetically, even personal notes. When she suggested he take a break, he'd smile faintly and say, "It's all about staying on schedule."

He was building a life where nothing, not a feeling, not a moment, could escape structure.

Inside that structure, his arrogance began to bloom. Rader believed his system made him untouchable. He saw himself as the embodiment of order in a disordered world. The city relied on him; the church respected him;

his family obeyed him. To the neighbors, he was strict but dependable. The image was perfect, the mask seamless.

But control carried its own decay. The tighter he wound his routines, the more brittle they became. His journals from those years, sparse but revealing, show a man measuring himself constantly, keeping score against invisible standards. He recorded how many citations he wrote, how many church meetings he attended, how many miles he drove. Even his leisure time was documented. "Mowed lawn 1.5 hours. Organized garage. 100% productive." The language was mechanical, the tone proud.

Behind that precision lurked fatigue. Maintaining perfection was its own addiction, one that required constant feeding. If he wasn't enforcing order, he felt anxiety. When he wasn't writing, he felt guilt. In his diary, one entry stands out: "Without tasks, I drift." It reads like a confession, though he would never admit it aloud.

He kept up appearances in church, serving as council president and leading committees. He enjoyed the structure of religion, the schedules, the bylaws, the minutes of meetings. But sermons about humility made him restless. He preferred the ones about obedience. To him, faith was another form of regulation, divine compliance. He quoted scripture the way he quoted city codes, as proof that rules defined righteousness.

Everywhere he went, Rader carried the quiet confidence of a man who believed he'd outsmarted fate. The BTK case had faded from public consciousness; even police rarely mentioned it anymore. He would occasionally hear jokes about the "old BTK days" and smile inwardly, the secret swelling like a private reward. "They never caught him," people would say. "He's probably dead."

He would nod. "Probably."

The longer he lived in that anonymity, the more he began to believe in his own legend. The killer was gone, the husband remained. He had divided himself so cleanly that the line between them no longer required effort. Yet deep down, the old impulses never vanished, they simply migrated. The thrill of dominance found new targets: subordinates at work, committee members at church, even his family.

His daughter, growing into adulthood, remembered her father's strange insistence on obedience. "He always wanted things done exactly his way," she said years later. "He'd make small rules just to make them." To her, it seemed like strict parenting. To him, it was the same system that had once governed life and death.

Rader's need for control began seeping into his private rituals again. He organized his photographs, his scouting memorabilia, his old crime notes, all labeled and stored in binders. Some were ordinary, others deeply incriminating. He believed his precision protected him. The binders were kept in hidden drawers, sealed in plastic, each marked with coded initials. In his mind, these weren't evidence. They were artifacts, proof of mastery.

Even in domestic stillness, the duality persisted. He could sit at the dinner table, quietly eating roast beef, while in another room the relics of BTK rested in tidy boxes. He liked knowing they were there, contained, catalogued, ready. He called them "the old days," as though referring to a chapter of history he had authored.

At work, his supervisors valued his discipline. He volunteered for additional duties, helped draft procedural manuals, and monitored employee conduct. He enjoyed inspecting others' performance. The more he enforced standards, the stronger his illusion of superiority became. He saw infractions everywhere, not moral failings, but inefficiencies. "People need rules," he said often. "They like knowing someone's watching."

That last phrase, in retrospect, was prophetic.

Through the late 1990s, Wichita remained peaceful. New neighborhoods grew where the old murders had once cast shadows. BTK had become folklore, his crimes receding into the city's collective amnesia. The silence comforted the public, and intoxicated Rader. He was the ghost among them, the man who had beaten time itself.

He kept reading about serial killers, Bundy, Dahmer, the Green River case, and measured himself against them. He believed he was superior. "They were sloppy," he wrote in a margin of one newspaper article. "They lacked discipline." He saw his restraint as proof of intellect, not morality.

He often fantasized about being remembered, not as a man, but as a design. The idea of legacy began to take hold. If BTK could not exist in action, he would exist in record. This thought was the seed of his eventual undoing.

As the millennium approached, Rader's world tightened further. Computers entered city offices, email replaced paperwork, and surveillance cameras became common. He watched technology change with curiosity but mistrust. He understood physical evidence, not digital traces. "Machines make mistakes," he told coworkers, dismissing computer systems as fads. But in private, he was unsettled. The new world no longer obeyed the same rules.

He wrote about it once: "Everything's being watched now. Everyone leaves marks. BTK never left marks."

The irony was already forming, he would be caught not by footprints, but by words and pride. Yet in those quiet years, he couldn't imagine exposure. The façade of his life felt impenetrable.

To the city, he was the embodiment of order. To his church, he was devotion incarnate. To his family, he was routine itself.

To himself, he was still BTK, silent, patient, waiting.

And waiting, as he had always believed, was not surrender. It was preparation.

By the early 2000s, Dennis Rader had built a life so structured it could almost pass for happiness. Every corner of his existence was boxed, labeled, and recorded. The system worked, until it began to devour itself.

He was fifty-eight now, gray at the temples, heavier, slower. But the neatness remained. His truck was immaculate. His desk drawers were aligned with military precision. His home office looked like an evidence locker, rows of binders, stacked logs, and carefully labeled disks. The world saw diligence; only he knew it was ritual.

And like every ritual, it began to crave renewal.

For years, his compulsion had been restrained by bureaucracy, the city ordinances, the church meetings, the paperwork that gave him daily doses of authority. But control without recognition eventually bored him. He could make people comply, yes. But no one *feared* him. Fear, he realized, had always been the true narcotic. The absence of it left a void.

It started with nostalgia. He began revisiting his old case notes, the yellowed clippings he'd kept hidden in a cabinet. He reread them late at night, the light from his desk lamp pooling over the brittle pages. He underlined old headlines, correcting reporters' mistakes in red ink. "False," he wrote beside one paragraph. "Did not happen this way."

He was reconstructing his legend.

The arrogance that had always simmered beneath his surface grew stronger. He'd beaten the system, outlasted the investigators, and watched the public forget. To him, that wasn't just survival, it was victory. He saw himself as the unseen genius of Wichita, the master of order in a world of chaos. And deep down, he wanted that mastery acknowledged again.

He wrote in his journal: *"The world moved on. They shouldn't have. They don't remember correctly."*

The statement marked a subtle but critical shift. For years, Rader's private writings had been about restraint, keeping the "system intact," maintaining balance. Now they began to focus on legacy. His compulsion was no longer just to control, but to be recognized for having controlled so perfectly.

He began testing boundaries again, the way he had done before every escalation. The first was emotional: he allowed himself to think like BTK again. He called it "reviewing the system." He mentally replayed the old "projects," not with guilt, but with fascination, the logistics, the planning, the precision of each.

Then came the behavioral tests. He started driving longer routes home from work, sometimes detouring near old neighborhoods. He told himself he was "inspecting property lines," but his destinations betrayed him. He was revisiting ghosts. He liked the feeling, the pulse of control returning in small doses.

Neighbors began noticing his restlessness. He talked more about crime, about police incompetence, about how "justice never really closes." He watched true crime shows obsessively and made notes during them, as if grading the killers. When one documentary claimed that "BTK had likely died or moved away," he smiled thinly and muttered to himself, "Not quite."

The seed of pride had sprouted.

Technology fascinated and unsettled him. He purchased his first computer in the early 2000s, a modest desktop, meant for word processing and reports. But once connected to the internet, it became a portal to his old obsessions. He searched for news about serial killers, about BTK, about the mythology that had formed in his absence.

He discovered entire forums dedicated to his crimes, amateur sleuths, crime historians, and armchair profilers who dissected his letters, debated his intelligence, speculated about his fate. Some called him brilliant. Others called him pathetic. Rader read it all.

And it consumed him.

He began printing online articles and filing them in new binders marked "BTK Review." He annotated them in his familiar precise handwriting, sometimes agreeing, sometimes correcting, sometimes arguing with the text like a man defending his thesis. He saw himself as misunderstood, a craftsman of control reduced to a footnote in crime history.

That, more than anything, offended him.

He wrote: *"They don't see the art. They don't understand the project system. They think it was random. It was never random."*

In his mind, BTK wasn't a monster; he was an architect, a man who had built a perfect design of control, one that lasted decades without collapse. He wanted history to remember that. The thought festered into an obsession: setting the record straight.

His home life remained unchanged on the surface. He attended church, cooked dinners, paid bills. But Paula began noticing small oddities, his distracted silences, his late nights at the computer, the sudden return of his old intensity. She assumed it was work stress. He had recently clashed with city officials over procedural changes. "They're sloppy," he told her. "No one respects structure anymore."

But the truth was simpler: he missed power.

He began keeping new notes, not of crimes, but of commentary. He described how "the modern world has lost discipline," how "people want freedom but can't handle it." He wrote about rules as salvation, about how "control keeps the world sane." It was the same tone he once used in his BTK communications, now softened by the years but unchanged in spirit.

His fantasy world never truly went away; it had just evolved. The self-bondage rituals returned sporadically, though modified to fit his age and caution. He documented them privately, photographing himself again, as he had decades earlier. He labeled the images "reflections", his word for the quiet reenactments that rebalanced his mind.

Each time, the rush lasted shorter. Each time, the emptiness afterward grew deeper.

By 2003, Rader had reached a crossroads he didn't consciously recognize. His life of control was no longer satisfying, and the legend he'd created was fading from memory. For a man who saw himself as a designer of history, oblivion was intolerable.

He began drafting letters again. At first, they were harmless, unsent notes addressed to newspapers and TV stations, written under pseudonyms. He wanted to see how it felt to communicate again, to remind the world that BTK still existed. The first draft began, "It's been many years. Did you forget me?"

He didn't send it. Not yet. But the act of writing rekindled something powerful. He called it "contact mode" in his notes, the phase he used to describe the period between fantasy and action. The language was clinical, as always. He wasn't describing emotion; he was describing procedure.

Every system he had ever built, every binder, every file, every photograph, had one flaw: it required acknowledgment. Without an observer, his order meant nothing. And for thirteen years, no one had been watching.

That realization became unbearable.

The following winter, as Wichita moved through another quiet year, Rader began rehearsing his reemergence. He read about police cold-case units reopening old files, and it thrilled him. "They're still looking," he wrote. "Maybe I'll help them."

He started assembling a new set of materials, old photos, copies of letters, typed notes. He placed them in envelopes, testing combinations of paper and typeface, just as he had done in the 1970s. It wasn't nostalgia. It was resurrection.

He told himself it would be harmless, just words, no action. A puzzle for the police, a game between equals. He convinced himself that BTK could return as a legend, not a killer.

But for a man whose every act was about control, reaching out again would be the ultimate loss of it.

He didn't know that yet. He believed he was still the architect.

Soon, he would learn he was only the exhibit.

The decision, when it came, was quiet. There was no rush of impulse, no dramatic breaking point. It arrived like everything else in Dennis Rader's life, planned, measured, justified by the internal logic of order.

By early 2004, he had spent months preparing what he called in his notes a "communication reactivation." The phrase had the sterile precision of an engineering term, not a confession. He outlined objectives, materials, and risk mitigation. To anyone else, it would have looked like a municipal project plan. To Rader, it was an awakening.

He convinced himself it wasn't dangerous. "Just correspondence," he wrote. "Information exchange. No contact." In his mind, he was not reigniting a crime spree, he was curating history. The world, he told himself, had gotten BTK wrong. He would correct it.

He began assembling the package at his desk late one January night. The house was still; his wife asleep in the next room. He worked by the thin cone of light from a desk lamp, his movements slow and deliberate. On the table before him lay relics from a vanished era: photocopies of his original letters, photographs of crime scenes clipped from old newspapers, and a fresh sheet of lined paper on which he began to write.

His handwriting was as careful as ever, slow, deliberate, a hybrid of engineer and clerk. He addressed the Wichita Eagle newspaper, the same outlet he had once taunted decades earlier. The words came easily, as if they had been waiting all along.

He opened with a question: *"Do you still remember me?"*

It was not a threat. It was vanity, the longing to be seen again, to have his myth restored. He imagined the city's confusion when the letter arrived, the police scrambling to confirm authenticity, the headlines resurrecting his name. He would be the phantom come back to life, the architect reasserting authorship over his legend.

He included a photocopy of an old crime-scene photograph and a few coded details that only BTK could know. Then he signed it in his familiar, looping way: **B.T.K.**

The initials looked both archaic and powerful, symbols of a past he alone understood.

He sealed the letter carefully, pressing the adhesive strip with his thumb. Then he sat back, studying the envelope like an artifact. It represented everything he'd built and everything he was about to risk.

He considered not sending it. The thought flickered briefly, a test of self-control. But the need to act had already surpassed the fear of consequence. For years, he had lived in a vacuum of recognition. Now, with one envelope, he could restore balance.

He waited until morning. Routine mattered even now. He shaved, dressed, packed his lunch, and drove his usual route through Park City. The envelope rested beside him on the passenger seat, tucked beneath a stack of inspection reports. To him, it didn't feel like evidence. It felt like continuity, the next entry in a perfectly ordered system.

He stopped at a public mailbox outside a hardware store. It was cold that morning, wind scraping across the flat Kansas streets. He looked around once, not in fear but in habit, the ritual glance of a man who had spent his life observing. No one was watching.

He took the envelope from his coat pocket and turned it over in his hands. The weight of it was almost nothing, paper and ink, history condensed to ounces. He thought briefly of the first letters, the thrill of those days when his name had terrified an entire city. He thought of the quiet since, the anonymity he had turned into a religion.

For thirteen years, he had hidden behind discipline. But discipline without acknowledgment had become emptiness.

He held the envelope between his fingers, feeling the faint texture of the paper. Then he slid it into the narrow blue slot of the mailbox. The sound it made, a soft rustle as it fell into darkness, was almost ceremonial.

The motion was small, unremarkable, invisible to everyone but him. And yet, in that instant, the silence of thirteen years shattered.

Rader stood there for a moment, hand resting on the metal edge of the box. The act was done. He felt calm, almost relieved. He told himself he was merely feeding history, not provoking it. He believed he could control what happened next, just as he had controlled everything else.

He walked back to his truck, started the engine, and merged onto the road. The morning looked ordinary, children walking to school, a jogger crossing the intersection, the sound of traffic blending with the wind.

But somewhere inside that mailbox, beneath the stack of ordinary correspondence, a killer's confession was on its way to the surface.

It would take only days for the letter to reach the newsroom, only hours after that for the Wichita Police Department to reopen a file thought long closed.

Dennis Rader didn't know it then, but that envelope, the product of his need for recognition, the proof of his pride, would be the first thread that unraveled his entire illusion of control.

He drove away without looking back, the blue mailbox receding in his mirror.

For thirteen years, BTK had been a ghost.

Now, with one quiet motion of his hand, the ghost was alive again.

Chapter Eleven
The Fatal Floppy Disk
The Byte That Betrayed Him; How Technology Caught the Master of Control

The city had almost forgotten him. For a generation, Wichita had moved on, new suburbs, new faces, new fears. The BTK case was a myth now, something told in half-remembered whispers or late-night television retrospectives. But in March 2004, an envelope arrived at the offices of the *Wichita Eagle*, and the myth exhaled again.

Inside was a single sheet of paper, typed and neatly folded. At the bottom was a signature no one thought they would ever see again: **B.T.K.**

The letter was brief, precise, and unmistakable. It referenced old crimes in exacting detail, facts never made public. It taunted the police with the same mix of arrogance and politeness that had defined the original BTK communications. It wasn't a hoax. It was him.

The newsroom froze. Within hours, detectives from the Wichita Police Department were inside the building, handling the paper like a sacred relic. The familiar handwriting was gone, replaced by typed text, but the rhythm of the words, the clipped phrasing, the peculiar self-importance, was the same. BTK had returned.

The letter contained a map leading to a cereal box hidden in a rural field outside town. When investigators followed the directions, they found another note inside, along with items connected to the old murders: a pendant, photographs, and references to the Otero case. There was no longer any doubt.

After thirty years, the ghost had decided to speak.

The task force that had once hunted him was long disbanded, but Wichita reassembled one overnight. Detectives who had retired were called back. Younger officers who had grown up hearing about BTK now found themselves inside the case. The cold file became hot again, and the chase that had defined a city reignited in the digital age.

But the killer they were chasing was not the same man they had hunted decades earlier. BTK had evolved. Or so he believed.

Over the following months, more packages appeared. They were left in parks, libraries, and drop boxes, each containing a mix of writings, puzzles, and relics from the past. Some were crude, others chillingly meticulous. One arrived in June 2004 at a local television station, an eight-page document filled with coded phrases, references to the "projects," and demands for recognition.

He was still trying to control the narrative, to write his own mythology. But his methods were anachronisms, floppy disks, Polaroids, photocopies, relics of a man who had stopped evolving in the 1980s. The modern world was moving too fast for him.

Investigators quickly realized that BTK wanted dialogue. He wasn't satisfied with being a relic. He needed validation. That need became their opportunity.

In one of his later letters, BTK posed a question to the police, one that would become legendary in criminal history. He asked:

"If I were to send you a floppy disk, could you trace it back to me? Be honest."

It was the kind of question only arrogance could produce. After three decades of control, he still believed himself untouchable. He wanted to trust them, to believe he could test the system without consequence. He thought the police were his audience, not his adversaries.

Detectives could hardly believe it. They saw the question for what it was: an open door.

The task force debated how to respond. If they lied too obviously, he might sense the trap. If they told the truth, they'd lose the chance to capture him. They decided on careful deceit. Through a coded message published in the newspaper, they assured BTK that the floppy disk would be safe, that it couldn't be traced.

It was a calculated gamble. They were betting on the one weakness he had never outgrown: his need to believe he was smarter than everyone else.

The ploy worked.

On February 16, 2005, a small padded envelope arrived at FOX affiliate KSAS-TV in Wichita. Inside was a purple 1.44MB floppy disk, labeled simply "BTK" in black marker. The return address was fake. The contents, however, were real.

When the disk was delivered to police headquarters, the room went silent. The air felt electric with disbelief. A floppy disk, one of the most traceable storage devices of the digital era, had come straight from the hand of a man who had eluded capture for thirty years.

Detectives immediately sent the disk to the forensics lab. They were careful not to open any visible files at first, copying the data and creating a protected clone. Then the analysts began to dissect the metadata, the invisible fingerprints of the digital age.

The first clue appeared almost instantly. Embedded in the properties of one deleted file were the words **"Christ Lutheran Church."**

Another tag followed: **"Created by: Dennis."**

The room froze.

For a moment, no one spoke. The analysts double-checked, running verification scans, ensuring the metadata hadn't been tampered with. But the data was clean. The disk had been used on a computer registered to Christ Lutheran Church in Park City, a congregation whose council president was a man named Dennis Rader.

It was almost too perfect, too careless, too human. The arrogance that had shielded him for so long had finally betrayed him.

Investigators didn't move immediately. They knew BTK's reputation for patience, for calculation. They needed to be sure. Surveillance was set up around Rader's home, his office, and the church. They monitored his movements, his routines, his communications.

He fit the pattern.

He was meticulous, organized, and eerily ordinary. He drove the same routes every day. He attended church with his family. He obeyed rules. And he lived less than fifteen minutes from several of the original crime scenes.

The irony was almost cinematic. For decades, Rader had hidden behind the illusion of order, the good neighbor, the church leader, the man who believed discipline made him invisible. But order, in the end, was what exposed him. The same precision that defined his life had left an unguarded trace in a line of code.

The task force moved cautiously, gathering more evidence. They needed something irrefutable, DNA, physical confirmation. But for everyone in that room, the outcome was already written. They knew they had him.

The man who once believed he controlled every variable had made the simplest mistake imaginable: he asked a question.

And the digital world, indifferent and exact, answered it.

The room at Wichita Police headquarters was silent except for the low hum of computer monitors. The digital forensic team had verified the evidence three times over. The metadata didn't lie.

The words were still on the screen, plain, unadorned, damning.

Author: Dennis. Organization: Christ Lutheran Church.

Detective Ken Landwehr, head of the BTK task force, leaned forward, reading it again as though his eyes might be deceiving him. After three decades, the ghost had finally left a fingerprint. It wasn't blood or fiber or handwriting. It was code, the quiet, unintentional confession of the digital age.

But Landwehr didn't celebrate. Not yet. BTK was cunning. He had played with them before, crafted false leads and red herrings just to watch them chase their tails. The name on the file could be another manipulation, another move in his ongoing game of control.

Still, something about this clue felt different. The arrogance was there, the belief that technology couldn't touch him, but the sloppiness wasn't. Rader had never been sloppy. He'd been precise, meticulous, calculating. For a man like that to trust a floppy disk meant one of two things: either he'd grown careless with age, or he was so confident in his invisibility that he believed no one could possibly see him anymore.

Both options led to the same conclusion.

They finally had him.

The next step was patience, the kind Rader himself had once practiced so well. The task force quietly began to build a profile around Dennis Rader. They gathered public records: his address, employment history, church involvement, vehicle registration, property taxes, even scouting affiliations. Each fact confirmed the impossible.

He lived in Park City, a quiet suburb of Wichita. He was a compliance officer, a man obsessed with order and regulation. He was married, with two children. He served as council president at Christ Lutheran Church. And he had lived in proximity to several of BTK's original murder sites during the 1970s.

Everything aligned.

Detectives began surveillance almost immediately. They parked unmarked cars on his street, monitored his routes to work and church, noted his daily routines. He was astonishingly predictable, leaving home at 7:45 a.m., driving the same route to city hall, returning home by five, attending church meetings midweek, mowing his lawn every Saturday at precisely 10 a.m.

The man who once moved through Wichita's nights unseen now lived in a glass box of his own making.

Agents from the Kansas Bureau of Investigation joined the task force, coordinating with the FBI's behavioral analysts. They discussed his personality, his habits, his likely response once confronted. Everyone agreed: Rader would not confess easily. He would try to control the narrative, even in his downfall.

But before they could move, they needed proof beyond the digital. They needed DNA.

BTK had left traces at his crime scenes, a drop of semen, a hair, biological fragments that had survived decades in sealed evidence containers. The technology of 2005 could now read those traces with precision unimaginable in the 1970s. What they needed was a modern sample from Rader or a close relative to make the match.

Obtaining it would be delicate. They couldn't risk alerting him, not yet. So they went after what he valued most: his family.

Investigators learned that Rader's daughter, Kerri, was a student at Kansas State University. Quietly, without her knowledge, they obtained a discarded pap smear sample from her recent medical visit, legally permissible through a sealed warrant. The lab compared it against the preserved DNA from one of BTK's victims.

Days passed in agonizing silence. Then the report arrived.

The results were conclusive. The sample from Rader's daughter was a familial match. Statistically irrefutable. The father of that young woman was the man who had terrorized Wichita for thirty years.

Detective Landwehr read the report twice, then set it down carefully, his hand trembling. He had spent most of his career chasing a phantom. Now, for the first time, the phantom had a face.

Dennis Lynn Rader.

The task force prepared the operation with the precision Rader himself would have admired. They wanted the arrest to be controlled, methodical, unambiguous, no chance for him to destroy evidence or turn the event into theater. Surveillance teams stayed on him constantly. Plainclothes officers were embedded at his office, his church, even his local grocery store.

They watched him for days. He showed no sign of awareness. He smiled at coworkers, attended a church council meeting, wrote city citations. He was living his ordinary life while an entire city's worth of law enforcement closed around him.

Rader's demeanor was almost serene. He had no idea the same system of order he worshiped, rules, records, traceability, was now his undoing. Every permit, every digital file, every entry in his city computer was another breadcrumb leading back to him.

Meanwhile, the FBI built an arrest profile. Rader was to be approached in public, away from his home, to minimize risk to his family. The goal: a clean, controlled takedown, not a chase, not a shootout.

They set the plan for February 25, 2005.

That morning, Rader left his house as usual. He wore his city-issued jacket, coffee thermos in hand, his clipboard on the passenger seat. He drove to a hardware store to eat lunch in his truck, a habit he'd developed over the years.

He didn't notice the unmarked vehicles that followed at a distance.

As he sat in the driver's seat, engine idling, a black SUV eased into the parking lot beside him. Two officers stepped out, calm but focused. They approached from both sides, their movements practiced and deliberate.

"Mr. Rader?" one said, voice steady.

He looked up, blinking behind his glasses. "Yes?"

They opened the door. "You're under arrest."

For a moment, he didn't react. The words seemed to drift past him like static. Then confusion flickered across his face, not fear, but disbelief.

"What's this about?" he asked.

No one answered. They moved him gently but firmly from the truck, cuffed his hands behind his back, and placed him in the waiting vehicle. Witnesses nearby saw nothing extraordinary, just another middle-aged man being quietly detained.

Inside the SUV, the reality began to settle. He looked at the officers, searching their faces for some indication, some confirmation of the unthinkable.

Finally, one of them said it.

"Dennis, we know who you are."

Rader's eyes narrowed. His voice was almost calm. "Oh," he said. "You found the floppy disk, didn't you?"

It was both confession and epitaph.

The line that had once defined his life, *Bind. Torture. Kill.*, had finally met its counterpart: *Pride. Data. Fall.*

The room was small, windowless, and humming with the faint electric buzz of the ceiling light. Dennis Rader sat at the metal table, his wrists cuffed loosely in front of him, the sheen of his city jacket dull under the fluorescence. He looked less like a monster than a man misplaced, the church president, the Scout leader, the father, trying to calculate what had gone wrong.

Across from him, Detective Ken Landwehr sat in silence. The air between them was almost reverent. For thirty years, Rader had been a phantom, a name on yellowing files, a ghost behind headlines. Now he was flesh and blood, breathing the same recycled air, blinking behind his glasses, waiting for an explanation.

Rader cleared his throat. His voice was thin but steady. "So," he said quietly, "this is about the floppy disk, isn't it?"

Landwehr didn't answer right away. He just studied the man in front of him, the contradiction he represented. Rader's posture was polite, his tone formal, but there was a flicker behind his eyes, something searching, defensive, desperate to regain footing.

"Dennis," Landwehr said finally, "you know why you're here."

Rader looked down at his hands. "I suppose I do." He tried to smile, but it faltered halfway. "I trusted you," he said. "You said it couldn't be traced."

Landwehr didn't respond. He let the silence hang. Rader filled it himself, because silence was one thing he had never tolerated.

"I asked," he went on, his voice tightening. "I gave you a chance to be straight with me. I said, could it be traced? You said no." He looked up suddenly, his composure cracking just slightly. "That wasn't very honest."

Landwehr leaned forward, his voice even. "You've spent your whole life controlling things, Dennis. That's over now."

The words hit him harder than he expected. For years, control had been the axis of his existence , his family, his job, his church, his crimes. He had always been the one who decided when to act, when to stop, when to vanish. The idea that someone else now defined the terms was unbearable.

Rader sat back slowly, eyes unfocused. "I just wanted the story to be right," he murmured. "They had it wrong. They forgot the details."

"That's what brought you back?" Landwehr asked. "The story?"

Rader hesitated. He seemed to shrink a little, the weight of his own reasoning collapsing inward. "I didn't mean for this," he said. "It was… it was just communication." He almost sounded like a man defending a bureaucratic error. "I wasn't going to hurt anyone. I just wanted to clear up the record."

Landwehr watched him carefully. He had seen this kind of rationalization before, but never in someone so composed. "You sent letters. You sent trophies. You bragged about what you'd done. You wanted to be seen again."

Rader's face twitched. "No," he said, too quickly. "It wasn't bragging. It was documentation."

The correction hung in the air, cold and absurd.

He looked around the room as if seeing it for the first time , the cinderblock walls, the stainless-steel corners, the faint reflection of himself in the tabletop. His breathing grew shallow. "I always kept records," he said softly. "That's what I do. I'm an organizer."

"Is that what this was?" Landwehr asked quietly. "Organization?"

Rader met his gaze, and for the first time, his eyes betrayed something raw. "Control," he said. "Always control."

The silence that followed was almost unbearable. The room felt smaller, the light harsher. The man across from Landwehr wasn't raging or crying or pleading, he was unraveling through realization.

He had been caught not by brilliance or bravery, but by his own question, by the thing he had spent a lifetime mastering.

He shook his head slightly, as if still processing the impossibility of it. "I was careful," he whispered. "Always careful." His lips tightened. "It's the system that failed. The rules changed."

Landwehr watched him sink into the machinery of his own logic. Every sentence he spoke was a thread leading deeper into a labyrinth of self-justification, a structure that had finally caved in on itself.

After a long pause, Rader spoke again. "How did you find me?"

Landwehr didn't elaborate. "You told us who you were," he said.

Rader frowned. "No. I didn't."

"Yes, you did." Landwehr slid a folder across the table, opening it just enough for the first page to show: the digital printout from the floppy disk, his name, the church, the file properties laid bare in black and white.

Rader stared at it for several seconds, unblinking.

The sound that escaped him was not quite a sigh, not quite a laugh, a strange exhalation that seemed to drain the room of air. "Well," he said finally, his voice faint, "there you go."

It was not confession, not yet. It was resignation.

Over the next hours, the conversation circled slowly inward. Landwehr didn't press; he guided. He asked about the letters, about the cereal boxes, about the codes. Each time, Rader answered with mechanical detachment, recalling events like minutes from a long-forgotten meeting.

But every so often, something cracked. A tremor in the voice. A flicker of pride fighting shame. When he spoke of "projects," he slipped into his old tone, the language of classification, control, and method. Then he would pull back, as if realizing how those words sounded now, here, in this sterile box of light and silence.

At one point, Landwehr asked him directly, "Do you feel any remorse?"

Rader looked at him blankly, searching for the right word. "I feel... disappointed," he said at last. "I should've stopped communicating. That was the mistake."

It was a chilling answer, the kind that left even seasoned detectives silent. His regret wasn't for what he'd done, but for losing the illusion of mastery.

As the hours passed, his calm returned, the same eerie composure that had fooled neighbors and friends for decades. But beneath it was something hollow, an echo of the man he'd been pretending to be.

When the interrogation ended, Rader asked one final question. "How did you know for sure?"

Landwehr looked at him for a long moment before answering. "Your daughter's DNA," he said quietly.

Rader blinked. "Kerri?" The name caught in his throat. For the first time, emotion flickered through the mask, shock, disbelief, maybe even grief. He looked down, his voice barely audible. "She didn't know."

"No," Landwehr said. "She didn't."

Rader nodded slowly, his composure cracking just enough for the air to shift. The control that had defined his life was gone, stripped away by technology, by genetics, by the world he thought he understood but never did.

He stared at the tabletop, tracing the reflection of the fluorescent light with his eyes. Then, with a voice that sounded smaller than it ever had, he said, "The floppy disk. I should've burned it."

Landwehr stood, gathering his notes. "You couldn't help yourself," he said. "That's what caught you."

Rader didn't look up. "I know," he whispered. "That's what scares me."

When they led him from the room, the hallway outside was lined with officers, men and women who had spent years chasing his shadow. Cameras clicked. The sound echoed like distant thunder.

For the first time in his life, Dennis Rader wasn't the one watching. He was the one being seen.

The next morning, the interrogation resumed in a larger room. Two cameras now watched from the corners, silent witnesses to the collapse of a thirty-year illusion. Dennis Rader sat in the same posture as before, hands folded, glasses polished, his tone polite, almost professional.

He had slept little. The shock of his arrest had hardened into something steadier, almost clinical. If control had been stripped from him, he would regain it the only way he could: by becoming the narrator of his own downfall.

When Detective Landwehr and Special Agent Otis returned, Rader greeted them like colleagues beginning a staff meeting. "I suppose we'll start from the beginning," he said, as if offering an agenda.

And he did.

For hours, he talked. Methodically. Calmly. Horrifically.

He described each murder in the same detached rhythm he used for city reports, organized, categorized, annotated with times and tools. There was no tremor in his voice, no sign of remorse. Only structure.

He referred to his victims as "projects." He spoke of "phases," of "preparation," of "execution." Each killing was an event to be managed, each mistake a "learning opportunity."

When he described the Otero family murders, his tone shifted slightly, not with guilt, but pride in precision. "I had it all planned," he said, as though presenting a case study. "I knew the schedule, the layout, the entry points. Everything was controlled. That's what mattered to me."

Landwehr watched him, taking notes, but mostly letting him talk. The more Rader spoke, the more he revealed, not just about the crimes, but about himself. His obsession wasn't merely sexual or violent; it was administrative. The structure was the point. The killing was a function of order, not chaos.

When he reached the 1977 Shirley Vian case, he paused, tapping his fingers lightly against the table. "The kids were in the bathroom," he said. "I told them to stay there. I gave them toys. They didn't see anything." He looked up briefly. "I'm not a monster."

The words hung in the room like a blade. Landwehr said nothing. There was nothing to say.

Rader continued, his voice monotone. "It was about control. Always control. Once it was achieved, the rest followed."

The hours turned to afternoon. Coffee cooled on the table. The air conditioner hummed. Every word he spoke was logged, timestamped, cross-referenced, his own precision now mirrored back at him by the system he'd once believed he could outwit.

At one point, when asked how he managed to hide for so long, Rader leaned back, a faint smile on his face. "Because I was ordinary," he said. "Nobody looks at the ordinary."

He was right. For thirty years, Wichita had lived beside him, neighbors, parishioners, coworkers, all fooled by his blandness. His disguise wasn't a mask; it was mediocrity.

But now, in this sterile room, that ordinariness had become terrifying.

When he finally finished recounting the murders, the detectives asked him why he came back after so many years. Rader's expression changed, just a flicker, a shadow across his face. "They forgot me," he said softly. "They got it wrong. I wanted to set the record straight."

"You wanted recognition," Landwehr said.

Rader hesitated. "I wanted the truth."

But the truth was what he could no longer control.

In the days that followed, his confession became public record. The news spread like wildfire across Wichita. Headlines screamed the unthinkable: *BTK Arrested. Church Leader in Custody.*

Television crews gathered outside the Park City home that had once seemed so perfectly ordinary. Neighbors stared in disbelief as police removed boxes of evidence, binders, trophies, Polaroids, sketches. The life of order he'd built had turned into an archive of horror.

Paula filed for an emergency divorce within days. His children refused contact. The congregation of Christ Lutheran gathered in shock, praying for understanding that would never come.

In the interrogation room, Rader continued to talk, granting interviews, writing letters, diagramming his crimes. He became his own archivist once again, the architect of the story's ending. He took satisfaction in detail, even in defeat. "You'll see the system now," he told detectives. "You'll understand how it worked."

But for the investigators who had spent their careers chasing him, the most chilling moment came when the cameras were off. Landwehr later recalled how, after hours of confessions, Rader looked at him and said almost conversationally, "Ken, you know, I always wondered what it would feel like to sit here."

Landwehr asked, "And how does it feel?"

Rader thought for a moment. "Strange," he said. "Like I'm still in control of the narrative."

It was delusion, but also truth. Even stripped of power, shackled and exposed, he clung to the illusion that his story was his to direct.

Yet the real control now belonged to the system he had mocked, the forensic science, the databases, the detectives, the city he once terrorized.

His reign of precision had been undone by precision. His legacy of control ended in a chain of custody report.

When the formal confession concluded, Landwehr stood and thanked him. It was standard procedure, a gesture of closure. Rader nodded politely, as if concluding a business meeting.

As officers led him away, the cameras followed. The hallway was lined with press. The flash of bulbs turned the air white. He flinched slightly but didn't hide.

When asked by a reporter, "Mr. Rader, are you BTK?" he paused, straightened his posture, and said evenly, "Yes, I am."

It was not pride. It was finality.

For a man who had built his identity on control, that single acknowledgment was both surrender and immortality. The name he had chosen decades earlier would now outlive him, etched into the mythology of American crime not as a symbol of power, but of hubris.

In the courthouse that afternoon, as the world learned the truth, Wichita fell silent. Churches tolled bells. Reporters swarmed. Survivors wept.

The man they had once trusted, the man who cited city codes, led prayers, and fixed fences, had been a ghost wearing flesh.

In his cell that night, Rader sat alone, writing in his notebook. He began to draft what he called *The BTK Story*, his final act of authorship. The words were small and neat, the handwriting familiar to investigators who would one day read it.

But for all his effort to reclaim the narrative, one truth had already escaped his grasp.

The floppy disk, the tiny, obsolete piece of plastic, had spoken louder than any confession.

It had answered the question he thought only he could ask: Who controls the story?

Not him. Not anymore.

Chapter Twelve

Confession Without Remorse

The Engineer of Evil; How BTK Turned Murder Into Method

The cameras were rolling again. The microphones caught every breath. Across the table, Dennis Rader adjusted his glasses, cleared his throat, and began to talk.

The detectives had expected resistance, denials, bargaining, or the defensive outrage that usually accompanied a serial confession. Instead, what they heard was a tone so casual it chilled the room.

"Let's start with the Oteros," he said, as though reciting minutes from an old meeting.

He leaned forward slightly, fingers intertwined, voice steady and unhurried. There was no tremor, no hesitation. Each word landed like a footstep on polished tile.

"I knew their schedule," he said. "I'd done the surveillance for weeks. I knew when they left, when they came home. I watched the mail, the curtains, even the dog's behavior. I liked to plan. Planning was the key."

He smiled faintly, proud of the sentence's precision. The detectives didn't interrupt. They barely breathed.

Rader continued, describing his entry into the home, the cut phone line, the quiet command of control. His tone never changed, even when he spoke of the family's terror. "I told them it was just a robbery," he said, as if clarifying a misunderstanding. "I needed them calm, cooperative. Things... didn't go as smoothly as I'd intended."

That word, *intended*, hung in the air like smoke.

He detailed the murders of Joseph and Julie Otero, then the children, step by step. He described the bindings, the sequence, the mistakes. His voice was clinical, analytical. When emotion entered, it was only self-criticism. "That one was messy," he said. "I should have used a different approach. Too many variables."

The detectives exchanged glances. One scribbled notes, another stared at the floor. They were trained to stay detached, but the dissonance of hearing such horror recounted in that polite monotone was like watching a surgeon dissect empathy itself.

Rader paused occasionally to clarify details, not out of conscience but accuracy. "I think the cord was white nylon," he said once. "No, wait, brown. Yes, brown. You should check that. It's important the record's correct."

It was this, the bureaucratic precision, the obsession with factual accuracy, that stunned the room more than the content. It wasn't just that he remembered every detail. It was that he cared about the details more than the lives they described.

He wasn't confessing. He was *archiving*.

Hours passed, and he moved from case to case, decade to decade, each one catalogued like a project review. He spoke of his "hit kits," of "target evaluation," of "control methods." He used these terms naturally, as if explaining a professional workflow.

In one moment, describing how he waited in closets or cars for victims to return home, he smiled faintly. "That was always the hardest part, waiting. But patience made the outcome clean."

"Outcome." Another word chosen like a craftsman describing a finished product.

When detectives asked how he selected victims, he explained the process in chillingly rational terms. "Some were random. Some were planned. I'd watch, evaluate patterns, decide suitability. I liked the ones that fit a type, neat house, predictable habits. It wasn't about who they were. It was about how they lived."

He referred to them not as women or people, but as "subjects," "types," "profiles." The humanity was scrubbed away, replaced with data points.

One detective later said listening to him felt like "reading a manual written by the devil."

But Rader didn't see it that way. He saw himself as an engineer of control, a man who had built systems that worked, until one didn't.

When he reached the middle years, he described the Kathryn Bright case. "That one almost went bad," he said. "The brother came home. Unexpected variable. Nearly ruined the project."

He frowned slightly, then looked up at the officers. "You know, I didn't like improvisation. That's where mistakes happen. Always stick to the plan."

It was the language of a manager, not a murderer.

Occasionally, he'd pause to make sure the stenographer was keeping up. "You got that?" he'd ask politely. "Don't want to misquote myself."

The detectives would nod numbly.

His tone shifted only when he discussed his own ingenuity, how he adapted to different homes, how he managed rope lengths, how he perfected knots. He described his self-made tools with pride, calling them "inventions," explaining how each device "served the purpose with maximum efficiency."

Efficiency.

He never mentioned mercy, or conscience, or fear. Only *efficiency*.

The most disturbing moment came when he explained his terminology. "I called them 'projects,'" he said calmly. "Not to be demeaning, but for structure. Each one had a phase: pre-stalk, capture, control, release."

"Release?" one detective asked.

"Termination," Rader corrected softly. "The conclusion of control."

There was no tremor in his voice, no darkness in his tone. He wasn't performing. He was explaining. And that, perhaps, was the most terrifying part, the absence of performance, the genuine belief that this was all logical.

When asked about emotion, he shrugged slightly. "I didn't feel much during," he said. "Too focused. Emotions cause errors. I preferred to analyze afterward."

He described returning to scenes, collecting items, photographing himself later to "revisit the system." He spoke of these acts not as grotesque indulgences, but as "documentation."

He even used the term "reconstruction," explaining how he sometimes re-created bindings or poses in photographs for accuracy. "I wanted to see how it worked," he said. "It was about perfection, not pleasure."

One detective, hardened by decades of homicide work, excused himself partway through. He said later that it wasn't the violence that broke him, it was the calm. "You wait for some flash of humanity," he said, "but there was nothing. It was like listening to a tax auditor describe a murder."

Rader, unaware or indifferent to their discomfort, continued speaking for hours. His sentences flowed with the confidence of a man finally being understood. He corrected misconceptions, adjusted timelines, and clarified false media reports.

When detectives asked if he felt relief in finally telling his story, he smiled slightly. "It feels… complete," he said. "Like closing a file."

Complete. The word hung in the air like the click of a closing drawer.

For Rader, this was not confession. It was completion, the satisfaction of final order restored. He wasn't unburdening guilt. He was balancing his own internal ledger.

By evening, his voice had grown hoarse, but his composure never faltered. He asked for water, thanked the officers, and resumed where he'd left off. Even courtesy had structure.

As the session ended, one of the detectives asked quietly, "Dennis, do you understand what this means? What you've just said?"

Rader nodded. "Of course," he said. "It means you'll have the facts right now. I wanted that."

He stood as they prepared to escort him back to holding. His expression was placid, even content. "You know," he said, "I always thought if this day came, I'd be nervous. But I'm not. It feels… organized."

He was right. It was organized, perfectly, terrifyingly so.

And for the men and women who had just listened to him recount death like data, that was what would haunt them most.

The next session began much the same way, Rader seated neatly at the metal table, posture straight, glasses gleaming under the fluorescent light. Before detectives could even begin, he was already speaking.

"I've been thinking about the diagrams," he said. "If you want, I can draw them again. More accurately this time."

He pulled a sheet of paper from the stack before him and began sketching floor plans, homes, rooms, doorways, furniture placement, each drawn with uncanny precision. The lines were crisp, the proportions exact, as though he were recreating architectural blueprints rather than murder scenes.

"These were my control zones," he said, pointing with the tip of the pen. "Entry point here, restraint here, observation here."

The detectives watched in uneasy silence. For Rader, the act of drawing wasn't a memory exercise; it was pleasure. Each line restored a sense of mastery. Each detail corrected the chaos that had crept into his mind since his arrest.

"This one bothered me," he said, referring to a layout from 1977. "There was a lamp here, too close to the bed. It made the lighting uneven. Harder to see the bindings properly."

He looked up, expecting acknowledgment. The detectives simply nodded, their faces pale.

He resumed drawing. "I learned from that. Afterward, I carried a small flashlight to control light direction. Simple adjustment."

Simple adjustment. As if he were troubleshooting a mechanical process.

He wasn't boasting for the sake of ego. To him, these weren't trophies of violence; they were examples of craftsmanship. The killings had become proof of concept, demonstrations of control executed to his internal standards.

At one point, he paused, tapping the pen against the table. "You see," he said, "people think it was about sex or rage. That's wrong. It was about order. Bringing everything into alignment. The ropes, the timing, the silence."

Landwehr, sitting opposite him, asked quietly, "And the victims?"

Rader blinked. "They were part of it," he said simply. "You can't have structure without variables."

Variables. The reduction of life to data.

When he ran out of paper, he gestured for more. The officers obliged, and he continued sketching. Each diagram became a visual echo of his obsession, neat lines containing unimaginable cruelty.

He annotated them as if preparing a presentation: *Entry through back door. Subject compliant. Time: approximately 8:45 p.m.*

He labeled victims by initials, distances by inches, time by seconds. There was no flourish, no emotional weight, only documentation.

To him, confession was not penance. It was reassertion. The act of recording reclaimed control, if only symbolically. He could no longer kill, but he could still categorize.

As he spoke, the investigators began to understand the true scope of his pathology. It wasn't merely the acts themselves that defined him , it was his relentless need to quantify them, to perfect the system that contained them.

He described how he kept records of everything: notes on bindings, lists of materials, coded references to each "project." He called them "study files." He wrote of learning from each attempt, refining his "methods" as though preparing an operations manual.

He leaned back and smiled faintly. "You probably think I'm crazy," he said. "But it all made sense to me at the time. You see, everyone has hobbies. Some people collect stamps." He gestured toward the drawings. "I collected data."

The words struck the room like a hammer.

No one responded. There was nothing to say that wouldn't sound futile against the vacuum of his logic.

He went on, unshaken. "The data was the important part. You can't improve without analysis. I'd look back, see what worked, what didn't. Evaluate efficiency."

Even his crimes, he explained, followed a formula. "Every good project has three stages: pre-plan, execute, evaluate. That's how I lived my whole life. Even my job followed the same pattern."

He said this with the same tone someone might use to explain a successful career strategy.

Landwehr broke the silence. "Dennis, do you ever think about them? The people?"

Rader's face stayed blank for a moment, as though parsing the question mathematically. Then he said, "Sometimes. But not in the way you mean. Once they were part of the system, they weren't individuals anymore. I couldn't think of them that way. That would have... disrupted things."

The statement was devoid of malice, just honesty, cold and absolute.

He turned another page and began writing names, not of victims, but of his self-created code words: "Project FOXTROT," "Project LIGHTHOUSE," "Project DOGHOUSE." He explained that each represented a separate fantasy, some acted upon, most not.

He listed them with satisfaction, as if presenting achievements.

Detectives glanced at one another, some averting their eyes. Even among seasoned investigators, the psychological weight of the confession was beginning to take its toll.

Forensic psychologist Dr. Mary Ellen O'Toole, who later reviewed transcripts of his sessions, described Rader's behavior as "a perfect storm of narcissism and detachment." He wasn't recounting pain. He was re-creating the architecture of control.

To Rader, words were blueprints. They rebuilt what handcuffs had taken away.

After several hours, Landwehr asked if he understood how people might see him now, as evil, monstrous, inhuman.

Rader tilted his head. "I don't think of myself that way," he said. "I think of myself as... methodical. I had my flaws, sure, but I wasn't random. I wasn't cruel without reason."

He said it as if defending a professional reputation.

When pressed on whether he ever felt empathy for the families, he seemed genuinely puzzled. "Empathy?" he repeated. "I didn't know them. I suppose I felt something after, maybe guilt, but not the crying kind. More like frustration. I'd say, 'Dennis, you let the emotions interfere again.'"

Even his guilt was procedural.

By evening, one detective sat outside in the hallway, head in his hands. "You think you've seen it all," he said later. "But this wasn't rage or madness. It was order. That's what scared me."

Back in the room, Rader asked for another notepad. He wanted to organize his confessions by timeline.

He spent the next hour drafting what he called his "BTK Index." Each murder had bullet points: date, location, method, lessons learned. He even added a section titled *Future Improvements*, an instinct so ingrained he couldn't suppress it even now.

When the notepad was full, he placed the pen neatly beside it and folded his hands again. "There," he said with quiet satisfaction. "Now it's accurate."

Accurate. That word again, his mantra.

For the investigators, there was no relief in hearing him speak. The more he explained, the less human he became. His mind was a filing cabinet; his conscience, an algorithm.

One officer later described it best: "He didn't confess like a man seeking forgiveness. He confessed like a man giving a tutorial."

And in that sterile room of order and documentation, Dennis Rader , husband, father, church president, and serial killer , achieved the last illusion of control he would ever know: the ability to narrate his own evil as though it were art.

By the third day of interrogation, exhaustion had become its own kind of silence. The detectives filed into the small room again, notebooks in hand, but the atmosphere was heavier now, thick with the invisible residue of everything they had heard before.

Rader sat waiting for them, already upright, already ready. He greeted them politely, as if they were continuing a seminar. "Morning, gentlemen," he said. "I reviewed some things last night. There are a few corrections I'd like to make."

The words landed like stones in water. Even his desire to amend horror came wrapped in bureaucracy.

He spoke first of timing discrepancies, then of "inconsistencies" in how his actions might have been recorded. "You'll want to get this right," he said. "It's part of the official record now."

The detectives nodded numbly, their pens moving without conviction. One of them, the youngest, had started to flinch at the sound of his voice. The cadence was too calm, too measured, the voice of a man describing process, not tragedy.

As he continued, something became clear: Rader was *enjoying* this. Not gloating, not boasting, simply reveling in the rhythm of explanation. For years, he had lived in silence, his secret world confined to the walls of his mind. Now, with every question, he was free again, speaking the language only he understood.

"I always figured people wouldn't get it," he said. "The organization behind it. The discipline. Everyone thought it was chaos. It wasn't. It was structured."

He leaned forward, almost earnest. "I suppose this is the only time anyone will ever really listen."

He wasn't wrong. For decades, no one had known the full extent of his system. Now, inside this gray room, every detail mattered to the people who once hunted him. And that knowledge, being heard, fed something deep inside him.

He corrected their terminology. "Not stalking," he said. "Preliminary surveillance. That's the proper term."

He even corrected their grammar once, mid-question, and then apologized with a polite nod.

Landwehr watched him carefully, the fatigue in his face giving way to something more complicated: fascination tinged with revulsion. There was no rage to fight, no guilt to expose. Rader's mind was an endless series of compartments, doors opening into smaller doors, none leading anywhere human.

When asked if he ever thought about the families, Rader tilted his head. "I know they hurt," he said. "That was part of the structure. Without pain, the narrative loses tension."

"Tension?" one detective repeated quietly.

Rader nodded. "The story has to build."

It was the closest he ever came to admitting motive: he wasn't seeking destruction. He was building narrative tension.

Every few hours, investigators rotated out. They would leave the room, step into the hallway, and stand in silence. Some stared at the floor. Others leaned against the wall, eyes shut. One officer vomited in the restroom after listening to Rader recount a killing like an engineering diagram.

No one said it aloud, but they all felt it, the slow, invisible erosion of empathy that came from listening to someone who had none.

Rader, meanwhile, was serene. Between sessions, he asked for coffee. He thanked the guards. Once, when his chair squeaked, he asked if maintenance should be notified. He was that composed.

His behavior unsettled even the most hardened among them. Landwehr confided later that it was like "watching a man dissect his own humanity with perfect posture."

When the detectives tried to shift the conversation toward remorse, Rader seemed confused. "Remorse?" he repeated. "I accepted accountability. Isn't that what this is?"

He genuinely couldn't separate confession from compliance. In his mind, obedience to procedure *was* morality. He believed that telling the truth, accurately, cleanly, fully, was his final act of discipline.

He looked proud of it.

At one point, a detective asked why he called his murders "projects." Rader smiled faintly, the kind of smile that never reached the eyes. "Because they were designed," he said. "Everything had parameters, variables, timing. I liked that. Projects have beginnings and endings. They can be improved."

He paused, as though hearing himself for the first time. "You know, I always liked improvement. It's what separates amateurs from professionals."

The room went cold.

He didn't notice. He was already reaching for the next folder, already returning to the numbers, the lengths of ropes, the distances between points on a floor plan. The precision kept him anchored. Emotion was noise; detail was peace.

Across the one-way glass, the observers watched in disbelief. Some took notes. Others just stared. The psychologists in the room debated quietly:

was this sociopathy or something deeper, a personality built entirely on control until control replaced conscience?

The answer, they realized, didn't matter. It was both.

As hours turned into days, the detectives began to develop coping rituals of their own. Some listened to music before entering the room. Some avoided eye contact with him entirely. A few began writing personal notes on the margins of their case files, phrases like *remember the victims*, or *don't normalize this*.

They had to remind themselves that they were listening to *testimony*, not *instruction*.

Rader never lost composure. He corrected small mistakes, asked for precise timestamps, sometimes paused mid-sentence to verify a date with eerie confidence.

"I'm glad it's all out now," he said once. "It means it's preserved. It won't get distorted by rumor anymore."

"Is that what this was about?" Landwehr asked. "Preserving your story?"

Rader nodded. "Every system deserves accurate documentation."

Landwehr didn't respond. He just looked at the man in front of him, the middle-aged bureaucrat who had terrorized a city and now sat there, serene and satisfied, as though he had just completed a successful audit.

Later that night, as the last session ended, one detective lingered in the empty room after Rader was escorted away. He stared at the chair where Rader had been sitting, the paper still on the table, the drawings of homes, of rooms, of ordinary spaces turned into diagrams of death.

He whispered to himself, almost involuntarily: "How do you listen to something like that and still believe in people?"

There was no answer.

In another wing of the building, Rader was eating a sandwich, neatly, efficiently, napkin folded in half. When a guard asked if he needed anything else, he said, "No, thank you. Everything's in order."

It was always in order. Even now, behind locked doors, surrounded by officers and walls, he found calm in structure.

But outside that room, the men and women who had hunted him were changed. They carried the weight of his words like a contagion, the sound of horror spoken in a voice too rational to hate, too empty to forgive.

When Dennis Rader finally stopped talking, the silence felt heavier than anything he had said.

For three days he had spoken without pause, describing murder as routine, horror as procedure. He left no mystery, no ambiguity, only structure. When the sessions ended, the detectives filed out one by one, each carrying a version of the same stunned expression. No one spoke. The air in the hallway felt stale, the hum of the lights too loud.

Rader was led back to his cell, his steps even, his shirt still neatly tucked. He thanked the officers escorting him, then asked what time he might expect dinner. His voice was calm, almost gentle.

"Everything's on schedule," one officer muttered, not looking at him.

Rader nodded with faint satisfaction. "Good," he said. "I like schedules."

That evening, the detectives gathered in the incident room. It looked like a war zone of paperwork, photographs, transcripts, diagrams spread across tables. The monitors replayed clips of his confession. His voice filled the room again, sterile and measured, explaining, clarifying, revising.

One detective switched the volume off mid-sentence. The sudden silence was unbearable.

Another, a veteran of twenty years, sat with his head in his hands. "He's proud of it," he said quietly. "Every word. It's not guilt. It's ownership."

They had all expected evil to look different, to rage, to weep, to justify. Instead, they had met something quieter: evil as routine, evil as calm.

Over the next weeks, the tapes were transcribed, catalogued, entered into evidence. Every word Rader spoke became part of the record. Prosecutors listened to them in private, sometimes pausing to catch their breath. Courtroom staff who later read the transcripts said it was like "reading blueprints drawn by a machine that knew it was human."

When the recordings were played in court, the spectators froze. Rader sat at the defense table, hands folded, listening to his own voice with the expression of a man auditing paperwork.

On the screen, his tone never changed. Even when describing the Otero children, his voice remained flat, steady, factual, without tremor. In the gallery, one juror pressed her hand to her mouth. A victim's relative left the room, trembling. The air was thick with the sound of his words echoing from the past.

When the audio stopped, Rader looked around the courtroom as if surprised by the silence.

"I wanted the record to be correct," he said softly, leaning toward the microphone. "Accuracy matters."

The words cut through the stillness like a blade.

For a moment, no one breathed. The judge's gavel came down hard, a sharp, human sound against the sterile rhythm of his voice.

Outside the courthouse, Wichita's summer air hung heavy with disbelief. People gathered on sidewalks, clutching newspapers, watching live coverage on television screens in shop windows. The face they saw wasn't a monster, but a neighbor, ordinary, middle-aged, polite.

Reporters described the mood as "collective vertigo." The city had been haunted by an invisible terror for thirty years. Now that terror had a face, and that face smiled when spoken to.

Inside the station, detectives replayed certain moments again and again. One in particular stayed with them: the moment Rader had been asked why he chose his victims. He'd answered, "They were available."

The simplicity of it, the absence of grand design, of ideology, of hate, made it worse. Evil without purpose. Calculation without passion.

After the verdict, when Rader was led away in shackles, one of the officers who had watched him for months felt his throat tighten. Not out of pity, but confusion. "He doesn't look broken," he said.

Another officer replied quietly, "He never breaks. He bends everything else."

In his cell, Rader began writing again. He drafted lists, outlines, and letters to himself. He titled one of them *The BTK Story: A Detailed Account by the Authorized Source.* He wasn't gloating, he was curating. Even stripped of freedom, he remained an archivist of his own control.

When the lights went out each night, guards sometimes saw him sitting on his bunk, staring at the wall, lips moving silently as though rehearsing sentences. One of them swore he heard Rader whispering to himself, "Details matter. Always did."

Meanwhile, those who had sat across from him during those confessions struggled to sleep. Some avoided interviews. Others spoke later, their voices heavy with exhaustion.

One said, "It wasn't the things he did that haunt you. It's how normal he sounded saying them."

Another remembered his final words before the last session ended. As he was being escorted out, he turned to Landwehr and said, "You'll take care of the files, right? They're important for history."

That was Dennis Rader's idea of legacy, not contrition, not forgiveness, but organization. He wanted his crimes to be remembered accurately.

To him, that was enough.

When sentencing day came, the courtroom was packed. Reporters filled the aisles. Survivors sat in silence. The families of victims spoke one by one, tears, fury, years of grief compressed into words. Rader listened, nodding occasionally, expression unchanged.

At one point, a mother's voice broke as she described her daughter's last moments. Rader blinked once, slowly, then adjusted his glasses.

The prosecutor turned to the judge and said, "Your Honor, this man has confessed to unspeakable acts with not one ounce of remorse. Not one."

Rader stood to address the court. He thanked the judge, the prosecution, even the police for their professionalism. Then he said, "I know what I did was wrong. I'm sorry for the hurt. But I was caught up in my own system. I see that now."

Caught up in his system.

He spoke of it as if it were machinery that had malfunctioned, not a life's worth of deliberate cruelty.

When the sentence was read, ten consecutive life terms without possibility of parole, he nodded politely. "That seems fair," he said.

The courtroom erupted in sobs, whispers, disbelief.

He was escorted out quietly, without resistance, the same way he had lived for decades, composed, measured, in control of nothing but his posture.

Afterward, the reporters called him "the calmest man ever sentenced." The phrase became shorthand for the enigma of BTK.

But to those who had sat across from him, there was no enigma left. They knew exactly what he was. Not a genius, not a phantom, just a man who mistook precision for purpose, control for meaning.

When the prison doors closed behind him, Wichita exhaled for the first time in thirty years.

But even then, somewhere deep in that sterile quiet, the echo of his voice lingered, the voice that had spoken of death as design, of human beings as data, of confession as completion.

And though the city moved on, the people who had heard that voice would never forget it.

Because the absence of remorse, they realized, was not a lack. It was a presence, something that filled every word, every pause, every breath he took.

Chapter Thirteen

The Family Torn Apart

The Last Victims; How BTK's Secrets Destroyed the People Closest to Him

It began on an ordinary morning.

Paula Rader was getting ready for work when she heard the phone ring, a neighbor, confused, saying police cars were outside, that Dennis had been taken away in handcuffs.

For a moment, she thought it was a mistake. Dennis was the last man in Wichita anyone would ever associate with handcuffs. He was the church council president, the code compliance officer, the man who mowed neighbors' lawns and volunteered with the Boy Scouts.

But when she stepped outside, the flashing lights were real. The officers were everywhere, in the yard, on the driveway, at the front door. She saw one of them carrying boxes toward the house. Another was speaking into a radio.

Her first thought was that something had happened at work. Some misunderstanding. Maybe an inspection gone wrong.

It wasn't until one of the agents gently took her aside that she heard the words that would destroy her life.

"Ma'am... your husband has been arrested. We believe he's the BTK killer."

The sentence didn't make sense. The syllables existed, but they didn't connect. BTK was a nightmare, a ghost that haunted headlines from the 1970s. BTK was cruelty, terror, faceless evil. Not Dennis. Not her husband.

But then she saw it, the line of officers carrying evidence from her home: boxes labeled *rope, camera equipment, documents*. The words printed in black marker cut through the disbelief.

Inside, the home was being dismantled. Drawers emptied. Files opened. His desk, once the neatest space in the house, was now covered with folders marked "City Inspections," "Church Materials," "Projects."

Everywhere, the same chilling intersection: order and horror.

That night, when the news broke, Wichita froze. Television screens across the city showed Dennis Rader's face, calm, bespectacled, middle-aged, above the headline: **"BTK ARRESTED."**

Neighbors who had shared barbecues and birthday parties stood in silence, watching the broadcast in disbelief.

The same man who had blessed their meals in church had been cataloguing death in his basement.

Paula sat in her living room, blinds drawn, as reporters gathered outside. She refused to speak. She didn't cry. She didn't move.

Her daughter, Kerri, tried calling, her voice breaking with every word. Her son, Brian, was stationed with the Navy in Connecticut, unreachable for hours. When he finally called back, he could barely form sentences. "Dad... what is this? Tell me it's not true."

But there was no answer that would make sense.

In the following days, the evidence made denial impossible. Police found his handwriting in the letters sent to newspapers. They found his old trophies, the stolen items, the Polaroids, the diagrams. DNA testing confirmed what no one wanted to believe.

Paula filed for divorce almost immediately, eleven days after the arrest. It was the fastest legal separation Kansas law would allow. In her filing, she cited "irreconcilable differences." The understatement barely hid the devastation behind it.

She refused all interviews. When journalists came to her home, she didn't open the door. Friends described her as "a ghost of herself."

For thirty-four years, she had lived beside a man she thought she knew, the father of her children, the man who read scripture at dinner, who kissed her forehead before leaving for work, who never raised his voice.

Now every memory felt poisoned.

The photographs on the wall, Dennis smiling in his uniform, Dennis at the church picnic, Dennis holding Kerri as a child, were no longer proof of a life shared, but evidence of how completely a lie can masquerade as love.

For Kerri, the shock was instant and physical. She vomited when she saw her father's mugshot on television. She told friends later that she "felt like the air had been sucked out of the world."

She tried to remember moments that might have hinted at something, odd silences, unexplained absences, but nothing fit. He had been attentive, even protective. He'd helped with homework, taught her to drive, written her letters while she was away at college.

He was just *Dad*.

Now the FBI wanted her DNA. They explained gently that they needed to confirm something from the evidence. She consented, not yet knowing that the sample she gave would become the proof that sealed his fate.

It was her blood, her innocence, that would close the case.

When she learned the result, she wept for days. Not for him, but for herself, for the unbearable collision of guilt and innocence. Her blood had helped end his freedom, but it had also tied her to his crimes forever.

Meanwhile, Brian, stationed overseas, watched the news unfold from a distance. Shipmates handed him copies of articles. Some didn't believe him when he said, "That's my dad." Others simply stared.

He withdrew from the world. His last name became a burden. Eventually, he asked to be stationed elsewhere, far from Kansas, far from the shadow that followed the word "Rader."

Back in Wichita, neighbors struggled to reconcile the man they knew with the monster in headlines. "He helped me fix my mailbox," one said, voice trembling. "He used to bring my trash cans in when I forgot."

At Christ Lutheran Church, where Rader had served as council president, the congregation gathered for a special service. The pastor spoke through tears, saying, "We do not know how such darkness can hide in the light, but we will not let it destroy our faith."

Some members couldn't bear to return. The pew where Rader had sat every Sunday, Bible in hand, became an open wound, a reminder that evil can smile, can sing hymns, can shake your hand at the door.

For Paula, the isolation deepened. Grocery trips became impossible. Cameras followed her car. Strangers whispered in aisles. She moved quietly, avoided eye contact, learned to live like a fugitive from her own name.

Friends offered help, but she refused. "I just want to disappear," she told one of them.

Her world had shrunk to walls and memories she couldn't trust. Every photograph, every note, every object in the house seemed to accuse her: *You didn't see.*

But how could she? Rader's compartmentalization had been perfect. His life of control extended even to the illusion of love. He had measured everything, tone, timing, gesture, with the same precision he used for his crimes.

And now, in the aftermath, the family he left behind bore the punishment for his deception.

Reporters called them "the forgotten victims." But to Paula and her children, the word *victim* didn't feel right. Victims receive sympathy. They received silence.

They would never escape him. Not truly. His name was their blood. His shadow, their inheritance.

As the days turned into weeks, the weight of revelation settled into something harder: permanence. The world knew his name, his crimes, his face.

And for Paula and her children, that meant their lives were no longer their own.

The shock did not fade with time, it multiplied.

Every morning brought new headlines, new footage, new commentary dissecting every corner of Dennis Rader's life. The home that once stood quietly on Independence Street was now the most infamous house in Kansas. Police tape fluttered in the wind where a picket fence used to be.

Neighbors couldn't look at it without shuddering. The curtains, the flower beds, the swing set in the backyard, everything had been ordinary once. Now it was an exhibit of the unimaginable.

Some tried to rationalize it. "He must have had some kind of breakdown," one said. "Something must have snapped." But the investigators' reports destroyed those theories. Rader hadn't snapped. He had planned. He had organized. He had maintained perfect normalcy for three decades while living a double life so meticulously crafted it fooled even those closest to him.

For the community, that realization was worse than the crimes themselves.

If Dennis Rader could be BTK, then anyone could.

The people of Wichita began to question their own neighbors, their coworkers, even their spouses. The boundary between normal and monstrous had dissolved.

At Christ Lutheran Church, parishioners gathered for a special Sunday service after the arrest. The sanctuary was packed, yet no one sang. The air was heavy, like a shared confession that no one could articulate.

Pastor Michael Clark stood at the pulpit, hands trembling. "We are all struggling to understand," he said quietly. "Evil often hides in plain sight, wearing the mask of decency. We can't let that mask define our faith."

But many couldn't return. The sight of Rader's seat near the front, the place where he had prayed, sung hymns, and helped count donations, was unbearable. Some avoided the building entirely. Others confessed privately that they felt violated, as if their trust in God itself had been used against them.

Church volunteers found his old handwriting on meeting notes. His neat, organized minutes now looked sinister, coded, wrong. His words, once mundane, seemed infected by the revelation of who had written them.

One woman who'd served beside him on the council broke down in tears when she discovered one of his old notes tucked into a hymnbook: *"Remember, order brings peace."*

It was a phrase that had once sounded comforting. Now it felt like a confession hiding in plain sight.

The shock rippled outward, reaching the edges of every life he had touched.

At City Hall, where Rader had worked as a compliance officer, coworkers stared at his empty desk. His files were immaculate, labels in neat block letters, drawers alphabetized. One folder contained complaint reports from local residents about grass height or broken fences. He had enforced order for a living, and now those same residents wondered what he had seen when he stood on their lawns, clipboard in hand.

The town's sense of safety, its sense of *knowing*, had been shattered.

Even his closest friends were paralyzed by disbelief.

Kevin Bright, the brother of one of Rader's early victims, had lived for decades with unanswered questions. When news broke that Rader had been arrested, Kevin sat in silence for hours before saying a word. "I knew he was still out there," he told reporters later. "I just didn't know he was sitting in church every Sunday."

For Paula's family, the news arrived like a secondhand explosion. Her relatives in another state turned on their televisions and saw her husband's face. They couldn't reach her, she'd stopped answering calls. One family member later said she "went somewhere inside herself and stayed there."

In Wichita, Kerri and Brian avoided interviews. But the media didn't stop calling. Television vans idled near their mother's house for weeks. Reporters shouted questions over fences. Every grocery store aisle, every gas station, every sidewalk was another stage for public curiosity.

"Did you know?" "Did he ever seem strange?" "What was he like at home?"

There were no good answers.

Kerri, still processing the role her DNA had played, withdrew completely from public life. She left Kansas for a time, trying to disappear under another name. Friends later said she carried an invisible guilt, as though her act of cooperation, something heroic in the eyes of law enforcement, felt like betrayal in the private corners of her heart.

In truth, her cooperation had been what finally closed the case. The sample she'd given, routine and unthinking, had matched DNA found on one of BTK's victims. That scientific thread, cold and irrefutable, had bound her blood to his forever.

The irony was unbearable: she had ended his power by giving up part of herself.

Meanwhile, Brian faced a different kind of punishment. In the Navy, fellow servicemen read about the case in the papers. Some stared, others whispered. A few treated him with open pity. "You can't outrun a name like that," one officer said. "It follows you into every room."

He stopped using his last name publicly. When asked about his family, he gave vague answers. The military became his only refuge, a world of structure and anonymity, a place where discipline meant safety, not horror.

Back in Wichita, the Rader house became a symbol, a monument to the city's trauma. Teenagers dared each other to drive by at night. Journalists called it "The House of Dual Lives." Police eventually sealed it, and years later, it was sold and demolished.

But even the demolition felt incomplete, as if the foundation itself still whispered reminders of the ordinary man who had fooled them all.

For Paula, the days turned into months of quiet isolation. She kept her blinds drawn and rarely ventured outside. She never gave a public statement, never appeared in court, never sought the spotlight that chased her name.

When a reporter mailed her a handwritten letter asking for her side of the story, she mailed it back unopened.

Her silence became its own kind of testimony, the only statement she could control in a world where her life had become public property.

Those who knew her said she lived "like someone trapped between two realities." On one side, the man she'd loved, the husband who folded laundry, read scripture, and kissed her goodnight. On the other, the stranger who had stalked and killed under her roof without leaving a trace of his darkness behind.

She had married one man and buried another without ever realizing they were the same.

When the anniversary of his arrest came, television stations replayed the footage again, his mugshot, his church photos, his house. Wichita's skyline looked unchanged, but the city itself wasn't the same.

People still avoided mentioning his name. At family gatherings, in offices, in schools, "BTK" remained a ghost syllable that carried too much weight to say aloud.

Even the police officers who had captured him confessed that they sometimes woke up hearing his voice, flat, polite, relentless.

And yet, amid that silence, one truth began to settle: for every victim whose name had been carved into the city's memory, there were others who lived, Paula, Kerri, Brian, haunted not by what they lost, but by what they never knew.

They were the last victims, the ones left to live with the echo of a man who had called them family.

In the official record, the detail appears simple: *a DNA match from a medical sample taken from the suspect's daughter confirmed paternity and established conclusive evidence linking Dennis Rader to the BTK crimes.*

But behind that sterile sentence lay the most devastating truth of all, that the act of catching him came at the cost of his own child's peace.

Kerri Rader, unaware at first that her routine medical procedure years earlier would one day lead to the unmasking of her father, became the final, unwitting instrument of justice. When investigators tracked down the sample and compared it to the biological evidence preserved from a 1974 murder scene, the result was immediate and undeniable.

It was her DNA that tied everything together. Her blood, her body, the same inheritance that once defined her as her father's child, became the evidence that exposed the family's greatest lie.

When the FBI called to inform her, they did it gently, cautiously. But there was no way to soften the sound of destiny colliding with truth.

She listened in silence. The words "DNA match" echoed through her head like a slow explosion. When the call ended, she sat alone for nearly an hour, unable to move, her mind replaying every childhood moment she'd ever shared with him, his smile, his calm voice, the way he'd say grace before dinner.

Then came the realization: every memory, every touch, every word was now linked to a man the world would call a monster.

In later interviews, she admitted that she hadn't cried at first. "It wasn't grief," she said softly. "It was disbelief. My brain couldn't put the two people together. They didn't fit in the same body."

But as the days passed, disbelief gave way to an unbearable guilt, the guilt of being the one who closed the circle. She had delivered justice, yet it felt like betrayal.

She wondered whether he knew. Whether he realized it was *her* DNA that had finally undone his perfect structure.

He did.

In one of his later letters from prison, Rader wrote about "the irony of the trail that led back home." He described it as "a neat symmetry", a phrase that horrified investigators who read it. To him, even his own downfall was orderly.

To his daughter, it was an unhealable wound.

The guilt ran deeper than logic could reach. She hadn't done anything wrong, she hadn't even been asked directly, but she still felt complicit in destroying her own bloodline.

Every mirror, every reflection reminded her of him. The shape of her face. The tone of her voice. The way people would glance twice when she gave her last name.

Eventually, she stopped using it altogether. She took her mother's name instead.

But names were paper; blood was permanent.

Paula, meanwhile, continued to fade from the world. After filing for divorce, she withdrew completely from public life. She stopped attending church, stopped visiting old friends, and rarely left her home except for errands done in silence.

When neighbors saw her, she was always alone, no makeup, no jewelry, moving quickly, as if presence itself had become dangerous.

She never spoke publicly about the marriage or the crimes. Not once. The silence was total.

But friends who had known her before the arrest said that her grief wasn't the grief of loss, it was the grief of *unreality*.

"She didn't know how to mourn him," one said. "Because the man she loved never existed."

Even the memories she tried to hold onto, vacations, anniversaries, moments of laughter, were poisoned. She couldn't trust any of them.

If he had fooled everyone else, he had fooled her most of all.

The police later confirmed that Paula had been fully unaware of his secret life. There had been no signs of violence, no hidden rooms, no suspicious behavior. His precision had been perfect.

And that perfection was what broke her.

In the months that followed his confession, she refused to see him, refused to take his calls, refused to open his letters. Prison officials confirmed that he sent several, each neatly handwritten, each carefully dated and signed. She never responded.

To the end of her life, she would not utter his name in public again.

When people asked about her husband, she would say quietly, "I don't have one."

For Kerri and Brian, the silence became their inheritance. They learned to live inside it, to avoid interviews, to stay far from Kansas, to disappear into lives where their father's name wasn't whispered like a curse.

But silence is never empty.

It hums. It echoes. It fills the space where truth should be.

There were nights when Kerri would wake up from dreams of her childhood home, the smell of coffee, the hum of the lawn mower, the sound of her father's footsteps in the hall.

She'd see his shadow pass the doorway, and for a moment, she'd forget. Then memory would snap back like a whip.

The illusion of safety. The lie of normal.

For Brian, the damage took a different shape. In the military, he thrived under structure, rules, hierarchy, order. It was his refuge. But even there, he couldn't escape. There was always someone who recognized the name, some whisper in the barracks, some headline taped to a bulletin board.

He avoided photos, social media, anything that could tie him to his father. But the world never forgets its monsters, or their families.

Years later, when he visited Wichita quietly for a relative's funeral, he didn't tell anyone he was coming. He left flowers at his grandparents' graves, said a short prayer, and left before anyone could see him.

He didn't stop at his childhood home. He couldn't.

For both children, the realization was permanent: their father hadn't just killed people. He had killed their history, their trust, their name.

Every family memory now had two meanings, the one they'd lived and the one they'd never seen.

The father who tucked them in at night was the same man who stalked others in the dark. The man who read the Bible at dinner was the same one who quoted scripture to justify murder.

It was unbearable symmetry, and it haunted them.

Outside their private grief, Wichita tried to move forward. The city repainted, rebuilt, and returned to its routines. But for those who had lived near the Raders, the healing never felt complete.

The block on Independence Street became a ghost of what it once was. Children grew up avoiding the sidewalk in front of the old Rader house. Neighbors moved away quietly, unable to bear the proximity to history.

Even after the home was demolished, the soil itself felt stained.

But perhaps the cruelest twist was that, in the eyes of the world, the Rader family could never truly separate from him.

Every article, every documentary, every retelling of BTK's crimes ended the same way, with his name, his family, his dual life.

Their pain was the epilogue no one asked to read.

And in that cruel symmetry, the same precision he once took pride in, the Rader family became what he had always wanted his victims to be: part of the story.

The years that followed were marked not by noise, but by absence. No trials for Paula to attend, no appeals, no television appearances. Just the slow, quiet unraveling of life as it used to be.

After the divorce was finalized, Paula moved away from Wichita. Public records show only the barest traces, utility accounts, a forwarding address in another county, a few property filings, but no one really knew where she went. Those who had once been her neighbors said she left before dawn, loading boxes into a moving truck with the blinds still drawn.

"She didn't say goodbye," one recalled. "Just disappeared."

And perhaps that was all she could do. In a world where her last name was now synonymous with horror, anonymity became her only safety.

She found work under her maiden name, quietly, away from the spotlight. The few who encountered her described her as kind but distant, polite but unreachable. Her eyes, one said, "looked like someone who lived behind glass."

She never remarried. Never spoke of Dennis. Never attended interviews, podcasts, documentaries, or anniversary specials. When letters arrived from journalists begging for her story, she shredded them without reading.

Silence was her rebellion.

If he had built a legacy on control and spectacle, she would erase herself from it completely.

For Kerri, silence worked for a time. She changed her name, moved states, started a family. For years she avoided television entirely, she couldn't risk hearing his voice in a documentary, or seeing his face appear suddenly between commercial breaks.

When her own daughter was born, she wept uncontrollably, holding the baby against her chest. "I realized I was finally building something new," she would say later. "Something that had nothing to do with him."

But the peace didn't last.

Whenever true crime shows revisited the BTK case, her father's face would appear again. Whenever new details emerged, letters, interviews, new books, reporters would reach out, asking for comment. She ignored them all.

Until one day, she didn't.

Nearly fifteen years after his arrest, Kerri Rawson (the name she now used publicly) agreed to write her own account. She said it wasn't for him, or for the media, but for herself, for her own sanity.

Her book, *A Serial Killer's Daughter*, told the story no one else could tell: not of the killer, but of the family that had lived beside him in good faith. She described the pain of discovery, the loss of faith, the years of therapy, and the struggle to forgive herself for surviving him.

"I didn't owe him forgiveness," she wrote. "But I owed myself freedom."

When she began speaking publicly, at schools, conferences, survivor groups, she did so with a trembling voice, unsure if people would understand. To her surprise, they did.

Victims' families embraced her. Survivors thanked her for speaking. The world that had once treated her as a shadow of her father now saw her as something else entirely: a person reclaiming her narrative from the ruin he had left behind.

Her bravery did what his crimes never could, it humanized the aftermath.

She spoke not of him, but of empathy, resilience, faith. She quoted her mother often, saying, "We don't live in his darkness; we walk in our own light."

For Brian, that light came more quietly. He remained in the military, serving with distinction, rarely granting interviews. His silence was not avoidance but protection, a wall built to keep the past from poisoning the present.

Privately, he and his sister reconnected over time. Their conversations were cautious at first, weighted by memories too heavy to name. But with each call, the silence loosened. They didn't talk about him, not directly. They talked about weather, work, holidays, their mother's health. The ordinary things, anchors in a world that had lost its shape.

When asked years later if he had forgiven his father, Brian's answer was simple: "You can't forgive something that isn't human."

In Wichita, the legacy endured in whispers. For a generation that had grown up under the terror of BTK, his name became shorthand for distrust. Parents still told their children to lock their doors. People still avoided certain streets at night. The fear had faded, but the lesson remained: monsters didn't live in the shadows, they lived next door.

And yet, the city healed in its own way. Memorials to the victims went up quietly, without fanfare. The police who had chased him for decades retired, their faces lined not from age, but from the weight of what they had carried.

Each anniversary brought brief media attention, then faded again into silence.

But for the Rader family, there were no anniversaries, no closure, only the quiet persistence of living.

Paula lived out her days privately, her name barely mentioned in the news again. She never sought to clear her reputation; she didn't have to. The investigators themselves had done that for her. One of them, speaking years later, said, "She was innocent. She was a victim, too. Maybe the purest one of all."

When she passed away quietly, it made only a small notice in the local paper. No reference to him. Just a name, a date, and the words *"beloved mother and teacher."*

Kerri attended the funeral in silence, standing over her mother's grave with a single white rose. She didn't cry. The tears had been spent years ago.

In interviews after, she said she still thought of her father sometimes, not as BTK, but as the man she once loved. The man who taught her to ride a bike. The man who read bedtime stories.

"I had to separate them in my mind," she said. "Because if I didn't, he'd take everything."

And that, perhaps, was the final act of survival: refusing to let him define what love meant.

The world had seen Dennis Rader as two people, a family man and a killer, but for those who bore his name, there was no division left. He was one thing, and one thing only: the source of their silence.

And yet, within that silence, something remarkable endured. Not vengeance. Not forgiveness. But endurance itself.

Paula, by vanishing, had reclaimed her peace. Brian, by serving, had rebuilt purpose. Kerri, by speaking, had transformed pain into witness.

Together, they became what he never could: human.

Years later, when asked what message she hoped people would take from her story, Kerri said, "That evil can wear a smile, but love survives it."

She paused, then added softly, "We're still here. That's our justice."

Outside, in the Kansas wind, the fields swayed under a pale sky. The town that once lived in fear now moved with quiet normalcy again.

And though the name "Rader" would forever carry the echo of BTK, it no longer belonged to him alone.

It belonged, finally, to those who survived.

Chapter Fourteen

Lessons From BTK
The Monster Next Door; How BTK Changed the Way We See Ordinary Evil

For thirty years, Dennis Rader believed he was smarter than everyone else.

That belief became his religion.

He had outlasted task forces, newspaper campaigns, and FBI profilers. He had watched other serial killers fall, Ted Bundy, John Wayne Gacy, Jeffrey Dahmer, and each time, he told himself the same thing: *They got sloppy. They wanted too much attention. They broke their own systems.*

He wouldn't make that mistake.

Until he did.

In the end, it wasn't a police sting, a dramatic chase, or even a confession that brought him down. It was a floppy disk, an obsolete piece of technology he believed was untraceable.

That single act of arrogance, born from decades of control and invisibility, exposed the fatal crack in his armor.

He couldn't resist the spotlight anymore. After twenty-five years of silence, he needed acknowledgment. He wanted the city to remember him, to whisper his name again with the same fear they had in the seventies.

And so, in 2004, BTK wrote to the Wichita Eagle, reviving his old persona with a question that would define his downfall: *"Can a floppy disk be traced?"*

The police, understanding his vanity, responded through the press: *No.* That lie was the bait that ended his illusion of perfection.

When Rader mailed the disk from a church computer, investigators traced it within hours to Christ Lutheran. A few more keystrokes revealed the author's identity: Dennis Rader.

The irony was almost biblical.

For a man obsessed with control, he had been undone by his need for recognition.

His mistake wasn't carelessness, it was ego. The same arrogance that fueled his crimes had led him to believe he was untouchable, even above technology itself.

The lesson was simple and eternal: evil, no matter how methodical, eventually overreaches.

But arrogance wasn't his alone. Law enforcement, too, had underestimated him for decades.

From the start, the Wichita Police Department had seen the early BTK killings as unrelated. The Otero murders in 1974 were treated as a family tragedy, not the work of a serial predator. Only when Rader himself sent a letter claiming responsibility, and detailing things only the killer could know, did investigators realize they were dealing with something far more terrifying.

Even then, the investigation suffered from missteps born of assumption. Wichita was a mid-sized city in the heart of Kansas, a place where people left doors unlocked, where neighbors mowed each other's lawns, where horror belonged to other places.

No one believed a serial killer could live among them, not *really*.

Detectives worked tirelessly, but their methods reflected the limits of the time. They collected fibers, shoe prints, and fingerprints, but BTK left none. They canvassed neighborhoods, interviewed hundreds, even looked into local servicemen and maintenance workers. But they were looking for a drifter, an outsider.

They weren't looking for a man with a wife, two children, a mortgage, and a seat on the church council.

That blind spot, the inability to see evil behind normality, became Rader's greatest weapon.

He blended into the landscape perfectly, and the city's belief in its own safety helped him disappear. He wasn't hiding in shadows; he was waving from driveways, sitting in pews, writing citations for overgrown grass.

Every time the investigation stalled, he grew bolder.

After his early murders, he taunted police through letters, daring them to catch him. He enjoyed watching them flounder. But as years passed and forensics advanced, he didn't adapt, he simply withdrew, convinced that time itself would protect him.

When the killings stopped after 1991, detectives assumed he had died, moved away, or lost the urge. In truth, he had merely shifted focus, building his reputation as a church leader, husband, and city employee while privately reliving his crimes through his notes and photographs.

His arrogance metastasized into complacency. He believed that if the police hadn't caught him by now, they never would.

The real tragedy is that, in some ways, he was almost right.

By the early 2000s, much of the original task force had retired. The new generation of officers had grown up hearing stories of BTK like campfire legends, warnings from the past, not an active threat.

When his letters began arriving again, the initial reaction wasn't panic. It was disbelief. The BTK killer was supposed to be gone.

That disbelief, shared by a community that had convinced itself the monster was history, became the final piece of the trap.

He needed to be seen again. To be relevant. To remind them that he was still there, invisible and clever.

The lesson was cruelly clear: evil thrives not in darkness, but in neglect.

The failure wasn't simply forensic; it was psychological. For decades, the assumption that monsters looked monstrous had blinded everyone to the possibility that they could look ordinary.

The "good neighbor," the "family man," the "helpful volunteer", these images were shields that protected him. People see what they expect to see, and Rader used that expectation like camouflage.

Even seasoned investigators fell for it. In the 1970s and 80s, the prevailing profiling models leaned heavily on stereotypes, loners, wanderers, social misfits. Rader was none of those things. He was methodical, articulate, gainfully employed. He didn't fit the template, so he slipped through its cracks.

He wasn't a drifter. He was the man next door.

That realization, too late for his victims, would forever change the way criminal profilers understood human darkness.

Rader's success at blending in exposed the fragility of what people call "normal." His life was proof that outward conformity means nothing. He obeyed traffic laws, paid taxes, attended worship, and murdered without remorse, all under the same roof.

For Wichita, that duality became a permanent scar. Parents began telling their children not just to beware of strangers, but to question the familiar. The city's collective innocence, the belief that evil had a look, a smell, a warning, was gone.

The BTK case forced America to confront something most people didn't want to believe: that horror doesn't need a mask.

And that the real danger isn't the monster who hides in the dark, It's the one who smiles in the daylight.

From the beginning, the media had been both his mirror and his fuel.

Every headline, every broadcast, every whispered conversation in Wichita became part of the theater Dennis Rader directed from the shadows. When he mailed his first letter to *The Wichita Eagle* in 1974, confessing to the Otero murders, it wasn't a mistake born of guilt, it was strategy.

He wanted the story printed. He wanted his name, *BTK*, spoken aloud. "Please make sure this gets in the paper," he wrote. "I can't stop myself."

He didn't want to stop. He wanted an audience.

For years, the newspapers and local TV stations gave him exactly that. They reported every message, every cryptic clue, every supposed sighting. To the public, it was a civic necessity. To Rader, it was applause.

The more the media chased him, the more elaborate his communication became. He sent poems, sketches, coded puzzles. He even wrote about other serial killers, comparing himself to Jack the Ripper and Son of Sam, weaving himself into their lineage of infamy.

What the public saw as horror, he saw as immortality.

The press, unwittingly, became his accomplice in ego. They couldn't help it, the story was too large, too monstrous, too strange to ignore. Wichita was a quiet city; BTK turned it into a national headline.

But while the newspapers spread fear, they also spread obsession, his obsession with how he was seen.

He cared about accuracy, about narrative. He corrected reporters' mistakes, scolded editors for misquotes, even provided "proofs" of his authorship to ensure the legend stayed authentic.

It was performative control, the same kind he used in his murders, but now applied to perception.

By the 1980s, however, the coverage faded. The letters stopped. Time moved on.

That silence wounded him.

He began to feel erased from the public record, forgotten by the very audience that had once given him purpose. His killings had given him power; obscurity took it away.

When he returned in 2004, he did so not because he needed to kill again, but because he needed to be *known*.

The media, cautious but hungry, picked up the story once more. News anchors spoke his name with reverent fear: "BTK returns." Headlines screamed *The Killer Is Back*. Wichita's collective nightmare resurfaced overnight.

And Rader, watching from his living room recliner, smiled.

He followed every broadcast. He cut out the new articles, taped them to pages in a binder. The killer who once controlled life and death now controlled headlines again.

That hunger to be seen was the beginning of his end.

In trying to manage his image, he exposed himself. His final letters, especially the one sent on the fateful floppy disk, revealed his growing obsession with control through communication. He wanted to dictate not just the story of his crimes, but the story of his capture.

The irony was perfect.

For decades, he had hidden behind the façade of ordinary life, untouchable. But once he reentered the conversation, once he invited the media back into his narrative, he stepped into a world transformed by technology.

The world had changed.

In the 1970s, forensic science was still limited to fingerprints and blood type. By 2004, DNA could reconstruct identities from the smallest trace of organic matter. Databases could cross-reference suspects across state lines. Metadata could map the digital footprints of anyone arrogant enough to leave one behind.

Rader never evolved with the world that had evolved to catch him.

He was a 1970s killer in a 21st-century world.

When detectives received the floppy disk and analyzed it, they discovered something Rader never anticipated, digital fingerprints. The file contained hidden metadata that revealed its origin: Christ Lutheran Church, and an author named Dennis.

It took less than three days for investigators to match that name to Dennis Rader, the church council president.

When his DNA, retrieved from his daughter's medical record, confirmed the connection, the myth of BTK collapsed in on itself.

All the structure, all the planning, all the meticulous control, undone by the arrogance of believing he understood a world that had moved beyond him.

That is the first great lesson of BTK: that evil, no matter how intelligent, eventually grows outdated.

Technology caught up to what arrogance refused to believe.

But beyond the digital trail and the forensics, BTK's capture reshaped something deeper, how law enforcement thought about monsters.

Before Rader, profiling was still an emerging science, built largely on patterns derived from the FBI's Behavioral Science Unit. Killers were categorized by method, compulsion, and pathology. Most were divided into "organized" and "disorganized" types, a binary that placed chaos and precision on opposite ends of a psychological spectrum.

BTK broke that model.

He was both. He planned meticulously, but his motives were impulsive. He had structure, but no conscience. He was emotionally cold, yet obsessed with emotional responses, fear, surrender, obedience.

He didn't fit the pattern because he *was* the pattern: order turned inward until it became madness.

For profilers, that duality was a revelation. It exposed the limitations of neat categories. Evil didn't need to be chaotic to be monstrous; it could be administrative, polite, and efficient.

Rader's case forced profilers to reexamine the relationship between ego, control, and fantasy. His crimes weren't about rage or necessity, they were about narrative control.

He wasn't killing for need. He was *curating*.

Modern profiling evolved because of him. Investigators began to look beyond the surface, beyond social dysfunction, to see how normalcy itself could be a disguise. The quiet man at the desk, the husband at the barbecue, the volunteer at church, all potential masks.

Psychologists studying Rader after his arrest coined the term "compartmentalized psychopathy" to describe his ability to separate his two worlds so completely. They compared his mind to a filing cabinet, each drawer neatly labeled, no emotion spilling from one into the other.

That model changed the way future profilers approached suspects who seemed "too normal."

The BTK case also redefined the balance between media and investigation. Law enforcement learned that public communication could not only shape perception but influence behavior. The decision to answer

Rader's floppy disk question falsely, telling him it was safe, was a calculated psychological trap, one of the first of its kind in the digital age.

The strategy worked because they finally understood what he wanted: acknowledgment.

That was the second great lesson of BTK, control isn't just about dominance. It's about visibility.

Every killer wants to be seen.

And the moment they demand it, they give themselves away.

When the news broke that the floppy disk had led police to his church, journalists marveled at the irony. But for investigators, it was less poetic than practical. They had learned how to weaponize a killer's own pride.

In the decades since, that principle has guided countless investigations. The idea that ego can be bait, that vanity can reveal truth, has become foundational in modern criminal psychology.

BTK's fall, then, wasn't just an ending. It was an education.

It showed that even the most controlled mind is vulnerable to its own reflection. That technology can illuminate the dark corners arrogance refuses to see.

And that sometimes, the most powerful weapon law enforcement has is patience.

For thirty years, BTK had believed the silence was safety. In the end, the silence was just the waiting breath of time catching up to him.

When the dust settled after Dennis Rader's arrest, the question that haunted both investigators and psychologists wasn't just how he'd gotten away with it for so long, it was how many others like him might still be out there.

Rader was unique, but he was also a warning: proof that obsession can grow in silence, hidden behind ordinary smiles and everyday rituals.

In his home office, police found binders filled with drawings, photographs, and notes detailing decades of stalking and fantasy. Many of those files referenced "projects" that were never completed, failed hunts, interrupted plans, ideas that never reached reality.

He had lived in a constant cycle of obsession and control, moving between fantasy and action with terrifying precision. Forensic psychologists later described this as a "closed-loop fantasy structure", a pattern in which imagination becomes its own substitute for violence until opportunity reawakens it.

Rader's ability to live inside that cycle for decades without exposure revealed a chilling truth about human psychology: the line between thought and action is thinner than most people want to believe.

He was not insane. He was deliberate. His fantasies were not random but systematic, cultivated like a hobby, organized like a job.

That organization, the methodical feeding of fantasy, was what made him dangerous.

He wasn't ruled by impulse; he ruled impulse itself.

And that, experts say, is the most frightening kind of killer, the one who doesn't need chaos to thrive.

After his capture, behavioral analysts studied his writings obsessively. What they found was not the typical stream of consciousness or mania seen in many killers, but something closer to a bureaucratic record of evil.

His journals documented not just what he did, but why he did it, and how he learned from it. "I adjusted the bindings," he wrote in one entry. "I improved control technique. Better next time."

Those words revealed the purest form of pathology: a man refining murder like craft.

But beyond the horror, those writings became a critical psychological case study. They helped law enforcement understand how fantasy-driven offenders operate in isolation, how imagination itself can become a rehearsal space for violence.

One FBI analyst put it simply: "BTK showed us that you don't need blood to practice evil. You just need time."

In the years that followed, criminal profilers used his case to develop early-warning models for fantasy-based offenders, men and women who fixate on control, domination, or ritual long before they commit crimes. They began studying collections of writings, drawings, and online activity not as eccentricities but as potential precursors.

Rader's legacy, in this dark sense, helped sharpen the psychological radar that protects communities today.

The internet, for example, became both a weapon and a window. Where Rader had relied on notebooks and Polaroids, modern fantasists could build entire secret lives online, digital worlds where their desires were shared, validated, and fed.

In online forums, investigators began to notice the same patterns: meticulous organization, coded language, and a detached fascination with "projects" or "scenarios."

The difference was scale. Rader worked alone, in the shadows of Wichita. His modern equivalents could exist anywhere, their fantasies shared across borders, their anonymity preserved by technology.

That realization sparked a new kind of vigilance in law enforcement, the understanding that the next BTK might never leave his house, might live entirely within the architecture of his imagination until something, somewhere, pushes him past the threshold of thought into action.

Rader's story became the psychological blueprint for that transformation, the moment where obsession stops being fantasy and starts becoming logistics.

His capture, therefore, wasn't just a triumph of police work, it was a warning about how complacency lets monsters evolve.

Even now, experts debate whether another BTK could exist today.

On the surface, technology seems to make such anonymity impossible. Surveillance cameras track faces, cell phones log movements, databases connect evidence within seconds. The tools that caught Rader have multiplied exponentially.

But psychology hasn't changed.

The need for control, the hunger for recognition, the dual life of the ordinary monster, those instincts are timeless.

What has changed is the arena. Where Rader once mailed letters, today's obsessive fantasists can feed their egos through screens. They can construct entire virtual lives around control and humiliation without ever leaving home.

The distance between thought and deed grows smaller when validation comes instantly.

That's what makes the BTK case more relevant now than ever. It isn't just about murder, it's about identity.

Rader's greatest disguise was normalcy, but his greatest weakness was vanity. He needed to be known.

That combination, hiddenness and hunger, defines modern criminal psychology in the digital age.

Social media has turned visibility into a currency. For someone like Rader, who fed on acknowledgment, platforms of attention would have been gasoline on his pathology. Investigators often speculate that if he'd been born twenty years later, he might have been caught sooner, or he might have become far more prolific.

In a world where self-documentation is constant, his compulsions would have found endless reflection.

The lesson, then, isn't that another BTK could exist. It's that the *potential* for BTK exists, in anyone who finds control more intoxicating than connection.

That's what still haunts psychologists today.

After Rader's conviction, forensic psychiatrists studied his brain scans, interviews, and behavior. They found no obvious neurological abnormalities, no tumors, no lesions, no chemical imbalances. His intelligence was above average. His emotional responses were measured but intact.

In short, there was nothing to "explain" him.

He wasn't broken by trauma or madness. He was built by choices.

He was the ultimate demonstration that evil doesn't require dysfunction, it can coexist with domestic life, civic order, and community respect.

That is the third and final lesson of BTK: evil doesn't always look extraordinary. Sometimes it looks like a neighbor waving from his porch.

That realization changed the way Wichita, and much of America, saw itself.

People learned to look twice, not just at strangers, but at the familiar. They learned that trust, once blind, must be earned.

Law enforcement learned something too, that catching monsters requires humility. That the belief in total understanding is as dangerous as ignorance.

Because arrogance, as BTK proved, belongs to both sides of the line.

For decades, he believed he couldn't be caught. For decades, police believed he couldn't still be out there. Both were wrong.

What broke that stalemate was not brilliance, but persistence, the simple, human refusal to give up the hunt.

That's how BTK was caught. That's how future killers will be.

In the end, the story of Dennis Rader is not just about one man's evil, it's about the fragile systems that allow evil to hide.

Technology, psychology, and law will continue to evolve, but the lesson endures: vigilance must be both forensic and moral.

Because somewhere, in a quiet neighborhood, there is always someone watching from behind the blinds. Someone ordinary. Someone unnoticed.

And sometimes, that is where the darkness waits.

Chapter Fifteen

Evil in the Everyday

The Banality of Horror; How BTK Turned Ordinary Life Into His Greatest Disguise

When Dennis Rader's identity was revealed, the first question everyone asked was simple, almost childlike: *How could it be him?*

That question, uttered in living rooms, churches, classrooms, and police stations, wasn't really about disbelief. It was about betrayal.

For decades, Wichita had been haunted by the faceless terror of BTK, a phantom who bound, tortured, and killed without warning. He was supposed to be a monster, a creature apart from humanity, a silhouette in the dark.

But when the mask finally fell, the face beneath it wasn't monstrous at all. It was ordinary.

That ordinariness was the most horrifying part.

Because BTK wasn't the drifter, the loner, the unwashed figure from nightmares. He was the neighbor who waved while mowing his lawn. The man who handed out candy on Halloween. The one who volunteered at church, led the Boy Scouts, and stopped to chat at the grocery store.

He wasn't hiding behind a disguise; he *was* the disguise.

What made Dennis Rader different from other serial killers wasn't his cruelty or even his intelligence. It was his ability to maintain two realities, one of perfect domestic normalcy, and one of unthinkable brutality, without ever allowing the two to collide.

He lived by a code of ordinary life. He kept schedules, made lists, attended meetings. He paid bills on time, called his mother, and helped his neighbors repair fences.

And in that pattern, those small, repetitive acts of civility, he found his perfect camouflage.

Rader's genius, if one can call it that, lay not in his crimes but in his control. He didn't live outside society's expectations; he lived precisely within them.

His neighbors saw punctuality. His victims saw precision.

He lived by rules, his own, and everyone else's. And that made him invisible.

In the annals of American crime, few killers blended so completely into their surroundings. Bundy charmed but drifted. Gacy hid behind performance and parties. Dahmer lived in isolation. Rader, by contrast, *thrived* in the daylight.

His evil was bureaucratic, domestic, procedural.

He didn't need chaos; he preferred order.

That order became the stage on which he played his two roles. At home, he was Dennis, husband, father, church leader. In secret, he was BTK, the planner, the watcher, the self-appointed "operator" of his own dark system.

The two weren't opposites; they were symbiotic. One made the other possible.

His public life offered him legitimacy; his private life gave him meaning.

It was the perfect symmetry of evil.

What made it more unsettling was how seamlessly he moved between those worlds. There was no visible tension, no slip of the mask, no confession whispered in sleep. He compartmentalized with the precision of an engineer, building walls between the two halves of himself and locking every door.

Psychologists later compared his mindset to that of a man maintaining two calendars, one public, one secret, each filled with appointments, obligations, and goals.

For Rader, the "banality of evil" wasn't an abstract concept, it was his daily life.

He wasn't a supernatural figure; he was the logical endpoint of a culture that values image over introspection, compliance over empathy, control over connection.

He lived the American dream: home ownership, steady employment, civic involvement. But beneath that veneer lay something corrosive, a hunger to dominate, to orchestrate, to be the unseen hand that decides who lives and who dies.

It wasn't madness that drove him. It was the cold comfort of routine.

He killed not out of rage, but because it fit within the architecture of his control. His crimes were scheduled, his fantasies filed, his trophies labeled.

Even his cruelty had structure.

That structure was what made him terrifying.

In his quiet suburb, Rader was surrounded by repetition, the hum of sprinklers, the clatter of trash bins, the rhythm of weekend errands. To him, those sounds were lullabies. They meant safety, predictability, invisibility.

He knew exactly how the world saw him: dull, dependable, forgettable.

And he weaponized it.

Neighbors later admitted that they couldn't remember ever seeing him angry. His voice rarely rose above a calm tone. He smiled politely, offered advice about city ordinances, and waved from his driveway.

It was that same driveway where police, decades later, would surround him, guns drawn, shouting his name. The shock on the faces of those neighbors wasn't fear, it was recognition warped into something unrecognizable.

Because when the world looked at Dennis Rader, it didn't see a killer. It saw itself.

That's what made his story so unnerving, not the violence, but the reflection.

Rader's existence forced people to confront a truth they'd rather ignore: that evil doesn't always announce itself. It doesn't always wear a mask. Sometimes it looks like a man with a clipboard, checking your fence for code violations.

He thrived precisely because the world is built to reward conformity.

At work, he enforced order. At church, he preached faith. At home, he maintained silence. Each sphere of his life reinforced the illusion that he was safe, stable, moral.

And society, trusting, polite, complacent, accepted it.

That trust was his camouflage.

It was also his addiction.

The comfort of being ordinary became his greatest pleasure. The more normal he appeared, the more powerful he felt. Every barbecue, every church potluck, every father-daughter event was another performance in his long-running play of deception.

His camouflage wasn't just physical, it was emotional. He mimicked empathy, rehearsed humor, adopted expressions that made others feel at ease.

He studied human behavior not to connect with it, but to hide within it.

He was a man who smiled without warmth, who asked questions without curiosity, who offered help without humanity.

And yet no one noticed.

That is the quiet horror of BTK. Not just that he killed, but that he was invisible while doing it.

The "banality of evil," a phrase coined decades earlier by philosopher Hannah Arendt to describe the bureaucratic mindset of moral indifference, found its modern embodiment in Dennis Rader.

He didn't see himself as a monster because he didn't feel monstrous. He was a man doing "projects." A man following rules, his rules. He measured morality not by empathy, but by efficiency.

He was evil reduced to process.

And that process thrived best in environments of comfort and routine.

Suburbia, the landscape of trimmed lawns, clean sidewalks, and familiar faces, was his hunting ground not because it was vulnerable, but because it was blind.

The illusion of safety became the perfect hiding place for danger.

He understood that better than anyone.

He knew that people see what they expect to see. And so he gave them exactly that: a reliable neighbor, a devoted husband, a man of faith.

He built his identity around their expectations and used it to disappear.

In doing so, he exposed the flaw at the heart of modern life, the belief that danger comes from the outside, that evil is foreign, that safety is earned through sameness.

But sameness was his mask.

His conformity was his weapon.

And every quiet, ordinary morning that he waved to his neighbors, the city unknowingly waved back at its own blindness.

Every mask requires an audience to believe in it.

And Dennis Rader's performance depended on an audience that wanted to believe in good neighbors.

The camouflage he built wasn't elaborate, it was painfully simple. A pressed shirt. A tidy lawn. A smile that said *trust me.*

He learned early that the more normal he appeared, the less people looked deeper. It became a kind of social magic trick: look long enough at the ordinary, and you stop seeing what's beneath it.

He didn't need to be charming. He only needed to be present.

The comfort of routine became his armor. He woke early, ate breakfast with his family, checked his inspection route, and drove a city-issued vehicle through quiet Wichita neighborhoods. To the residents, he was the enforcer of order, the man who made sure lawns were trimmed, cars registered, fences compliant.

It was a role he relished. Power without suspicion. Control under the guise of public duty.

The same control he sought in his private fantasies was mirrored in his professional life. When he wrote citations or enforced ordinances, he felt the same authority he felt when he planned his "projects." The only difference was that one was sanctioned by the city, and the other by his own pathology.

He had turned conformity into cover.

At church, he read scripture about obedience and righteousness, and his congregation nodded in approval. No one thought to question the precision of his moral vocabulary, the way he spoke about "rules" and "discipline" with almost military zeal. To them, he was a man of conviction. To himself, he was a man of control.

Even his wife, Paula, who knew his routines better than anyone, saw nothing strange. He was reliable, attentive, occasionally distant, but what husband wasn't? He kissed her goodbye in the mornings, helped with chores on weekends, attended Scout meetings with his son.

He didn't hide bodies in the basement or bloodstains under the carpet. His evil left no visible trace. That was the point.

In the end, his camouflage worked because it aligned perfectly with what society wanted to see, a quiet man leading a quiet life.

The horror wasn't that he pretended to be normal. It was that he *was* normal, at least in every visible way that mattered.

The sociopathic brilliance of Dennis Rader wasn't in his cruelty; it was in his comprehension. He understood the human desire for safety, for pattern, for reassurance. And he built himself around that.

He embodied the idea that danger always looks different, that it wears dark clothes, avoids church, mutters to itself, lives on the edge of town. He was none of those things.

He was the edge of town.

The ordinary man with extraordinary cruelty, that was the paradox.

Even now, when investigators replay his interviews, what strikes them isn't his lack of remorse, but his calm. He spoke about murder the way one might describe a job completed on schedule. "I had a plan," he said. "I followed it."

No rage. No confusion. Just process.

He saw himself as a technician of death. A man perfecting a system, not committing a sin.

And the system required normalcy.

He couldn't exist without it. It was the ecosystem that sustained him, the polite hell of routine where no one asked questions too personal, where the neighbor's name mattered more than his nature.

When Wichita tried to make sense of it afterward, there were endless interviews with friends, coworkers, neighbors, all repeating the same refrain: *He seemed so normal.*

That phrase, repeated in documentaries, newspaper retrospectives, and television specials, became his epitaph.

He seemed so normal.

What no one said out loud was the deeper truth: they wanted him to be normal. They needed him to be. Because if he wasn't, then what did that say about everyone else who trusted him?

Society's reluctance to see the warning signs wasn't stupidity, it was self-preservation. To admit that a killer could be sitting beside you at church or fixing your mailbox was to admit that safety itself was a myth.

So people turned away from their own unease. They explained away the small oddities, the controlling tone, the fixation on rules, the cold detachment, as quirks, not clues.

That denial is what he counted on.

He didn't just hide in plain sight, he built his camouflage from everyone else's refusal to see.

And in that sense, BTK was less an individual aberration than a mirror reflecting something societal: our collective blindness to quiet authority, to conformity mistaken for morality.

The lessons he left behind weren't just for law enforcement. They were for everyone who still believes that monsters announce themselves.

Because they don't. They fit in. They learn the language of comfort, mimic decency, and disappear into the routines of daily life.

That's why his story is still relevant today, not because it's about one man's crimes, but because it dismantles the illusion of the safe world we think we live in.

Rader's life is a map of how evil functions when it wears the clothes of normalcy. Every step, every ritual, every polite smile was a step away from conscience.

He wasn't an exception to humanity; he was a product of it, proof that moral blindness can coexist with civility.

The uncomfortable truth is that he didn't invent his disguise. Society gave it to him.

We live in a world that rewards composure, manners, order, and appearances. We prize those who keep things "under control." And Rader understood that control is the easiest virtue to fake.

The lesson of BTK isn't that monsters hide among us. It's that they *are* us, until the moment they decide not to be.

His story endures because it challenges the narrative of safety. It forces us to question the spaces we trust most, homes, schools, churches, neighborhoods, and the assumptions that govern them.

When people say "it could never happen here," they are reciting the same lullaby that let Dennis Rader sleep peacefully for three decades.

The danger of forgetting him isn't that we'll forget his crimes, it's that we'll forget what made them possible.

Even now, psychologists studying the BTK case use his life as a cautionary framework in criminology courses. They call it the "ordinary mask", a behavioral model that warns against equating appearance with truth.

Students are told: Don't look for the monster in the shadows. Look for the man who never breaks routine.

Rader's case remains the most haunting example of that paradox because he wasn't the bogeyman of folklore, he was the man you trusted to fix your porch light.

His legacy, if it can be called that, is a question that won't go away: how well do we really know the people around us?

And perhaps the more haunting question, how well do we know ourselves?

Because every system he exploited, the politeness, the privacy, the reluctance to pry, still exists today. We build fences to protect our homes but not our awareness. We teach our children to fear strangers, not to question the familiar.

We still live in a world built for his kind of camouflage.

That's why his story is not just history, it's prophecy.

In every quiet neighborhood, behind every manicured hedge, there are lives we assume are as harmless as they appear. Most of them are. But some are built, brick by brick, from the same stillness that once hid BTK.

Evil doesn't need chaos to survive. It just needs to be ignored.

And that brings us to the final reflection, the watcher himself.

For decades, Dennis Rader watched his community. He watched windows, schedules, patterns. He watched people go about their lives, unaware they were part of his theater of control. Watching was his true addiction.

But in the end, when the world turned its gaze back on him, when cameras, reporters, and neighbors all looked, finally, into the quiet life he had built, he crumbled.

The watcher could not bear to be watched.

That is the ultimate inversion of the BTK story. The man who lived unseen could not survive the light of recognition.

It was never the exposure of his crimes that broke him, it was the exposure of his ordinariness.

When the mask fell, there was nothing underneath.

Just a man. Just a neighbor. Just a reminder that evil doesn't always roar. Sometimes, it whispers from across the fence.

And sometimes, we wave back.

Chapter Sixteen
The Names in Silence
The Victims of BTK

*T**he lives behind the headlines. The names that endure when the voice of the killer is finally silent.*

When the noise of the headlines fades, only names remain.

The case files close. The television lights dim. But somewhere, a photograph still sits on a dresser, a child's drawing curls at the edges of an old refrigerator, a church pew stays empty.

This is where the story ends, not with the man who took, but with those who were taken.

The Otero Family

January 15, 1974 – Wichita, Kansas

Morning sunlight through kitchen curtains. A family breakfast never finished. A dog barking into the quiet.

Joseph Otero Sr., 38, retired Air Force master sergeant; Julie Otero, 34; their children Joseph Jr., 9, and Josephine, 11. Four lives bound together by love and by the hands of a man they had never met.

The Oteros were the beginning. The blueprint. The test of control that would become BTK's signature.

Rader entered their modest home on East 13th Street, cut the phone line, and turned routine into nightmare.

Julie's devotion, Joe's discipline, Joseph Jr.'s curiosity, Josephine's laughter, each now survives only in family memories. Two older siblings, away at school that morning, returned to find the house still, the air heavy with something no child should ever see.

The Oteros' deaths shattered Wichita's sense of safety. They also revealed a truth that the city, and later the world, would spend decades trying to understand: evil can walk through an unlocked door at breakfast time.

Kathryn "Kathy" Bright

April 4, 1974 – Wichita, Kansas

An apartment on East 13th Street. Afternoon light. The hum of a stereo. Two siblings arriving home together.

Kathryn Bright was 21, a Wichita State University student, part-time secretary, and dreamer saving for art school. Her brother, Kevin, 19, walked in with her that day, unknowingly into an ambush.

Rader had waited inside. What followed was chaos, a struggle, gunfire, desperate movement through the small rooms of the duplex. Kevin was shot twice but managed to escape. Kathryn fought until the end. She was stabbed and strangled.

Police officers at the scene described the silence afterward as "suffocating."

Her death confirmed that the Oteros had not been an isolated tragedy. Wichita now had a predator who planned.

Kevin Bright lived, scarred in body and mind. For years he carried guilt no survivor deserves, the weight of having seen and survived.

Kathryn Bright is remembered not for her death but for her fight. In every retelling of that day, there is one constant detail: she never gave up.

Shirley Vian

SILENT WATCHER

March 17, 1977 – Wichita, Kansas

A modest home on South Hydraulic Avenue. A kitchen table with cereal bowls still half-full. Children whispering behind a locked bathroom door.

Shirley Vian was 24 years old, a mother of three, recently separated, working to build a new life.

That morning, a stranger knocked.

Rader entered under the pretense of needing to use the phone. What happened next became one of the most haunting chapters of his violence.

He forced Shirley's young children, aged six, four, and five, to hide in the bathroom, tying the door shut before killing their mother in the next room.

He left quietly, as if leaving an ordinary house. The children emerged to find the world changed forever.

Neighbors remember Shirley as warm, kind, protective, a woman who worked too hard and loved even harder.

Her family declined nearly every interview after Rader's arrest; their silence said everything.

In police files, the word *mother* appears again and again beside her name.

It remains the most accurate description of who she was, and what was stolen.

Nancy Fox

December 8, 1977 – Wichita, Kansas

A small duplex. Christmas lights glowing from a nearby window. A cat waiting at the door.

Nancy Fox was 25, worked at a jewelry store by day, sang in her church choir at night.

Independent, private, self-reliant, she represented everything Rader both envied and sought to control.

He broke in through a rear window while she was out, waited, and confronted her when she returned.

Later, in his confession, he described it clinically, as if recounting a task. But the detail that investigators remember most is what he did afterward: he called 911 from a pay phone to report her death himself.

"I'm BTK," he said. "You'll find her at 843 South Pershing." Then he hung up.

That phone call marked the apex of his arrogance. For the first time, his voice, steady, almost polite, entered the case record. Nancy Fox became his self-chosen proof of control.

To her friends and coworkers, she remains the woman who loved to laugh, who kept her home immaculate, who sang even when no one was listening.

The city still remembers her address.

The names continue. Each one a break in the pattern of ordinary days. Behind every date, a life that touched others, a voice that deserved to be heard longer.

The years between 1978 and 1985 brought a deceptive calm. Wichita exhaled, believing the nightmare had passed. But the silence was only intermission.

Marine Hedge

April 27, 1985 – Park City, Kansas

A calm spring night. Porch lights flicker out one by one. Crickets, then silence.

Marine Hedge was fifty-three, a mother, grandmother, and Rader's next-door neighbor. She tended her yard with care, spoke softly, trusted easily. She lived less than a mile from the man who watched her for years.

That night she vanished from her home. Neighbors thought she'd gone out of town. She hadn't.

Rader took her from her own bed, killed her elsewhere, and returned her body under cover of darkness to leave it near a rural ditch.

Police later realized he had used a church meeting as his alibi, slipping away between prayers.

Forensic teams found almost nothing. The quiet street where she lived still looks the same; only the memory of her absence lingers.

She was buried with family beside her. The people who knew her speak of gentleness, of evening walks, of kindness returned to every greeting.

Vicki Wegerle

September 16, 1986 – Wichita, Kansas

A weekday morning. A camera on a kitchen table. The sound of a vacuum cleaner stops abruptly.

Vicki Wegerle was twenty-eight, a musician and mother. Her husband, Bill, was suspected for years, until BTK resurfaced decades later, revealing he had kept Vicki's driver's license as proof of his crime.

She was strangled in her home, photographed afterward by her killer. Those photos, recovered later, ended any doubt that BTK had continued during his supposed dormancy.

Her family endured decades of suspicion and silence. When Rader was finally caught, Bill Wegerle said quietly to reporters, "Now they can rest."

Vicki's friends remember her singing at church and playing piano late into the night, windows open, the sound carrying into the street. In every retelling, people mention her hands, graceful, musical, alive.

Dolores E. Davis

January 19, 1991 – Park City, Kansas

The edge of town. A bridge over frozen water. Wind rattling through dry grass.

Dolores Davis was sixty-two, a widow who loved gardening and her small dog. Rader knew her from the neighborhood.

That night, he attended a Scout leader meeting, left early, changed clothes, and drove to her home.

She was strangled and her body hidden beneath the bridge for days before being found.

Her murder marked the end of BTK's known killings. After that, he vanished again into normal life, church duties, city inspections, fatherhood.

For Wichita, her death closed the circle but left no closure. Investigators often say her case still feels unfinished, not because evidence is missing, but because her quiet dignity resists being reduced to a "final victim."

Neighbors still place flowers near the bridge each January. They don't speak her name loudly. They simply remember.

The Survivors and the Missed Projects

Sometimes survival is a lifetime sentence of memory.

Kevin Bright, who survived bullets and trauma, carried testimony that eventually helped define BTK's early pattern.

The Vian Children, locked in the bathroom, grew up and built lives far from Wichita's headlines.

Others, women identified only by initials in Rader's notes, were watched, photographed, or nearly attacked before circumstance intervened: a doorbell, a phone call, a passing car.

In his writings, Rader called them "missed projects."

The world calls them survivors.

Their lives, though forever touched by what might have been, are proof that evil can be interrupted by the smallest accident of grace.

The Unknowns

In the margins of Rader's journals, there are codes and partial names. Some will never be solved.

Investigators suspect additional stalking cases between 1979 and 1984, break-ins, stolen clothing, cut phone lines, that match his pattern but lack proof. Whether those incidents were rehearsals, fantasies, or forgotten crimes remains uncertain.

Rader hinted in interviews at "a few more projects," then retracted. Forensic teams scoured old reports, but time erases traces more efficiently than guilt.

What endures is the possibility, the haunting sense that his story might not be complete.

For the families of unsolved disappearances in Kansas during those years, that uncertainty is its own life sentence.

About the Author

Miles Donovan is an investigative nonfiction writer whose work explores the dark intersections of psychology, crime, and the human condition. Known for his cinematic yet meticulously factual style, Donovan examines how ordinary lives conceal extraordinary secrets and how society's pursuit of order can sometimes hide the most disturbing truths.

Drawing on years of research into criminal profiling, behavioral psychology, and archival case documentation, Donovan's writing moves beyond sensationalism to reveal the human patterns beneath horror. His works challenge readers to confront not just the nature of killers, but the blindness of the world that allows them to exist.

In *Silent Watcher*, Donovan dissects the myth of the suburban predator, exposing how normalcy itself became the perfect mask for one of America's most methodical murderers. With a journalist's precision and a storyteller's empathy, he restores the focus to the victims, the names in the silence, and the community that endured long after the headlines faded.

Miles Donovan writes under the imprint **Quantum Quill Media**, where his investigative titles continue to explore the hidden, the unspoken, and the human cost of evil.

Printed in Dunstable, United Kingdom